THE IMF AND GLOBAL FINANCIAL CRISES

The International Monetary Fund's response to the global crisis of 2008–9 marked a significant change from its past policies. The IMF provided relatively large amounts of credit quickly with limited conditions and accepted the use of capital controls. This book traces the evolution of the IMF's actions to promote international financial stability from the Bretton Woods era through the most recent crisis. The analysis includes an examination of the IMF's crisis management activities during the debt crisis of the 1980s, the upheavals in emerging markets in the 1990s and early 2000s, and the ongoing European crisis. The dominant influence of the United States and other advanced economies in the governance of the IMF is also described, as well as the replacement of the G7 nations by the members of the more inclusive G20, which have promised to give the IMF a role in their mutual assessment of policies while undertaking reforms of the IMF's governance.

Joseph P. Joyce is a professor of economics at Wellesley College and serves as the faculty director of the Madeleine Korbel Institute for Global Affairs. Professor Joyce's research deals with issues in financial globalization. He has published articles in many journals, including the *Journal of International Money and Finance, Open Economies Review, Review of International Economics, Journal of Development Economics*, and *Economics & Politics*, and he is a member of the Editorial Board of the *Review of International Organizations*. He received his Ph.D. in economics from Boston University.

The IMF and Global Financial Crises

Phoenix Rising?

JOSEPH P. JOYCE

Wellesley College

Department of Economics

CAMBRIDGE
UNIVERSITY PRESS

32 Avenue of the Americas, New York NY 10013-2473, USA

Cambridge University Press is part of the University of Cambridge.

It furthers the University's mission by disseminating knowledge in the pursuit of
education, learning and research at the highest international levels of excellence.

www.cambridge.org
Information on this title: www.cambridge.org/9781107436862

First published 2013
First paperback edition 2014

A catalogue record for this publication is available from the British Library

Library of Congress Cataloguing in Publication data
Joyce, Joseph P.
The IMF and global financial crises : Phoenix rising? / by Joseph P. Joyce.
p.   cm.
Includes bibliographical references and index.
ISBN 978-0-521-87417-5 (hardback)
1. International Monetary Fund.   2. Financial crises.   3. International finance.
4. Global Financial Crisis, 2008–2009.   5. International Monetary Fund –
Developing countries.   I. Title.
HG3881.5.I58J69   2013
332.1′52–dc23   2012023656

ISBN 978-0-521-87417-5 Hardback
ISBN 978-1-107-43686-2 Paperback

The phoenix hope can wing her flight
Thro' the vast deserts of the skies,
And still defying fortune's spite,
Revive, and from her ashes rise.

Miguel De Cervantes,
Don Quixote (Motteux, trans.)

Contents

List of Figures, Tables, and Boxes

Figures

Tables

Boxes

Preface

The year 1973 was a transitional one for the global economy. Attempts to revive the Bretton Woods system of fixed exchange rates were abandoned; increases in oil prices led to the occurrence of higher prices and falling output, which was labeled "stagflation"; and it was the last year that the U.S. government maintained restrictions on capital flows. There was one other event of somewhat lesser significance: my graduation from Georgetown University's School of Foreign Service, where I developed an interest in international economics. After two years of work in New York, I entered Boston University's graduate program in economics. I subsequently was fortunate to receive an appointment to the faculty at Wellesley College, where I have remained ever since.

I began my professional academic life, therefore, during the post–Bretton Woods era of currency regime and financial liberalization. The removal of capital controls by the United States was followed by financial deregulation in other developed economies in the 1970s, and by many Asian and Latin American countries during the following decades. Capital flows rapidly expanded, and by the end of the century it was possible to refer to the integration of financial markets across borders as the latest manifestation of globalization (Mishkin 2006). But it was also a period of economic volatility and upheaval, which included the debt crisis of the 1980s, the financial crises in the emerging markets of the 1990s, and, most recently, the global crisis of 2008–9.

At the center of all these events was the International Monetary Fund. I was drawn to the study of the IMF because it provided a focus on the twists and turns in the international economy. The IMF was often the subject of criticism: sometimes misinformed and unfair, sometimes well deserved. In my research I sought to substantiate the record of the IMF's activities and their impact. In one of my first postdissertation research papers, I investigated the economic characteristics of countries that sought the IMF's assistance. Subsequent works dealt with the repeated occurrence of IMF programs, the implementation of the policy conditions attached to them, the impact of Fund programs on poverty, the IMF's status as a provider of public goods, and the IMF's stance on capital account deregulation. In all of these studies I learned something about the IMF and about the economic conditions of its member countries.

Like others, I was caught off guard by the outbreak of the financial crisis in 2008 but greatly interested by the response of the IMF. The Fund, which had laid off staff members earlier in the decade because of a lack of lending programs, answered its members' requests for assistance by providing large amounts of credit with relatively limited and focused conditionality. The IMF was labeled a "phoenix" and seen as "back in the game," and its rapid and energetic reaction allowed its reputation to recover from the criticisms it had received for its previous crisis management activities, particularly those undertaken during the East Asian crisis of 1997–8. But the IMF was soon involved in the European debt crisis, while the emerging market nations pressed the IMF to investigate the role of capital controls in containing the impact of financial flows.

This book examines the IMF's attempts to promote the international public goods of economic and financial stability from the end of the Bretton Woods system in 1973 through the 2008–9 crisis and the subsequent events in Europe. This account demonstrates how the IMF changed its policy prescriptions in response to the financial turbulence of this era. The IMF learned to respond more quickly when necessary and to distinguish between crisis conditions that require major adjustments in domestic policies and those that are due to external shocks that should be financed. This shift matched a growing awareness of the instability that can arise in financial sectors and an evolution in the IMF's position on the advantages and disadvantages of unregulated capital accounts.

In telling this story, this book also surveys the IMF's relationship as an agent with its principals, the member governments. For many years the IMF's membership was divided among the advanced (or upper-income) economies, emerging market (or middle-income) nations, and developing (or lower-income) countries. This stratification was not rigid, and countries did rise and fall among the categories. But during the post–Bretton Woods era the advanced economies that dominated the IMF and other international agencies did not need to borrow from the Fund, while the emerging markets with much less clout were forced to turn to the IMF for credit whenever they experienced one of their recurrent financial crises.

The IMF's poorer members were cut off from private financial flows and depended upon the IMF and other multilateral agencies for assistance. Consequently there was friction between those nations that directed the IMF's governance and those that borrowed from it.

The financial shock that shook the world economy in 2008, however, originated in the United States, and the advanced economies were particularly hard hit by the ensuing crisis. Moreover, these nations could no longer claim any superiority in their regulatory systems once the activities of the "shadow" banking systems came to light. The emerging markets, on the other hand, suffered only mild slowdowns before their growth resumed its impressive pace. The change in the relative positions of the IMF's members was made clear when the G7 group of nations transferred its role as the chief forum for international economic policy making to the G20, which includes many emerging markets. This changeover was accompanied by promises to overhaul the governance of the IMF.

The IMF, which for thirty-five years sought to find its place in the era of financial globalization, must reinvent itself again. No one expects a return to a Bretton Woods–style system of universal exchange rate and capital account regimes. But the transition to a world where the advanced economies cope with mounting debt and the emerging markets and developing economies seek to continue their rapid growth without exposing themselves to financial volatility will require a reappraisal of the international monetary system by the IMF and its members as profound as that which occurred at the Bretton Woods conference in 1944. My hope is that this book contributes to that debate.

Acknowledgments

This work has benefited from conversations with many colleagues. Among those who have discussed these issues with me are Rawi Abdelal, Jeffrey Chwieroth, Onno de Beaufort Wijnholds, Domenico Lombardi, Kenneth A. Reinert, Lorenzo Bini Smaghi, Thomas Willett, and Ngaire Woods. Special thanks are due to my former coauthors Graham Bird, Ilan Noy, Raul Razo-Garcia, and Todd Sandler. Scott Parris of Cambridge University Press has shown great patience as this book has gone through multiple drafts, and an exceptional reader explained how to separate the wheat from the chaff. Several Wellesley College students, including Virginia Ritter, Leslie Shen, and SuiLin Yap, provided valuable research assistance.

The completion of this book owes much to the patience of my wife, Catherine Clark. She tolerated without reproach many hours of my absence while maintaining the household. My children, Caroline and Alison, also accepted as part of a normal childhood their father's many disappearances to work on the book. I am very fortunate in having a wonderful and supportive family.

Abbreviations

ASEAN	Association of Southeast Asian Nations
BCBS	Basel Committee for Banking Supervision
BIS	Bank for International Settlement
CCL	Contingent Credit Line
CMI	Chiang Mai Initiative
CMIM	Chiang Mai Initiative Multilateralization
CPSS	Committee on Payments and Settlement Systems
EC	European Community
ECB	European Central Bank
EFF	Extended Fund Facility
EFSF	European Financial Stability Facility
EMS	European Monetary System
ERM	Exchange Rate Mechanism
ESAF	Enhanced Structural Adjustment Facility
ESF	Exogenous Shocks Facility
EU	European Union
FCL	Flexible Credit Line
FDI	Foreign Direct Investment
FSAP	Financial Sector Assessment Program
FSB	Financial Stability Board
FSF	Financial Stability Forum
FSSA	Financial System Stability Assessment
G5	Group of Five
G7/8	Group of Seven/Eight
G10	Group of Ten
G20	Group of Twenty
G24	Group of Twenty-Four
G77	Group of Seventy-Seven

GAB	General Arrangements to Borrow
GFSR	*Global Financial Stability Report*
GNI	Gross National Income
HAPA	High Access Precautionary Arrangement
IAIS	International Association of Insurance Supervisors
IEO	Independent Evaluation Office
IFI	International Financial Institution
IFIAC	International Financial Institution Advisory Commission
IGO	Intergovernmental Organization
IMF	International Monetary Fund
IMFC	International Monetary and Financial Committee
IOSCO	International Organization of Securities Commissions
IPG	International Public Good
LIBOR	London Interbank Offer Rate
NAB	New Arrangements to Borrow
OECD	Organisation for Economic Co-operation and Development
OPEC	Organization of Petroleum Exporting Countries
PRGF	Poverty Reduction and Growth Facility
SAF	Structural Adjustment Facility
SBA	Stand-By Arrangement
SDR	Special Drawing Rights
SDRM	Sovereign Debt Resolution Mechanism
SLF	Short-Term Liquidity Facility
SRF	Supplemental Reserve Facility
WEO	*World Economic Outlook*

1

Introduction

Among the many surprising features of the global financial crisis of 2008–9 was the emergence of the International Monetary Fund (IMF) as a leading player in the response to what has become known as the "Great Recession." The news that the IMF was "back in business" was remarkable in view of the deterioration of the IMF's reputation after the crises of the late 1990s and the decline in its lending activities in the succeeding decade. The IMF had been widely blamed for indirectly contributing to the earlier crises by advocating the premature removal of controls on capital flows, and then imposing harsh and inappropriate measures on the countries that were forced to borrow from it. The number of new lending arrangements approved by the IMF had fallen from twenty-six in 2001 to twelve in 2007 (Figure A.2), and all but two of the latter went to the IMF's poorest members, which had little access to private sources of finance.

Moreover, the IMF, the intergovernmental organization assigned the task of promoting international economic and financial stability, initially had no direct role in dealing with the crisis. Finance ministers and central bank heads in the United States and Western Europe, where the financial institutions most affected by the crisis were located, sought to contain its impact by easing credit conditions and rescuing distressed financial institutions. The IMF was relegated to the sidelines as government officials in the advanced economies coordinated their responses to the crisis.

All this changed in the fall of 2008, however, after a series of financial failures in the United States. Global financial markets froze as lenders drew back in response to the uncertainty over which borrowers were still viable. The collapse of the financial system led to an economic contraction that spread outside the original group of crisis countries. World trade fell and capital flows slowed and in some cases reversed, as nervous banks, firms, and investors sought to reallocate their money to safer venues.

The financial crisis also triggered an upheaval in international economic governance. The Group of Seven/Eight (G7/8) was replaced by the Group of Twenty (G20) nations as the appropriate forum for international economic coordination, and the leaders of the broader set of countries met in Washington, D.C., to formulate a joint response to the crisis.[1] They announced their support of the IMF and agreed to boost its financial resources significantly so that the Fund could meet the demands for its assistance. In response, the IMF provided loans to a range of countries, including the Ukraine, Hungary, Iceland, and Pakistan (Chapter 10). In addition, the IMF restructured its lending programs, cutting back in many cases the policy conditions attached to its loans and increasing the amount of credit a country could obtain. The Fund also introduced a new credit line without conditions for countries with records of stable policies and strong macroeconomic performance. Moreover, the IMF pledged to work with national governments and other international organizations after the crisis receded to continue the economic recovery and improve the regulation of global financial markets. Consequently, many commentators hailed the rejuvenated IMF as a "phoenix" (Beattie 2010).

This book contends that the IMF's response to the Great Recession marked a significant break from its policies during previous global financial crises. These had taken place during an era when the IMF's membership was stratified by income and whether or not a country borrowed from the Fund.[2] In addition, the IMF had actively encouraged the deepening and widening of global finance. The IMF's previous responses to financial crises, therefore, reflected the dominance of its upper-income members as well as an ideological consensus in favor of financial globalization. Its lending programs had sought to restore countries in crisis to the global capital markets.

---

[1] The members of the G7 are Canada, France, Germany, Italy, Japan, the United Kingdom, and the United States. The G7 became the Group of Eight (G8) when Russia joined in 1997. However, the G7 finance ministers continue to meet separately from the Group of Eight national leaders. The G20 includes the countries of the Group of Eight and Argentina, Australia, Brazil, China, India, Indonesia, Korea, Mexico, Saudi Arabia, South Africa, Turkey, and the European Union. See Chapter 3 on the formation of the G7 and Chapter 10 on the G20.

[2] The World Bank classifies countries by their gross national income (GNI) per capita. In 2011 low-income nations were those with a GNI of $1,005 or less; middle-income countries those with GNI per capita of $1,006 to $12,275; and upper-income countries those with GNI per capita of more than $12,276 or higher. The middle-income countries were divided into lower and upper middle-income nations at a GNI per capita of $3,975. These thresholds have risen over time, and countries have moved among categories. The three main groups correspond to what we call the advanced economies, the emerging markets, and the developing countries.

But the crisis upended those circumstances. The shock to the global economy originated in the upper-income countries, and the recovery of many of these nations has been relatively sluggish. The emerging economies, on the other hand, rebounded from the global economic contraction more quickly, in turn contributing to the recovery of the developing nations. Moreover, the crisis demonstrated that financial instability can be a systemic condition, confirming the need for prudent oversight and the regulation of financial markets and capital flows.

While the Great Recession provided the IMF with an opportunity to demonstrate that it has learned the lessons of its past mistakes, there are fundamental economic and political transformations under way that will affect the ability of the IMF to counter future financial instability. The replacement of the dominance of the G7/8 by the G20 should lead to a more equitable governance structure within the IMF, although inertia has slowed the pace of reform. Moreover, the European debt crises pose new challenges to the IMF. The Fund is caught in the crossfire among Eurozone governments and their citizenries over how to deal with members in financial distress. Fiscal burdens will mount in other advanced economies with aging populations and rising health care and public pension costs. The emerging market governments, which face a different set of challenges as they seek to continue their rapid growth, will be suspicious of IMF programs if these appear to be less demanding than those extended during earlier crisis periods.

This book examines the evolution of the policies and programs of the IMF with respect to the global financial markets and crises in these markets.[3] We show how the IMF's activities during the period of 1973–2008 reflected the influence of its dominant members as well as the IMF's own commitment to capital market integration and evaluate the effectiveness of the IMF in its roles as crisis preventer and crisis manager. The challenges of the future are also addressed, as well as the steps the IMF must take to solidify its reputation.

The consequences of the changes in the IMF's own governance extend beyond the IMF itself. Similar relationships between the IMF and its members exist in other international agencies, where the need to accommodate the aspirations of the emerging market countries must be met. We draw

---

[3] Other research deals with related aspects of the IMF's work. Histories of the IMF include works by Boughton (2001b) and James (1996). Bird (2007) has provided an overview of the professional literature. Political analyses of the IMF's activities have been undertaken by Copelovitch (2010), Stone (2011), Vreeland (2007), and Woods (2006). Boughton and Lombardi (2009) offer an assessment of the IMF's dealings with its low-income members.

upon agency theory to explain how the advanced economies exercised a collective leadership to influence the IMF and other multilateral agencies, and how that control has been replaced by wider but perhaps less effective direction by the G20.

This account also illustrates the importance of viewing both economic and financial stability as international public goods. Financial stability was once seen as an outcome or accompaniment of economic stability. But the asset booms of the last decade, following the technology boom of the 1990s and the Japanese property bubble of the preceding decade, demonstrated that asset prices could veer for years from values justified by fundamental factors. The subsequent reversals have had serious consequences for economic activity that persist over many years and extend over national borders.

The remainder of this chapter presents a synopsis of the basic concepts that will guide our analysis. The next section provides an overview of the status of international economic and financial stability as international public goods (IPGs). It is followed by a description of the activities of intergovernmental organizations (IGOs) such as the IMF. The following section presents the theoretical perspectives of agency theory, which provides a valuable perspective on the Fund's relations with its member governments. The last section contains an outline of the main arguments of the book.

1.1 IPGs and Financial Stability

Crises have been a constant of market capitalism – from the bursting of the British South Sea bubble and the French Mississippi in 1720, ... to the depressions of the 1870s and 1930s in the industrial economies, to the debt crises of middle-income Latin American countries and low-income African countries in the 1980s, the collapse of output in the formerly socialist economies in the 1990s, and the East Asian financial crisis in 1997–1998. (Easterly, Islam, and Stiglitz 2001: 191)

The devastating impact and wide scope of the recent crisis provide ample evidence of the status of financial stability as an IPG. Public goods constitute a type of market failure, as characterized by the features of nonexcludability in their supply (once a good is provided, it is available to all) and nonrivalness in their consumption (a good can be used by more than one individual simultaneously) (Olson 1965, Cornes and Sandler 1996). Consumers have no incentive to purchase an item if they think that others may pay its cost and they can also enjoy it, a phenomenon known as "free riding." A government, however, can compel its citizens to contribute to the provision of a good that will benefit all.

Impure public goods are partially nonrival or nonexcludable. In the case of a club good, the good is excludable but partially nonrival, and a charge (such as a toll) can be imposed to ensure the efficient amount of the good is provided. A joint product has a combination of outputs that vary by their degree of nonexcludability and nonrivalness, such as a public good that is provided with a club good (Sandler 1977).

Market failures take place on an international as well as a national basis. If the benefits of a public good transcend national borders, it is an international public good (Kaul, Grunberg, and Stern 1999b, Kaul *et al.* 2003, Sandler 1997, Sandler 2004). Climate change, for example, cannot be addressed adequately on a national or regional basis. Similarly, the rapid spread of communicable diseases demonstrates the need for international coordination to offset threats to public health. But the same problems exist with IPGs as with domestic public goods. Market incentives to provide the goods do not exist or are distorted, and private producers will not supply them. The problem is compounded on the international level, since the rewards to providing an international public good are diffused among many nations, and there may be little incentive for a single country to supply it.

Axelrod and Keohane (1986), however, pointed out that the long-term horizons – the "shadow of the future" – of economic relationships could contribute to the willingness of nations to engage in collective actions. Another situation that can promote the provision of IPGs is the emergence of a hegemonic nation that receives most of the benefits of the good. The hegemonic nation may decide to provide the good unilaterally and allow smaller countries to share the benefits. Great Britain played a hegemonic role in the nineteenth century, and the United States held a similar position after World War II.[4]

An additional characteristic of a public good is the determination of its supply, or its aggregation technology (Cornes and Sandler 1984). The available amount of most public goods is based on the summation of the contributions of the individual units. In the case of a "weakest-link" technology, however, the smallest contribution determines the availability of the public good. The prevention of disease, for example, is dependent on the efforts of the state with the least-effective controls, which can motivate other nations to contribute to the provision of the good in that state (Sandler 2004). A related technology is the "weaker link," where the smallest contribution has the largest impact on the overall level of the public good, followed by next

---

[4] Eichengreen (1989), however, questions the extent of hegemonic domination by the United States.

smallest, and so on. Other possible technologies include the "best shot," where the amount provided of the public good depends on the efforts of the most-qualified or largest contributor. Cures for diseases are typically discovered within countries with the financial resources to support drug development and testing. With "better shot" public goods, the largest contributor provides the largest contribution, followed by the second largest, and so forth.

Financial stability (or the lack of instability) has historically been viewed as a public good. While there are many descriptions of what constitutes financial stability (Houben, Kakes, and Schinasi 2004), many analysts would agree with Crockett's (1997) claim that stability includes the ability of key financial institutions to meet their obligations, and movements in the prices of financial assets that reflect changes in fundamental factors. When financial stability prevails, Crockett (1997: 14) points out, "it creates a more favorable environment for savers and investors to make intertemporal contracts, enhances the efficiency of financial intermediation, and helps improve allocation of real resources." The absence of financial stability results in instability, defined by Allen and Wood (2006: 159) as "episodes in which a large number of parties, whether they are households, companies, or (individual) governments, experience financial crises which are not warranted by their previous behavior, and where these crises collectively have seriously adverse macro-economic effects."

The international aspects of financial stability have received more attention in recent years due to the rise in cross-border capital flows and the occurrence of crises with global consequences (Griffith-Jones 2003, Wyplosz 1999). The integration of financial markets contributes to the rapid spread of shocks across frontiers, thus making their prevention an international task. The occurrence of crises in several countries simultaneously or in rapid succession may be due to a common external shock, or trade or financial links among the crisis countries (Claessens and Forbes 2001).

Financial crises can take different forms (Reinhart and Rogoff 2009). A currency crisis occurs when there is a wave of selling of a currency that is fixed in value by a central bank. If the central bank's efforts to preserve the pegged value are unsuccessful, it is forced to devalue the currency. The depreciation raises the cost of imports and servicing foreign debt and may induce a contraction in output in the short run as well as higher inflation rates. A successful defense of a currency peg can be costly if the central bank is forced to raise interest rates or spend its foreign currency reserves to preserve the pegged rate (Eichengreen, Rose, and Wyplosz 1995).

A bank crisis occurs when the financial intermediary is not able to meet its obligations to its depositors. In the case of a liquidity crisis, a solvent bank lacks sufficient liquid assets to cover its liabilities. If the bank's assets decline in value, however, resulting in negative net worth, then the bank is insolvent. Bank crises are usually resolved by government intervention, which has a fiscal cost. The total fiscal cost of bank crises in the developing economies during the twenty-five-year period before the latest global crisis had been estimated to exceed $1 trillion (Honohan and Laeven 2005).

The simultaneous occurrence of a currency crisis with a bank crisis has been named a "twin crisis" (Kaminsky and Reinhart 1999). Most bank crises in emerging markets and developing countries are accompanied by currency crises, although not all currency crises are tied to bank crises. A "sudden stop," which is the reversal of capital flows from inflows to outflows, can also occur during a bank crisis. Another form of crisis is a sovereign debt crisis, which occurs when a government or government-sponsored agency is unable to make payments on its debt and either asks its borrowers for relief or defaults on its obligations. Emerging markets that borrow in the international capital markets often issue debt denominated in a foreign currency, and their default can lead to a currency crisis.

Bordo *et al.* (2001: 72) studied the frequency of currency, banking, and twin crises in a sample of countries during the period of 1880 through 1997 and concluded: "Since 1973 crisis frequency has been double that of the Bretton Woods and classical gold standard periods and matched only by the crisis-ridden 1920s and 1930s. History thus confirms that there is something different and disturbing about our age." These authors also noted that there has been a rise in the frequency of twin crises, which are more disruptive than banking or currency crises alone. Kindleberger and Aliber (2005: 278) confirmed that the dominant pattern of recent financial crises "was one of banking and foreign exchange crises occurring at the same time."

These crises impose costs on economies in terms of lost output. Bordo *et al.* (2001) found that financial crises over the preceding one hundred years were followed by economic downturns lasting on average two to three years and costing 5–10 percent of GDP. Similarly, Hutchison and Noy (2005) examined the output costs of currency and banking crises in a group of countries over the period of 1975–97 and reported that currency crises reduced output by 5–8 percent over a two- to four-year period, while banking crises lowered GDP by 8–10 percent.[5] In addition, Baldacci, de

---

[5] Boyd, Kwak, and Smith (2005) and Hoggarth, Reis, and Saporta (2002) offer analyses of the costs of banking system instability.

Mello, and Inchauste (2002) reported that financial crises are associated with an increase in poverty. The negative repercussions of financial crises extend past the time of their occurrence, imposing intergenerational effects. Cerra and Saxena (2008) reported that currency, banking, and twin crises have persistent negative effects on output. They also contribute to macroeconomic volatility, which has a negative impact on long-term growth. Hnatkovska and Loayza (2005) found that this inverse relationship of growth and volatility has become larger in recent decades and was exacerbated in the poorer countries. Another channel of transmission from crises to lower growth results from the fall in investment expenditures following bank crises (Joyce and Nabar 2009).

Financial stability has often been treated as synonymous with economic stability. However, they are related but different phenomena, and since the Great Recession the linkages between them have become the subject of scrutiny and analysis. Economic stability has traditionally referred to consistent rates of growth in output and low and stable inflation rates. It had traditionally been assumed that financial and price stability were linked, but the record of the last two decades has demonstrated that low inflation rates are not a sufficient condition for stability in asset prices (Borio and Lowe 2003).

1.2 IGOs and the IMF

The provision of IPGs can be promoted by IGOs. The IGOs are associations of national governments with permanent secretariats that perform the work of the organization (Archer 2001). IGOs exist because they provide (or assist national governments to provide) IPGs and are a relatively recent phenomenon in international governance. The first was the International Telegraphic Bureau, founded in 1865, which still functions as the International Telecommunication Union. There are currently approximately 240 such associations (Union of International Associations 2008).

IGOs can be viewed as elements of regimes, which are a form of IPGs. Keohane and Nye (2001: 17) described regimes as "sets of governing arrangements," and Krasner (1983: 2) defined them as "sets of implicit or explicit principles, norms, rules and decision-making procedures around which actors' expectations converge in a given area of international relations." Kaul, Grunberg, and Stern (1999a) view regimes as intermediate public goods that contribute to the provision of final IPGs. In the international sphere there are regimes governing shipping, health standards, air traffic, communications, and many other areas.

Keohane and Murphy (2004: 914) have described IGOs as the external manifestations of these regimes: "We can think of the regime as an overall set of rules and practices, and the IGO as the purposive bureaucratic organization that monitors and reacts to activity." An IGO is well suited to provide IPGs (Abbott and Snidal 1998, Martin 1992, 1999, Russett and Sullivan 1971). The organization can provide information and resolve problems of cooperation among its members, thus lowering the transaction costs to collective action. In addition, an IGO can undertake activities for its members that may be difficult for individual governments to perform.

International organizations differ from each other in a number of aspects (Koremenos, Lipson, and Snidal 2001, Sandler and Cauley 1977). For example, IGOs can operate on a regional or a global basis. The optimal size of the IGO is based on the principle of subsidiarity, which states that the size of an organization should be based on the size of the geographical area it serves. IGOs also vary in the number of their activities. If there are economies of scope, then one organization can provide more than one public good more efficiently than separate institutions.

Another important aspect of an IGO's operations is its governance. In some cases, such as the General Assembly of the United Nations, all member nations have an equal vote. In other settings, such as the IMF, votes are weighted in some manner. There may also be rules on voting procedures, such as the need for a supermajority in some circumstances. All these features affect the ability of the IGO to formulate and implement common policies, and to respond to new crises and challenges. Fratianni and Pattison (1982), for example, pointed out that consensus is less likely to be obtained when the number of members of an IGO increases.

The IMF has been the primary IGO to be assigned the responsibility of promoting international financial stability. Kindleberger and Aliber (2005: 293) noted that the IMF was established in response to the financial instability of the 1920s and the 1930s. While the first Article of Agreement of the IMF, which lists its goals, does not specifically mention financial stability (Chapter 2), it does refer to "exchange stability" and "orderly exchange arrangements." The revised Article IV, which was adopted in 1973, refers to "financial and economic stability" as an objective (Chapter 3). The G7 governments expanded the IMF's responsibilities in this area after the capital account crises of the 1990s.

Stanley Fischer (Fischer 2000), a highly respected economist and former first deputy managing director of the Fund, in a description of the nature of the public good provided by the IMF, claimed:

It is worth going back briefly from time to time to first principles and asking why one needs an institution like the IMF. The basic fundamental reason is that the international financial system left to itself does not work properly, and it is possible to make it work better for the sake of the people who live in that system....

Our goals are to prevent crisis, to create stability and to promote economic growth. Those have been our goals for over 55 years now.

The IMF fulfills its IPG mandate by providing joint products with different degrees of publicness, such as multilateral surveillance and crisis lending (Joyce and Sandler 2008). In the post–Bretton Woods era, the IMF has sought to identify those weaker-link economies that pose a threat to international financial stability in order to strengthen their macroeconomic policies and financial regulatory structures (United Nations Industrial Development Organization 2008). When a crisis in a country does occur, the IMF acts with other multilateral agencies and governments to provide financial credit and other forms of assistance as the domestic government implements policies to address the crisis.

While there was agreement on the IMF's key position in this area during the era of the Bretton Woods system, new organizations, called collectively the international financial institutions (IFIs), have been established also to deal with the maintenance of international financial stability. Many of these are based in Basel; they include the Bank for International Settlements, which actually predates the IMF, and the Basel Committee for Banking Supervision. The Financial Stability Forum was established in 1998 to coordinate activities intended to promote stability across national boundaries. In 2009, this body was expanded to an organization with a larger membership, the Financial Stability Board, and the relationship of the new organization with the IMF is one of the outstanding issues in the postcrisis era (Chapter 11).

1.3 Principals and Agents

Agency theory provides a framework for analyzing the relationships of governments and IGOs (Copelovitch 2010, Hawkins, Lake, Nielson, and Tierney 2006). In a principal-agent relationship, the agent is a person, firm, or organization that performs a task for others, the principals. The delegation of authority to the agent can be constrained by rules of conduct, or the agent may have discretion in performing its job.

If there is a divergence between the interests of the principal(s) and those of the agent, then there is a possibility that the agent may act to further its own interests. This type of situation, known as "slippage," arises because of asymmetric information. Problems with asymmetric information occur whenever one party to a transaction has relevant information that the other does not. To minimize the occurrence of slippage, the principal(s) must monitor the actions of the agent and provide incentives to obtain the desired results.

In the case of a democratic state, the principals are the voters who choose government officials (mayors, presidents), who in turn hire civil servants (teachers, soldiers) to supply public goods. This constitutes multistage agency, as the electorate monitors the behavior of their representatives, who in turn oversee the performance of the bureaucracy. If the amount or quality of the public good is inadequate, the voters can notify the appropriate elected officials, who direct the civil servants to adjust their actions. If the electorate continues to be dissatisfied, it can replace the elected officials with new ones who will issue revised directions or hire new civil servants.

The principal/agent relationship in international governance differs from that of domestic governance along several dimensions (Vaubel 2006). In the case of an IGO, there is extended multistage agency: the electorate of a country votes for a national government, which then chooses to join the intergovernmental organization. Consequently, there are more delegations of authority than there are with domestic bodies, and more opportunity for the slippage of control from electorates to the international agency. In addition, international nongovernmental organizations that seek to advance some issue or policy goal attempt to influence the oversight of the domestic governments in order to promote their policy agenda.

In an IGO, the member governments must share control over the organization. Lyne, Nielson, and Tierney (2006) differentiate between situations where there are multiple principals, who act independently in their relationship with bureaucratic agents, versus collective principals, where the principals must make joint decisions. The second type of arrangement is common with IGOs such as the IMF. As the number of principals of an IGO increases, however, the coordination of their preferences becomes more difficult to achieve. This provides the IGO agent with more scope for independent action if preference heterogeneity regarding the goals of the organization prevails among the principals.

The public good or service provided by the IGO may be directly supplied to the international population (data standards, research), but in some cases the organization works with a government in providing the good within a country (infrastructure projects, public health programs). In these circumstances there is reciprocal agency: the government retains its authority with other states over the IGO, while the IGO needs to ensure that the actions of the government with respect to the provision of the public good are appropriate. The existence of reciprocal agency explains some of the controversies that surround the actions of the IGOs. There are inherent differences between the IGOs, which base their policies on their assessments of global benefits and costs, and the domestic governments, which are concerned with national benefits and costs.

Alternative interpretations of the behavior of IGOs appear in other schools of analysis. Public choice analyses of IGOs, for example, concentrate on the activities of the individuals within the organization. Public sector bureaucrats at the IGOs are assumed to maximize their own interests, which include income and prestige, as measured by the size of their budget and staff. The IGO bureaucrats implement policies for national governments in exchange for their continued support of the organization.

Vaubel (1986), for example, has claimed that domestic officials transfer the responsibility for unpopular policies to international agencies in order to evade the response from voters for their imposition. Domestic politicians can also use the IGOs to satisfy the demands of interest groups. The international agencies have more opportunities for undertaking these activities because of voter ignorance about their actions and a lack of transparency. Frey (1997) points out that monitoring international organizations is difficult because of the multidimensional nature of their output.

Another perspective on these issues is offered by those who adopt the social constructivist position in international relations theory. Barnett and Finnemore (2004), for example, also view the IGOs as bureaucracies. However, they point out that these bureaucracies have expertise in their respective fields, which allows them to define problems and devise solutions. The bureaucrats classify knowledge, fix meaning, and establish rules and norms of behavior. While their authority is delegated by the sovereign states, the IGOs' mandates are often broadly defined. Consequently, the staffs of the IGOs have a large degree of latitude in deciding how the mandate will be carried out. Their autonomy increases when the delegated tasks involve specialized knowledge that outsiders do not possess.

It is interesting to compare these two perspectives on a common issue, such as the growth over time of the IMF. A public choice analysis attributes such expansion to the bureaucrats' desire to control more resources in order to increase their influence. The oil price shocks of the 1970s and the international debt crisis of the 1980s, for example, provided opportunities for the international economic organizations to devise new tasks and responsibilities (Chapter 4). Vaubel (1994: 44) has claimed that "the international debt crisis in 1982 provided the IMF officials with an opportunity to secure the survival and growth of their organization."

Barnett and Finnemore (2004: 43) agreed that IGOs tend to expand over time. However, they claimed that such expansion in international organizations (IOs) "is often not the result of some imperialist budget-maximizing impulse so much as a logical extension of the social constitution of the bureaucracy.... IOs tend to define both problems and solutions in ways that favor or even require expanded action for IOs." But Barnett and Finnemore also believe that there are self-imposed limitations to bureaucratic expansion. These occur "when staff believe that new goals are only marginally related to the primary mission" (Barnett and Finnemore 2004: 64). They cite the alleviation of poverty as an example of a goal that receives a mixed response from the IMF's staff.

1.4 Overview

In the following chapters we will draw upon these concepts – international financial and economic stability as IPGs, the IMF as an IGO, and agency theory as a tool of analysis – in our examination of the evolution of the IMF's response to global crises. This section provides an overview of the following chapters.

In Chapter 2 we describe the operations of the Bretton Woods international monetary system. The postwar arrangements, which were a response to the disorder of the prewar years, were based on a fixed exchange rate regime and restrictions on capital flows. The IMF was assigned the tasks of promoting monetary cooperation among its principals and extending credit to member countries with balance of payments disequilibria. The Fund's staff formulated economic models to design the policy conditions that were attached to its lending programs, and these often called for cutbacks in fiscal expenditures and credit creation.

The stability of the Bretton Woods system depended on the acceptance by the IMF's principals of the rules governing the system. The IMF as an agent could monitor, but not compel, compliance. Once the United States was no longer willing to fulfill its central role within the system, the IMF was unable to prevent its breakdown. The reemergence of private capital flows contributed to the collapse of the rule-based system.

New institutional arrangements were devised in the post–Bretton Woods period to govern international transactions, and these procedures and organizations are reviewed in Chapter 3. The revision of Article IV of the IMF's Articles of Agreement allowed governments to choose the exchange rate regime they found appropriate for their economies but also stipulated several provisions to ensure that national choices would be consistent with international stability. The revised article assigned the IMF the task of surveillance of its members' compliance with their new responsibilities, although the scope of the IMF's oversight powers was vague.

The responsibility of supervising international banking in the Euromarkets, on the other hand, was entrusted to a new agent, the Basel Committee on Banking Supervision, which included the governments of only the advanced economies as members. The lending activities of private banks were amplified by increases in oil prices that resulted in increased borrowing by developing economies. The IMF responded to the growth of international financial intermediation by developing a niche as a lender to the poorest countries. But by the end of the 1970s, flexible exchange rates and private capital flows seemed to have eliminated the need for IMF lending, while new, more focused IGOs provided more effective forums for intergovernmental consultations.

The international debt crisis of the 1980s represented a major threat to financial stability, and Chapter 4 deals with the IMF's involvement in the crisis. In the early years, the IMF worked with the banks and the debtor countries to reschedule loan repayments while providing new credit. Its policy conditions were consistent with currency crisis models that attributed the breakdown of exchange rate pegs to expansionary monetary policies. The IMF's intervention prevented a complete disruption of international financial flows, but it did not resolve the crisis. While the IMF dealt with the management of the crisis, the upper-income countries, operating through the Basel Committee on Banking Supervision, established a regulatory response through the adoption of uniform standards for bank capital requirements.

The debt crisis was eventually resolved through a conversion of the commercial banks' loans to bonds. The IMF emerged from the crisis as a "crisis manager" as well as a lender. The IMF was criticized for favoring the interests of the private banks, and using the crisis as a justification to expand its own activities. But the G7 governments circumscribed the scope of the Fund's actions during the crisis, and the IMF could only implement strategies countenanced by those governments.

The resolution of the debt crisis was followed by a resurgence of capital flows during the 1990s, and a synopsis of the IMF's activities during this period is provided in Chapter 5. The IMF saw no conflict between encouraging capital liberalization and its mandate to promote economic stability and growth. The Fund supported the removal of regulations on capital flows in its dealings with members and sought to use its own loans as a catalytic agent to promote private financial flows. However, during the late 1980s and early 1990s the IMF provided little guidance on how to pace the implementation of financial deregulation or deal with procyclical capital inflows.

The IMF also attempted to establish an institutional role for itself in the international financial markets though an amendment to the Articles of Agreement that would have established capital account liberalization as a goal for its members. This change would have extended the mandate of the IMF to include assessing compliance with the new obligation. The IMF initially had the support of its most powerful members for the amendment but was forced to shelve the proposal after the outbreak of the Asian financial crisis.

The eruption of currency crises during the 1990s in Europe and Mexico, and the IMF's role (or absence) in their resolution, are examined in Chapter 6. The European countries dealt with their crisis without involving the IMF, thereby contributing to the division between those IMF members that borrowed from it and those that did not. The events in Europe prompted the development of new models of currency crises, which allowed for the possibility of self-fulfilling speculative attacks in the occurrence of currency crises.

On the other hand, the IMF was extensively engaged with the United States in the resolution of the Mexican crisis. The events in Mexico demonstrated that capital outflows could undermine an exchange rate peg and disrupt a country's domestic financial sector. The IMF's activities were subsequently criticized again for serving primarily the interests of foreign creditors, and for signaling investors that the IMF would bail out a country in the event of a financial crisis.

Mexico proved to be a precursor of more instability. The East Asian crisis and the IMF's response are described in Chapter 7. The East Asian countries had prospered in the early 1990s, and foreign capital flowed to those economies that had decontrolled their financial sectors. The capital inflows fueled asset price booms and furthered the economic expansion. But foreign investors became concerned about the sustainability of the boom and the viability of fixed exchange rate pegs. Capital flight, exacerbated by contagion, spread throughout the Asian countries, resulting in the breakdown of currency pegs and the widespread failure of domestic financial institutions.

The IMF provided assistance to Thailand, Indonesia, and South Korea. However, the IMF was harshly criticized for imposing contractionary conditions and inappropriate structural conditionality on the governments that adopted Fund programs. The IMF was also blamed for indirectly precipitating the crises through its encouragement of capital account deregulation. Malaysia followed a different path and enacted capital control measures.

The East Asian crisis was followed by more crises in other emerging markets, confirming their status as the "weaker links" in the international financial markets. The principal financial emergencies of this period are described in Chapter 8. In the case of Russia, the IMF responded to the mandate of the G7 leaders to support its new government. But continuing fiscal imbalances resulted in a default by the Russian government on its debt and a breakdown in its pegged exchange rate in the summer of 1998. The IMF, on the other hand, was successful in backing the Brazilian government's response to capital outflows in 1999. The country's financial sector proved to be relatively robust and was not disrupted by the currency's depreciation. The IMF also sought to support the Argentine government despite misgivings over the sustainability of its monetary policies. But the continuing worsening of that government's fiscal position, reinforced by investor concerns, caused the IMF to cease providing credit in late 2001. The Fund was blamed within that country for the ensuing crisis.

Chapter 9 deals with the response of the IMF and its members to the instability in global financial markets. The IMF undertook a self-review and changed some of its policies. The IMF became more cautious in its stance on capital account decontrol and reduced the scope of its conditionality. On the other hand, the IMF embraced its role as a global lender of last resort, which included the rapid provision of credit in the event of a crisis.

Meanwhile, the split among the IMF's principals continued. The upper-income governments saw a lack of transparency and weak regulatory controls within the emerging markets as responsible for the run of financial crises. They established the Financial Stability Forum to oversee the establishment of financial and economic standards and assigned the IMF and the World Bank the task of reviewing the implementation of the new guidelines. The emerging markets, on the other hand, sought to bolster their positions by accumulating foreign exchange reserves and devising regional arrangements to provide liquidity in the event of another crisis.

An account of the period leading up to the Great Recession and the IMF's involvement in that crisis is offered in Chapter 10. The relative economic stability of the early and middle 2000s masked growing financial instability in the advanced economies. The IMF was concerned about the negative consequences of capital flows to advanced economies with current account deficits, but not as aware of the growing fragility of their financial markets as a result of deregulation. The IMF sought, without success, to broker an agreement among its largest members to address the phenomenon of "global imbalances."

When financial failures in the upper-income nations resulted in a global crisis, the IMF effectively took the role of an international lender of last resort. It moved quickly to provide large amounts of credit to those members most affected by the disruption of trade and financial flows. The IMF also revised its programs in order to enhance their effectiveness and showed a willingness to reconsider its positions on capital controls and other issues. The G20 leaders, after taking over from the G7/8, promised to involve the IMF in future mutual policy assessments while reorganizing its governance to raise its credibility.

The IMF did not have a respite from its crisis management duties after the global crisis eased. The postcrisis period, surveyed in Chapter 11, has been one of uneven recovery, with the emerging markets and developing economies showing much stronger and more sustained growth than the advanced economies. Fears of insolvency in several European governments led to higher borrowing costs and volatility in the markets for sovereign bonds, and the IMF has joined other European nations in providing financial assistance to the most indebted nations there. Moreover, the challenge of mounting debt levels, compounded by demographic trends toward older populations, affects virtually all upper-income nations. The IMF's contributions to the bailouts of indebted governments will be controversial with its other members.

The emerging markets must deal with capital inflows and the task of developing their financial sectors to match the growth of their economies. The governments of these economies expect the IMF to contribute to the development of tools to control financial volatility. In response, the IMF has shifted its position on capital controls and now considers them as an instrument of macroprudential policy. More generally, these governments must decide how far to go in integrating their financial markets and institutions with global markets. These issues are relevant not just for the emerging markets but also for those developing economies that aspire to join them, and they will look to the IMF for guidance.

The IMF's ability to provide assistance to its members in meeting these challenges as well as the new crises that undoubtedly will occur is constrained by its own governance procedures. The basis of the post–Bretton Woods' stratification of the IMF's membership has disappeared, and the IMF must respond if it is to retain its newly won credibility. The IMF's member governments have begun to redistribute quota shares to reflect more accurately the growing size of its middle-income members, but many substantive issues remain. There are also aspects of the international monetary system that require reform if the reemergence of global imbalances and growing reserve holdings are to be avoided. The IMF can provide the means to avoid or at least minimize a recurrence of the global crisis, but in the end the IMF's principals must decide whether they will engage in collective decision making to achieve financial and economic stability. We will never again see universal fixed exchange rates and managed capital flows, but the formation of the Bretton Woods system – which we examine in the next chapter – provides a model of collaboration among governments that is still quite relevant.

2

Bretton Woods

The IMF is the IGO that has been entrusted with the responsibility of promoting the IPGs of international economic and financial stability. This chapter deals with the establishment of the IMF after World War II and its responsibilities within the Bretton Woods system that lasted from 1945 through 1973. In succeeding chapters we will contrast the record of the IMF's activities within this rule-based system with its actions during the post–Bretton Woods era.

The first section provides an account of the founding of the Bretton Woods system and the specific responsibilities of the IMF. The Allied victors of World War II established a new international monetary regime to prevent a repeat of the economic chaos of the 1930s. The system was based on fixed-but-adjustable exchange rates and the removal of restrictions on current account transactions. The IMF monitored the observance of its members of these commitments while providing credit to those with balance of payments disequilibria. The Bretton Woods system differed from the Gold Standard (1870–1914) in its reliance on controls on capital flows to provide members with the ability to use monetary policy to achieve full employment.

The second section describes the governance structure of the IMF, which was shaped by the United States, the postwar hegemonic power, and its West European allies. These countries devised a voting system based on economic size that allowed them to dominate the actions of the IMF and its policies. The new organization created lending programs that required members that borrowed from it to implement policy measures before credit was disbursed.

The IMF's economists developed economic models to analyze the determinants of balance of payments disequilibria and serve as the basis of the conditions attached to its lending programs. The third section provides an overview of these models and the macroeconomic policy conditions derived from them. The models placed the burden of adjustment to a deficit on the government borrowing from the IMF, regardless of its source.

The performance of the new system depended on the willingness of its principals to observe its rules, and the fourth section describes how this consensus broke down. The United States faced special constraints because of the use of the dollar as the reserve currency and the pledge of the United States to exchange gold for dollars held at central banks. But foreign monetary authorities became less willing to accept dollars once their holdings exceeded the amount of gold owned by the United States. The U.S. government, concerned about a wave of redemptions of dollars for gold, ended its gold conversion in 1971. The United States and the West Europeans sought to restore the system but could not achieve agreement, and the Bretton Woods system ended in 1973.

The last section reviews the record of the IMF during this era. The Bretton Woods system was an intermediate IGO that contributed to the economic growth of the 1950s and 1960s. The IMF served a valuable role by providing a mechanism to verify conformance with the obligations of the system and provide financial support to countries with disequilibria. But the continued operation of the system depended on the agreement of the IMF's principals to adhere to its rules. Once that willingness disappeared, the system was no longer viable.

2.1 New Order

The representatives of the forty-four nations who met at Bretton Woods in New Hampshire in 1944 sought to prevent the recurrence of the economic and financial instability of the interwar period. Attempts to reestablish the Gold Standard after World War I had been unsuccessful (Eichengreen 2008). Governments engaged in currency devaluations during the 1930s to mitigate the impact of the Great Depression and placed restrictions on capital flows in order to defend against what was seen as destabilizing speculation (League of Nations 1944). Moreover, protectionist policies became widespread and contributed to a decline in world trade. Debtor countries in Latin America that faced declines in the terms of trade for their exports of primary products defaulted on their debt, as did governments in Southern and Eastern Europe (Eichengreen 1991, Eichengreen and Fishlow 1998).

The chief architects of the new international monetary system were Harry Dexter White of the U.S. Treasury Department and John Maynard Keynes, who led the United Kingdom's delegation to the conference. They had begun negotiating their competing plans for the reconstruction of international monetary relations while the war was still being waged. Keynes proposed the establishment of a new international currency, the *bancor,* which would be administered by a global central bank and used by countries to settle their outstanding balances with each other. White, however, feared the inflationary consequences of a new source of international liquidity and insisted that the amount of credit available to countries be based on national deposits of gold and domestic currencies. The eventual agreement, which became the basis of the document signed at Bretton Woods, was largely based on White's proposal, an outcome consistent with the hegemonic position of the United States at that time (Boughton 1998, Eckes 1975, Moggridge 1992, Skidelsky 2000).

Under the Bretton Woods arrangements, central banks maintained fixed values for their currencies vis-à-vis gold or the U.S. dollar, while the United States stood ready to buy or sell gold to them at a fixed price of $35 an ounce. The dollar was used as the intervention currency, and central banks held their reserves in dollars as well as gold. A member government could change the par value of its currency to correct a "fundamental disequilibrium" (never defined) in the balance of payments after consultation with the IMF, and approval was supposed to be automatic if the adjustment did not exceed 10 percent. However, competitive "exchange alterations" were explicitly forbidden in the original Article IV of the IMF's Articles of Agreement.

The new system needed a monitor to verify compliance with the requirements of the new system, and the IMF was created to serve this purpose.[1] The Fund's Articles of Agreement listed several tasks for the IMF, including the promotion of international monetary cooperation, the facilitation of international trade, the promotion of exchange stability, and the establishment of a multilateral system of payments for current account transactions (Box 2.1). These were intermediate IPGs, designed to contribute to the "primary objectives of economic policy," which were listed as "the promotion and maintenance of high levels of employment and real income and ... the development of the productive resources of all members" (IMF 1993, Article I (i)).

---

[1]   The International Bank for Reconstruction and Development, also known as the World Bank, was also established at the conference.

Box 2.1. IMF Article of Agreement I

Purposes

The purposes of the International Monetary Fund are:

(i)   To promote international monetary cooperation through a permanent institution which provides the machinery for consultation and collaboration on international monetary problems.

(ii) To facilitate the expansion and balanced growth of international trade, and to contribute thereby to the promotion and maintenance of high levels of employment and real income and to the development of productive resources of all members as primary objectives of economic policy.

(iii) To promote exchange stability, to maintain orderly exchange arrangements among members, and to avoid competitive exchange rate depreciation.

(iv) To assist in the establishment of a multilateral system of payments in respect of current transactions between members and in the elimination of foreign exchange restrictions which hamper the growth of world trade.

(v)   To give confidence to members by making the general resources of the Fund temporarily available to them under adequate safeguards, thus providing them with opportunity to correct maladjustments in their balance of payments without resorting to measures destructive of national or international prosperity.

(vi) In accordance with the above, to shorten the duration and lessen the degree of disequilibrium in the international balances of members.

The Fund shall be guided in all its policies and decisions by the purposes set forth in this Article.

The IMF was also assigned the specific function of providing financial resources to member countries with "maladjustments in their balance of payments" in order "to shorten the duration and lessen the degree of disequilibrium in the international balances of payments" (IMF 1993, Article I (v) and (vi)). The availability of official credit would allow countries to avoid "measures destructive of national or international prosperity" without depending on potentially volatile private capital flows. Obstfeld and Taylor

(2004: 37) point out that "the IMF's founders viewed its lending capability as primarily a substitute for, not a complement to, private capital inflows."

The Bretton Woods planners also sought to promote the resumption of international trade, and Article VIII of the IMF's Articles of Agreement prohibits restrictions on current account payments. A member could delay accepting the responsibilities of Article VIII through a transitional arrangement, which is permitted via Article XIV. On the other hand, governments were expected to control short-term capital flows, which had frustrated the prewar attempts of domestic policy makers to stabilize their economies. Article VI forbade the use of the Fund's resources to meet an outflow of capital and gave the IMF the authority to request a member to utilize capital controls to prevent such usage.[2]

The Bretton Woods arrangements represented a consistent response to the "impossible trinity," which limits the independence of policy making. A government can only choose two of the following features of a monetary system: a fixed exchange rate, unregulated capital flows, and/or control of the domestic money supply.[3] Under the gold standard, central banks had been committed to buying or selling gold at a fixed price, which tied together the values of the different currencies. Capital flows were unconstrained, and the United Kingdom financed growth in the emerging markets of that era, including the United States. To maintain the system, governments relinquished the use of monetary policy to achieve domestic goals such as full employment.

The new system provided an alternative to the Gold Standard: it replaced capital market integration with capital controls and allowed governments to use monetary policies to tame business cycles. Ruggie (1982), in explaining the differences in the postwar system from its predecessors, coined the term "embedded liberalism" and claimed that "unlike the liberalism of the gold standard and free trade, its multilateralism would be predicated upon domestic internationalism" (Ruggie 1982: 393). Ruggie (1992: 592) also pointed out that "the United States after World War II sought to project the experience of the New Deal regulatory state into the international arena." The Roosevelt administration established new government agencies, such as the Securities and Exchange Commission and the Federal Deposit Insurance Corporation, to promote domestic recovery from the Great Depression. The establishment of the IMF to oversee the new international

---

[2]   However, Article VI never served as a check on the IMF's ability to lend, since a capital account disturbance will have an impact on the current account (Boughton 2001a).

[3]   This relationship is derived from the Mundell-Fleming model. See the following discussion for the background of the model.

system and facilitate its operation was consistent with this institutional template, as well as Keynes's belief in the need for explicit management of the global economy to ensure stability (Vines 2003).

One key difference between the Gold Standard and the Bretton Woods system lay in their respective treatments of countries with balance of payments surpluses. The gold flows of the Gold Standard triggered an increase in spending in these countries, which reduced the imbalance. The IMF's Articles of Agreement contained a "scarce currency" clause, Article VII (3), which allowed members to impose controls on transactions with countries with chronic surpluses, but it lacked the obligatory response of the Gold Standard. The policy was designed to deal with a postwar shortage of dollars but was never invoked because the shortage became a glut.

2.2 Administrative Arrangements

The Fund began its operations in 1946, with forty members and an aggregate quota of $7.8 billion. The governance of the new organization was clearly dominated by the victors of World War II. The headquarters of the IMF were located in the United States at the insistence of its government, while the Europeans chose the new organization's chief administrative officer, its managing director – a tradition that has remained in place until the present day.[4] Camille Gutt of Belgium was appointed the first managing director and was followed in that position in subsequent years by other Western Europeans (Table A.1). The placement of the IMF in Washington, D.C., marked the establishment of a "Washington Hub" consisting of the IMF, the World Bank, other IGOs, and various nongovernmental organizations that wielded a powerful influence on international economic issues.

Each member of the IMF was assigned a quota based on the country's economic size and openness. The quotas are used to determine the size of a member's subscription to the Fund, its voting power in the IMF's weighted voting arrangements, and the amount of credit that the country can receive. A member paid one-quarter of its quota to the IMF in the form of gold, and the remainder in its domestic currency. After the passage of the Second Amendment to the Articles of Agreement in 1978 (Chapter 3), gold was replaced by widely used currencies such as the dollar and later

---

[4]   The United States, in turn, claimed the privilege of naming the head of the World Bank. In addition, the deputy managing director of the IMF was a U.S. citizen after that position was established in 1949. In 1994 three additional deputy positions were created, but the first deputy managing director is a citizen of the United States.

the *euro*. The actual calculation and assignments of the national quotas at the time when the IMF was founded were undertaken by the U.S. Treasury Department and reflected political decisions as much as objective criteria (Mikesell 1994).

While overall control of the IMF is vested in a Board of Governors with representation from each member, the daily operations of the IMF are supervised by an Executive Board. In the original configuration of the board, the five countries with the largest quotas appointed their own executive directors, while the remaining nations were grouped into constituencies that choose directors.[5] The managing director acts as chairman of the board but does not have a vote. Voting power is based on both a member's quota and its basic votes, which are allocated evenly among the members. The dominant share of voting power held by the United States fell over time as the number of member countries rose, but it retained a preponderant proportion of the total votes (Figure A.1). A stipulation that major changes could only be passed with an 85 percent majority effectively gave the United States a veto.

The IMF functioned as a type of credit union for its members: nations paid their quotas so that they could draw upon the common resources of the IMF's General Resource Account when they faced a crisis situation (Kenen 1986). A member that borrows from the IMF purchases reserve assets with its own currency; consequently, the IMF's holdings of reserve assets fall while its holdings of the member's currency rise. When the country repays the credit, it buys back its own currency with a reserve currency, and the IMF's holdings return to their original levels. Since members of all income levels borrowed from the IMF, it was in their collective interest to ensure that the Fund had adequate financial resources.

During the early years of the IMF's existence, there were debates over whether the Fund could limit the amount of borrowing of its members or impose conditions. A compromise solution emerged in the early 1950s that has prevailed with some modifications to the current day. A country could draw the first 25 percent of its quota (called the "gold tranche" and later renamed the "reserve tranche") without restrictions (Dell 1981). However, to receive larger amounts a government needs to present a plan of policy measures that will remedy the imbalance in the external sector.

These conditions are contained in a Letter of Intent signed by government officials of the borrowing country. The IMF monitors the country's implementation of the agreed-on policies through the use of prior

---

[5] In recent years China, Russia, and Saudi Arabia have also appointed their own executive directors.

actions, quantitative performance criteria, and structural benchmarks (Fritz-Krockow and Ramlogan 2007). Prior actions are policy measures to be taken before an agreement is approved or a review completed. Performance criteria are measurable variables or conditions that must be met, while the structural benchmarks are treated as markers or indicators to assess progress. The IMF only disburses credit if the performance criteria are met, a practice known as "conditionality." If the conditions are not met and there are no extenuating circumstances, then the program can be suspended. The IMF defends the use of conditionality as necessary to ensure the repayment of the loan extended to a borrowing nation.

The lending programs of these years were Stand-By Arrangements (SBAs) and disbursed credit over a one-year period. Many of these early programs were precautionary: that is, they were established to ensure a country's access to credit if needed but never actually used. There was a sliding fee scale, based on the duration of a drawing and the amount of a country's quota borrowed (Horsefield *et al.* 1969). The number of lending arrangements rose as the membership expanded (Figure A.2).

The recognition of an economy as a "weaker link" in the global economy occurred when a balance of payments crisis occurred and the IMF lent to a member. While the United States and Western European nations controlled the governance of the IMF during the Bretton Woods era, there was no systemic stratification of Fund membership based on whether a country had borrowed from the IMF. Members of all income levels borrowed from the IMF. The United Kingdom, for example, obtained Stand-By Arrangements in 1964, 1967, 1969, and then again in 1975 and 1977.[6]

2.3 Adjustment versus Finance

Under fixed exchange rates, a deficit in the balance of payments forces a central bank either to use its foreign exchange reserves to maintain the fixed exchange rate (financing the shock) or to adopt policies to reestablish balance of payments equilibrium (adjustment) (Bird 1980, Bryant 2003). Adjustment to a negative shock to the balance of payments by lowering domestic expenditures or devaluing the currency imposes costs on the residents of an economy in terms of a lower living standard. Financing the shock incurs an opportunity cost from running down the central bank's stock of

---

[6] The United Kingdom had also entered into arrangements during the 1950s and early 1960s but did not draw upon them.

foreign reserves or borrowing foreign exchange. Moreover, financing a permanent shock only delays the inevitable; eventually the country will run out of reserves and then it must make the necessary adjustments. On the other hand, if a shock is temporary, then full adjustment may impose unnecessary hardship. Therefore, a mix of the two is often optimal.

When a country finances all or part of a deficit, it first draws upon its own reserves. If it does not possess sufficient foreign currency, it can obtain more by borrowing either from international banks or from an IFI, usually the IMF. Borrowing from the private banks carries explicit borrowing costs, and the costs may escalate over time if there is a floating interest rate on the loan. In the case of a severe balance of payments disequilibrium, the private market may not be willing to lend to the country on any terms. The IMF, on the other hand, can serve as a lender of last resort but will insist that the country implement adjustment policies.

If the country engages in adjustment, then it must choose between expenditure-reduction and expenditure-switching policies. The former includes the use of contractionary monetary and fiscal policies to lower the domestic demand for imported goods. Expenditure-reducing policies have the undesirable side effects of lowering output and raising unemployment. Moreover, the brunt of the cutback in private domestic spending often falls on investment expenditures, which has negative long-term consequences for long-term growth.

Expenditure-switching policies, on the other hand, attempt to keep total output at the full-employment level but change its composition from foreign to domestic goods. This is accomplished through depreciations of the exchange rate and other measures, such as export subsidies or import tariffs, to encourage exports while discouraging imports. One adverse effect of this type of policy is its impact on inflation. The prices of domestic goods may rise in response to the higher prices of imported intermediate goods. Workers can demand higher wages to pay the higher costs of imports they consume, pushing prices up further.

Balance of payments deficits, therefore, involve difficult decisions for a government. First, it must choose between financing or adjusting to a deficit. If it chooses the latter, it must decide between expenditure-reducing or expenditure-switching policies. Each of these choices involves benefits and costs, which must be balanced against each other. Expenditure-switching and reduction are part of the policies that accompany IMF-sponsored programs. By providing foreign exchange, the IMF allows a country more time to formulate and implement the proper adjustment policies.

During the 1950s, the Fund's economists developed open-economy macroeconomic models to aid them in formulating appropriate stabilization policies.[7] The model that served as the economics profession's standard open-economy model for many decades, the Mundell-Fleming model, was developed while one of its authors, Marcus Fleming (Fleming 1962), was a member of the Research Department of the IMF in the early 1960s (Boughton 2003). In addition, Robert Mundell (Mundell 1963) also joined the IMF at this time. However, it appears that their work was done independently of each other, and Mundell had begun his analysis before he went to work for the Fund. The synthesis of their work, the Mundell-Fleming model, analyzes the relative effectiveness of macroeconomic policies under different exchange rate and capital account regimes.

Financial programming was developed at the IMF by Jacques R. Polak (1957, 1998), who served as director of the Research Department and later on the Executive Board. The model links balance of payments deficits under fixed exchange rates to domestic monetary policy (Box 2.2).[8] It is based on two behavioral equations (the demand for money and import demand), two identities (the supply of money and the balance of payments), and an equilibrium condition (money market equilibrium). Capital flows were assumed to be fixed in the short run and therefore could not accommodate an increase in a current account deficit. The model's simplicity was an asset in the postwar era, when data limitations were a constraint on policy formulation.[9]

Box 2.2. Financial Programming

The demand for money is based on national income:

$$M^D = k\Delta Y \tag{2.1}$$

where M^D is the demand for money, k is the inverse of the income velocity of money, and Y is national income.

Changes in the supply of money are based on the central bank's holdings of foreign reserves and domestic credit assets:

$$\Delta M^S = \Delta FR + \Delta DC \tag{2.2}$$

---

[7] De Vries (1987) reviews the intellectual history of these models.
[8] Agénor (2004) and IMF (1987) provide presentations of the model.
[9] Easterly (2006), however, undertook an empirical analysis of financial programming that did not find evidence in support of many of the assumptions of the model.

where M^S is the supply of money, FR represents the central bank's holdings of foreign reserves and DC its holdings of domestic credit assets, and the money multiplier is assumed to equal 1. Equilibrium in the money market prevails when the demand and supply of money are equal:

$$\Delta M^D = \Delta M^S \qquad (2.3)$$

The demand for imports depends on national income:

$$\Delta IM = m\Delta Y \qquad (2.4)$$

where IM represents imports and m is the marginal propensity to import;

The balance of payments includes the current account and the capital account as well as changes in the central bank's holdings of foreign reserves:

$$BP = (X - M) + K - \Delta FR = 0 \qquad (2.5)$$

where BP is the balance of payments, X is exports, X – M is the current account, and K is the capital account. The change in foreign reserves is equal to the current and capital accounts, with exports and the capital account exogenous:

$$\Delta FR = (\overline{X} - IM) + \overline{K} \qquad (2.6)$$

By substituting 2.1 into 2.6, the model can be used to express the determinants of changes in the central bank's holdings of foreign reserves:

$$\Delta FR = k\Delta Y \quad \Delta DC \qquad (2.7)$$

Changes in foreign reserves in the long run reflect any imbalance between the demand for money and the change in the central bank's domestic credit assets. The model can also be used to establish ceilings on the increase in the domestic credit assets. If there are a target level for the change in foreign reserves, ΔFR^*, and a projected change in national income, ΔY^P, then the maximum allowable change in domestic credit, ΔDC, can be calculated:

$$\Delta DC = k \, \Delta Y^P - \Delta FR^* \, (2.8) \qquad (2.8)$$

Sources: Agénor (2004), Polak (1957, 1998).

In the model, a rise in the central bank's holdings of domestic credit leads to a rise in national income and therefore imports. The immediate results are a current account deficit and a loss of reserves. In the long run, the change in domestic credit is completely offset by the change in foreign reserves. The solution to a balance of payments disequilibrium, therefore, lies in cutting back the growth of domestic credit. This is often tied to the government's fiscal position, since in many countries a fiscal deficit will be financed by the central bank, so that an expansionary fiscal policy is accompanied by an expansionary monetary policy.

The other model developed at the IMF is the absorption model, which links the balance of payments to domestic demand and output (Alexander 1952). In this model, the current account (X – M) reflects the difference between domestic output (Y) and the domestic demand for goods and services, absorption (C + I + G): a surplus is recorded when output is higher than demand, and a deficit in the opposite situation.

$$Y - (C + I + G) = X - M$$

This approach focuses more directly on fiscal policy, since an increase in government spending leads to an increase in absorption, and therefore a current account deficit. The emphasis on fiscal policies led to the claim that the letters IMF actually stand for "It's Mostly Fiscal."

IMF-designed policies were based on these models. Fund programs usually included a tightening of monetary and fiscal policies in order to reduce total expenditures, and performance criteria included limits on domestic credit expansion and government borrowing. In addition, the IMF could also recommend a depreciation of the exchange rate in order to switch expenditures to domestic goods and stimulate exports. The IMF's policy analysis was compatible with mainstream economic theory of this era. Cooper (1983: 571), summarizing the discussion of a conference devoted to IMF conditionality, suggested that almost any group of economists who were asked to devise an economic adjustment program for a country would come up with a policy program that "would not differ greatly from a typical IMF program."

However, the use of these models to devise policies assumed that the burden of dealing with a disequilibrium rested with the domestic government, regardless of the source of the imbalance. Countries that faced fluctuations in their terms of trade or declines in imports due to a cyclical contraction in their trading partners were expected to adopt measures to lower domestic spending as much as those with governments that had engaged in expansionary policies. Barnett and Finnemore (2004: 56) point out that the models "led Fund officials to become more concerned with the workings of domestic economies than the Bretton Woods founders would have anticipated." The subordination of the IMF to its principals was partially reversed when the IMF could decide whether or not to disburse credit to a borrowing nation.

In retrospect, the models have a limited treatment of financial variables. Money is the only domestic asset, and reserve flows equilibrate the demand and supply of money. International capital flows are fixed in the model by government controls. The lack of emphasis on financial variables is consistent with both the macroeconomic theories of the 1950s and 1960s, as well as the government regulation of financial markets and institutions in those periods. The eventual development of financial markets and the decontrol of capital accounts would require more sophisticated treatment of financial flows.

2.4 Collapse of Bretton Woods

While 1946 marked the initiation of the IMF's operations, the beginning of the Bretton Woods system is often assigned to the year 1959, when many European nations accepted the obligation of Article VIII to allow the convertibility of their currencies for current account transactions. Other countries followed, and by 1961 two-thirds of the IMF's membership allowed their residents to use foreign currencies for the purpose of current account transactions (James 1996). But while the Bretton Woods system worked reasonably well through the 1960s, it was based on an unstable foundation.[10]

Foreign central banks were willing to hold their reserves in dollars as long as the U.S. government would exchange these for gold. However, the postwar shortage of dollars became a glut during the 1950s as U.S. balance of payments surpluses became deficits. By the mid-1960s, the holdings of dollars in foreign central banks exceeded the value of the U.S. gold holdings, and the gold coverage (the value of the U.S. holdings of gold as a proportion of its liabilities to foreign central banks) continued to decline for the rest of the decade. This situation was known as the Triffin dilemma, named after the economist Robert Triffin, who first drew attention to it.

The continuing supply of dollars was criticized by other countries, particularly those in Western Europe, as an abuse by the United States of its

---

[10] Bordo (1993), Eichengreen (2008), James (1996), and Solomon (1982) offer accounts of this period, while the IMF's historians, Horsefield *et al.* (1969) and De Vries (1976), provide the Fund's perspective.

special position within the Bretton Woods system. The French in particular sought to return to the use of gold as the primary reserve medium. In an attempt to find an acceptable compromise, the U.S. government supported a proposal to create a new reserve asset that would be issued through the IMF, Special Drawing Rights (SDRs). In 1968 the IMF's members approved the use of the SDR, and the First Amendment to the Articles of Agreement was accepted the following year. However, a number of limitations were placed on the use of the SDR, including a restriction that it could only be held by governments and not private holders. The initial allocations of SDRs took place during 1970–2, but the new reserve asset did not gain acceptance as an alternative to the dollar.

The dispute over the use of the dollar as a reserve currency produced a political stalemate. The United States was not willing to subordinate its domestic policy goals in order to provide stability to the global monetary system, and no other country was in a position to take its place. International tensions among governments increased as the United States was blamed for exporting inflation. In August 1971, President Richard Nixon unilaterally ended the commitment of the United States to exchange gold for the dollar reserves of central banks. The United States and the major European nations subsequently undertook negotiations to realign their currencies, but the political will to negotiate a revised version of the Bretton Woods system was missing, and attempts to revive the system ended in failure in 1973.

The responsibility for the collapse of Bretton Woods is usually placed on the United States for not accepting the obligations of maintaining gold convertibility. However, the system was becoming unstable for other reasons. International capital flows were beginning to emerge after their postwar interruption (Chapter 3). A generation had passed since the depression, and capital transactions were no longer viewed as destabilizing. But the emergence of private financial flows violated the Bretton Woods solution to the constraint of the impossible trinity. A fixed exchange rate system was incompatible with the increasing movement toward capital movements and national autonomy over macroeconomic policies (James 1996). The system may have continued to be viable for some period if the United States had attempted to live within the rules, but other developments were precipitating the end of the rule-based system.

2.5 IMF and Bretton Woods: Appraisal

The years of the Bretton Woods system are generally viewed as an era of growth and stability, a "golden age of capitalism." Living standards rose in

Western Europe, North America, and Australia, while many developing economies also experienced high rates of economic growth. Increases in per-capita income exceeded not only those of the pre–World War II era but those of the Gold Standard as well. It was also a period of relative financial stability, with a total of thirty-eight banking, currency, and twin crises occurring in industrial countries and emerging markets during the period of 1945–71 (Bordo and Eichengreen 2003), a decline from the forty-nine crises of the 1919–39 period.[11] If the objective of the Bretton Wood system was to achieve financial and economic stability, then its planners were successful.

How much credit does the IMF deserve for this record? Dominguez (1993) pointed out that while the Fund was not able to preserve the par value system, it was successful at the task of collecting and disseminating information. She drew the conclusion that "evidence suggests that international organizations can effectively promote cooperation by providing their members with a credible monitoring technology" (Dominguez 1993: 392). Similarly, Eichengreen (1993: 643) concluded that "The Fund surely facilitated efforts to monitor the actions of the smaller players and thereby helped minimize the free-rider problems that otherwise might have resulted from the large-numbers problem."

This view of the IMF's role is consistent with Martin's (1992) analysis of the role of international organizations in situations that require strong surveillance. An active organization was needed to monitor compliance with the agreement to adhere to the common exchange rate regime, since there was an incentive to devalue in the event of a balance of payments deficit. However, countries did not always obtain Fund approval before they instituted changes in their exchange rate pegs. Finch (1989: 5) pointed out that "in fact decisions were made on national authority and the IMF Executive Board had little choice but to rubber-stamp approval on short notice – usually over a weekend – on the basis of hastily prepared staff papers." The Executive Board had no source of authority to overturn a policy unless IMF lending was involved.

The IMF's own historian claimed that "the major contribution of the Fund was to facilitate among its members the development of harmonious cooperation on monetary and fiscal policies" (De Vries 1985: 93). The cooperation, however, was achieved through the indirect means of adhering to

---

[11] The crises of the Bretton Woods era were virtually all currency crises, with only one twin crisis recorded by Bordo and Eichengreen (2003). The decline in banking crises reflected domestic regulation of this sector as well as controls on capital flows.

the rules of Bretton Woods. Kahler (1995: 49) noted that "the idea of central policy coordination bargains was not part of the Bretton Woods scheme." Similarly, Guitián (1992: 5) explained the basis of this coordination:

> It is not coordination based on continuous bargaining among countries; rather, it is coordination based on their a priori willingness to adhere to mutually agreed norms of behavior and to constrain their domestic policies to the discipline imposed by those norms.

The Bretton Woods system, therefore, served as an intermediate IPG in support of financial and economic stability. The IMF facilitated its operations by supervising national adherence to its standards. Moreover, the Fund's lending gave member governments the opportunity to implement measures to restore balance of payments equilibrium without invoking measures with negative repercussions for other nations. While individual nations were forced to turn to the IMF for emergency lending, the control of capital flows contributed to the absence of global financial crises.

There were limits on the Fund's powers of oversight, however. Dornbusch (1993) observed that the IMF did not have a leading role in developing new international monetary policies and institutions. He raised the question of why the Fund did not take on this task and after speculating that it may have been due to the proximity of the U.S. Treasury, added, "Another hypothesis is that, as an organization, the Fund declines to be anything but the arm of its constituency and certainly rejects the notion that it was invented to push ahead international financial integration" (Dornbusch 1993: 103).

This opinion is consistent with the view of the IMF as an agent that has latitude in operational matters but is constrained by its members in formulating new policies. The rules of the system were established at Bretton Woods essentially by the United States, and subsequently modified and adapted to particular circumstances. But when the time came to rewrite the rules, the principals who had the power to change the system chose to deal directly with each other.

3

Transitions

The end of the universal system of fixed exchange rates and capital controls gave governments the ability to choose new responses to the "impossible trinity" in the post–Bretton Woods era. This chapter describes the institutional arrangements that arose as new exchange rate arrangements and capital account regimes were adopted and the impact of these choices on the IMF. The IMF's revised duties in the post–Bretton Woods period were vaguely defined, and it was no longer the only IGO that dealt with economic and financial issues.

The IMF's dominant members led the negotiations over the revision of the IMF's Article of Agreement IV. The revised article, summarized in the first section, gave the membership the freedom to choose the exchange rate arrangement they found most suitable for their economies. This choice was constrained, however, by new obligations, and the IMF was given the responsibility to oversee compliance with these through its surveillance operations. However, the nature of its oversight powers was left ambiguous.

The growth of private capital flows occurred with much less planning or oversight. The second section explains how central bankers of the advanced economies where the major financial markets were located set up new organizational structures based at the Bank for International Settlements to monitor capital flows, exchange information, and discuss regulatory responses. But there was no consensus among the IMF's membership regarding the deregulation of capital accounts, and the IMF itself played no role in these developments.

The IMF had a minor role in the responses to the oil price shocks of the 1970s, which is examined in the third section. The revenues of the oil exporting nations were often deposited in private banks in Europe and the United States. The deposits were then lent to oil-importing developing economies, as well as oil exporters such as Mexico where spending outstripped their revenues. The IMF set up Oil Facilities for members with large import bills and established special arrangements for its poorer members. But the private recycling of oil revenues dwarfed the IMF's actions in this area.

The emerging divisions among the IMF's members resulted in the establishment of organizations with smaller memberships and more homogeneous policies, and these are described in the fourth section. The United States organized the G7 meetings to give the leaders of the largest economies opportunities to hold regular discussions and to provide direction for the international economy, including the work of the IMF. Organizations of upper-income nations such as the Organization for Economic Co-operation and Development also dealt with economic issues. The middle- and low-income nations, frustrated by their exclusion from these groups, responded by establishing their own bodies.

By the end of the 1970s, nations no longer subscribed to a common understanding of how the world economy should function. There were agreements in some areas, such as the need to avoid current account restrictions, but governments chose different configurations of exchange rate and capital account arrangements. The last section points out that the need for the IMF seemed to have diminished as other organizations offered forums to coordinate governmental actions in areas of common concern, while private capital markets provided funds to countries that sought to finance balance of payments disequilibria.

3.1 New Responsibilities

In 1972, the IMF's Board of Governors established a special committee, the Ad Hoc Committee of the Board of Governors on Reform of the International Monetary System and Related Issues, better known as the "Committee of Twenty," to address the reform of the international monetary system.[1] But the committee's deliberations were overshadowed by the oil price increases that occurred in 1973, and the committee ended its deliberations in 1974 without any consensus on whether a new fixed exchange rate regime should be established.

While the interim committee continued the work of its predecessor, the countries with dominant positions in the IMF met to plan new monetary arrangements. The United States retained its hegemonic status among the

---

[1] The size of the committee was based on the twenty seats that constituted the Fund's Executive Director Board at that time.

non-Communist countries, but the growth of the West European nations in the post–World War II era forced it to negotiate the framework of a new international regime with their governments. Negotiators from France and the United States agreed on a compromise proposal that included elements that each side thought essential (De Vries 1985). The Fund's interim committee, meeting in Jamaica in 1976, accepted this proposal as the basis of the Second Amendment to the IMF's Articles of Agreement. The revised Article IV attained the required threshold approval of the Fund's total voting power in April 1978.

The amended article represented a significant departure from past practices. The first section (Box 3.1) lists the general obligations of the members, which include collaboration with the Fund and other members "to assure orderly exchange arrangements and to promote a stable system of exchange rates." A stable system, however, is not the same as a stable rate. The wording of the section was a product of the compromise between the United States and France and emphasized the need for both stable domestic economic policies (the U.S. position) and exchange rate policies consistent with the obligations of members (the French position).

Section 2 of the revised article gives members the latitude to adopt any exchange arrangement consistent with their obligations under the previous section. The section specifically mentions fixed rate and cooperative agreements but also recognizes "other exchange arrangements of a member's choice." The section allows the Fund's members to choose a new general arrangement at a future date, but governments could retain the exchange rate regime they thought best-suited for their economies. Similarly, the article's fourth section allows for the resumption of a "widespread system of exchange rate arrangements based on stable but adjustable par values." However, such a move needs the approval of an 85 percent voting majority, thus effectively granting the United States a veto over such an arrangement. In addition, a member could fix its currency in terms of SDRs or any other member's currency, but not gold, which was removed from its place as one of the IMF's reserve assets.

In the article's third section, the IMF is assigned the task of ensuring that the members fulfill their responsibilities: "The Fund shall oversee the international monetary system in order to ensure its effective operation, and shall oversee the compliance of each member with its obligations under Section 1 of this Article." The section specifically gives the IMF the right to exercise "firm surveillance over the exchange rate policies of members" and requires the members to provide the IMF with the information

---

Box 3.1. IMF's Revised Article of Agreement IV

Obligations Regarding Exchange Arrangements

Section 1. General obligations of members

Recognizing that the essential purpose of the international monetary system is to provide a framework that facilitates the exchange of goods, services, and capital among countries, and that sustains sound economic growth, and that a principal objective is the continuing development of the orderly underlying conditions that are necessary for financial and economic stability, each member undertakes to collaborate with the Fund and other members to assure orderly exchange arrangements and to promote a stable system of exchange rates. In particular, each member shall:

(i)   endeavor to direct its economic and financial policies toward the objective of fostering orderly economic growth with reasonable price stability, with due regard to its circumstances;

(ii) seek to promote stability by fostering orderly underlying economic and financial conditions and a monetary system that does not tend to produce erratic disruptions;

(iii) avoid manipulating exchange rates or the international monetary system in order to prevent effective balance of payments adjustment or to gain an unfair competitive advantage over other members; and

(iv) follow exchange policies compatible with the undertakings under this Section.

---

it needs to carry out this duty, as well as meeting with the Fund to discuss these policies. Previously, only countries that had not accepted Article VIII's provision for current account convertibility were required to consult the IMF.

On one level, this responsibility was an extension of the IMF's activities under Bretton Woods, when it had supervised compliance with the requirements of the fixed exchange rate regime. The IMF could extend the informational role it had exercised then to accommodate the new rules. However, there were limitations on the Fund's ability to carry out this task. There was no clear explication of which national economic policies were *not* consistent with the obligations listed in the article's first section, although the grant of authority in the third section stated that the IMF would "adopt specific principles for the guidance of all members with respect to those policies."

Moreover, if the IMF found a country not in compliance with its obligations under the revised article, nothing in the article indicated how the IMF should respond. If the IMF was not disbursing credit to a government through a lending arrangement, it had no powers over its sovereign members. James (1996: 273) claimed that "the provisions of Article IV with regard to exchange rate policy represented more of a pious code filled with a hope of liberalization than a serious attempt to change countries' policies by specific intervention on the part of the Fund."

The IMF's Legal Department (2006a: 3) later acknowledged in a candid admission that the ambiguities in the wording and interpretation of the article reflected the divisions among the principals who negotiated it:

The substance of Article IV was effectively negotiated by a small group of members outside the Executive Board and represented a delicate political compromise among those members. When the text was presented to the Executive Board by these members, it was generally understood that the scope for substantive change was very limited, notwithstanding the fact that a number of Executive Directors – and staff – expressed concern regarding the vagueness and ambiguity of its terms.

The IMF sought to address the ambiguity regarding exchange rate policies in 1977 when the Executive Board issued its *Decision on Surveillance over Exchange Rate Policies* (IMF 1977), which included "Principles for the Guidance of Members' Exchange Rate Policies." The first of these stated that "a member shall avoid manipulating exchange rates or the international monetary system in order to prevent effective balance of payments adjustment or to gain an unfair competitive advantage over other members" – wording almost identical to that which appeared in the first section of the new Article IV. The second principle asserted that a member should intervene in the exchange market "to counter disorderly conditions," while the last principle added that such intervention should take into account the interests of other members. The board did not have enough experience with the new exchange rate arrangements to provide a comprehensive list of indicators that would signal whether a member was abiding with the principles and allowed itself discretion in its reviews. The board committed itself to biennial reviews of this decision, but it would take thirty years before a new set of guidelines were issued, and this revision would result in a rift between the IMF and China (Chapter 10).

The IMF, then, emerged from the remains of the Bretton Woods system in an uncertain position. The IMF's role as the guardian of a fixed exchange rate system had been replaced with the responsibilities of surveillance. But the description of the policies it was to monitor was imprecise, as were its powers to induce members to comply with the Fund's view of what was needed to achieve economic and financial stability (Lombardi and Woods 2008). The IMF was still nominally the global economy's emergency lender, but the prevalence and nature of balance of payments disequilibria in a world of mixed exchange rate regimes were unknown.

These ambiguities reflected a fundamental disagreement among the member nations regarding the future of international monetary affairs, and whether they would be guided by a rules-based system or a regime of discretionary behavior by governments. The IMF, as an agent with its own agenda, could seek to use this divergence to establish new roles for itself. But it would need to establish that it could provide a service that no other private or public organization could serve, and its ability to do that was constrained by external circumstances as well as the policy preferences of its members.

3.2 Euromarkets

While the choice of an alternative to Bretton Woods' fixed exchange rate regime was widely debated, the status of controls on capital flows was handled on an ad hoc basis in response to changes in global finance. International capital transactions had never totally ceased under Bretton Woods, although they were sometimes hidden under the "errors and omissions" component of the balance of payments. After the lifting in 1958 of exchange controls in European nations for current account transactions, the use of dollar balances for business dealings became more common.

Eurodollars were dollar-denominated deposits held at banks outside the United States (including the foreign branches of U.S. banks). A transnational market, where these deposits could be lent out, emerged in London and became known as the Euromarket (Rolfe and Burtle 1973, Sampson 1981). The government of the United Kingdom, hoping to reestablish London as an international finance center, encouraged the development of this market. The U.S. government supported the activities of U.S. banks there, since their branches could pay a higher return than they could at home, which encouraged foreigners to hold onto dollars (Rajan and Zingales 2003).

The Euromarkets recorded a boost in activity in 1963 when the U.S. government began to tax foreign borrowing within its borders, driving borrowers to look elsewhere for credit. This movement was reinforced by restraints on the foreign lending operations of U.S. banks, which were introduced on a voluntary basis in 1965 and made compulsory in 1968. Private firms and governments, including those of developing economies, discovered that they could raise funds in the Euromarket through Eurodollar bank loans. Over time, the loans were denominated in other currencies, such as the West German mark, and participating banks included institutions from all over the globe; nonetheless, the markets continued to be called the Euromarkets.

The banks that participated in this market initially existed in a regulatory limbo, with no clear line of supervisory authority over them. The central bankers of the Group of Ten (G10) countries (Section 3.4) had been meeting at the Bank for International Settlements (BIS) since the 1960s and in 1971 formed a Eurocurrency Standing Committee to monitor the expansion of the Eurocurrency market.[2] Its initial focus was the macroeconomic consequences of the Euromarkets (Johnson and Abrams 1983). In 1974, however, concerns about the stability of these markets arose in the wake of bank failures in Germany and the United States, and the Committee on Banking Regulations and Supervisory Practices, based at the BIS at Basel, was established.

In 1975, this committee, which became known as the Basel Committee on Banking Supervision (BCBS), issued a concordat with basic principles for the supervision of the activities of multinational banks. The Concordat stated that the supervision of foreign banks should be the joint responsibility of the regulators of the home country where a bank's head office was located and the host country where the foreign branches were set up. Subsequent revisions and extensions of these guidelines shifted more responsibility for overseeing the consolidated activities of the banks to the regulators of the home country and recommended that the banks provide consolidated statements of their activities (Kapstein 1994, Wood 2005).

No consensus had emerged in the pre-Jamaica discussions regarding the use of controls on capital movements. Many governments were concerned about the impact of capital flows on their ability to conduct macroeconomic policies, and the Committee of Twenty had established a technical group to explore the impact of disequilibrating capital flows and measures to counteract them (Lamfalussy 1981). The group reported that such flows were likely to become more frequent as the global economy grew and endorsed the use of regulatory mechanisms to contain them. However, the group also found that controls were not totally effective and could hinder constructive capital movements. There was no agreement in favor of changing the status

[2] In 1999 the committee was renamed the Committee on the Global Financial System.

quo, and Article VI of the IMF's Articles of Agreement, which allowed controls, remained intact. Lamfalussy (1981: 201) summarized the status quo at this time: "The end of the Bretton Woods par value system coincided with what may be considered to have been a reaffirmation by the membership of the Fund of the broad philosophy about capital controls embodied in Article VI of the Fund agreement."

However, the first section of the revised Article IV states "that the purpose of the international monetary system is to provide a framework that facilitates the exchange of goods, services, and capital among countries." This implies that capital flows are not only permissible, but are an integral part of the international economy. This clause would be cited in 1997 to justify proposed Fund oversight of capital account practices (Chapter 5).

While discussions regarding international capital flows were taking place, individual countries were taking advantage of the breakdown of the Bretton Woods system to make their own decisions regarding the use of capital regulations (Abdelal 2007). The United States abandoned its controls in 1974 and was followed by the United Kingdom in 1979 and West Germany, Japan, and Switzerland in 1980. International capital movements grew in size as the Bretton Woods consensus over capital regulations came to an end.

The establishment of the BCBS and the passage of the Concordat marked the beginnings of the creation of an institutional structure for the regulation of the international financial markets. Decisions on these arrangements, however, were made by the countries where the major international banks were located and reflected the domination of the global capital markets by the advanced economies. Moreover, individual governments were undertaking capital decontrol with little, if any, international consultation. The IMF was not directly involved in either the movement to capital account deregulation in the advanced economies or the establishment of cross-border policies to govern the growing international movement of capital. This would be a significant gap in the scope of the IMF's newly assigned surveillance activities.

3.3 Recycling

Another event that contributed to the rise in international financial capital flows occurred in 1973 when the Organization of Petroleum Exporting Countries (OPEC) cartel quadrupled the price of oil. The oil-exporting nations recorded significant surpluses in their current accounts that were matched by deficits in the balance of payments of the oil-importing nations.

Table 3.1. *Oil Exporters' Revenues*

Period	Percent of Own GDP	Percent of World GDP
1973–1976	48%	1.5%
1978–1981	31%	1.4%
2002–2005	40%	1.0%

Note: Ratios are relative to GDP in first year of each period
Source: Nsouli (2006).

In 1974, for example, the aggregate current account surplus of the major oil exporters amounted to $68 billion, which equaled one-third of their GDP. The surplus was offset by deficits in the industrial countries of $31 billion, which represented 0.8 percent of their GDP, and $34 billion in the oil-importing developing nations, which equaled 10.5 percent of their national income (Boughton and Kumarapathy 2006).

The transfer of resources from oil consumers to oil producers after the first oil shock has been estimated at 1.5 percent of world GDP (Table 3.1). Oil producers with large populations and absorptive capacity, such as Indonesia and Nigeria, increased their spending and their current account surpluses soon shrank. However, those with smaller populations, particularly Saudi Arabia and Kuwait, continued to record large surpluses. These governments, therefore, needed to find suitable uses for their surplus funds. Initially, they chose short-term liquid instruments, such as Eurodollar deposits as well as deposits at banks in the United Kingdom and the United States. Over time, the oil-exporting nations diversified into longer-term investments, including government bonds issued by the United Kingdom and the United States.

A difference emerged between the oil-importing developing nations and the upper-income countries over how they responded to the deficits precipitated by the higher oil prices. A recession in the latter group initially led to a compression in their imports and a combined current account surplus by 1975, and a cumulative deficit over 1974–9 of $44 billion. The drop in their imports from the non-oil-importing developing countries, however, worsened the position of this group, which recorded a cumulative current account deficit of $139 billion during the 1974–9 period (Boughton and Kumarapathy 2006).

These deficits had to be financed by inflows of capital. The IMF's managing director, H. Johannes Witteveen, who had taken office in 1973, proposed that the IMF provide credit to the oil-importing nations through a new Oil Facility. The United States opposed the establishment of the new program, and the U.S. executive director at the IMF stated that his country preferred to use private intermediaries to arrange the financing of the deficits (De Vries 1985: 341). The European countries did not support this position, and the Oil Facility was set up, but on a restricted scale.

The first Oil Facility was financed through a special IMF borrowing of $3.6 billion, almost all of it from oil exporters (James 1996). A second Oil Facility program, which followed in 1975, made $4.7 billion available. Ten developed countries, including Italy and the United Kingdom, and forty-five developing nations borrowed from the IMF through these facilities. There were few conditions, but the interest rate charged by the IMF, which ranged between 7 and 8 percent, depending on whether a country borrowed through the first or second facility and the length of the loan period, reflected the rate that the IMF itself had to pay its lenders.

The Fund also set up an Oil Facility Subsidy account to reduce the cost of borrowing for its poorest members; eventually twenty-five nations benefited from this provision. This account was the first Fund arrangement to differentiate explicitly between the developing countries and other members (De Vries 1985) and represented an attempt by the IMF to establish a niche that the private sector would not serve. In addition, in 1974 the IMF set up a new lending facility, the Extended Fund Facility (EFF), to extend credit over a three-year period. The new program was established to assist members with balance of payments imbalances due to structural impediments. The target recipients were the poorer members, which needed more time to address these issues.

However, most of the lending to the developing countries was done through private capital flows, primarily by banks in the Euromarkets (Helleiner 1994). They "recycled" the funds they had accumulated from the oil exporters by lending them to oil-importing developing nations. The lending rate was linked to the London Interbank Offer Rate (LIBOR) and periodically adjusted, thus transferring the risk of increased costs to the borrowers. The banks diversified their exposure to the risk of nonrepayment by forming syndicates of twenty or more banks to pool their funds. The lead banks that arranged the syndication were large, international banks in Europe, the United States, and Japan (Table 3.2). The remaining banks in the syndicates included smaller, regional banks that were attracted to the loans by their rates of return and the belief that the loans were safe. The lead banks received large fees (Makin 1984) and spread the risks of nonpayment among the other members of the syndicates. This represented an agency problem for the other banks in the syndicate, since their interests were not perfectly aligned with the lead banks'.

Table 3.2. *Main Lender Banks to Developing Nations: 1970s*

Home Country	Banks
France	Banque Nationale de Paris, Banque Paribas, Crédit Lyonnais, Société Générale
Japan	Bank of Tokyo, Dai-Ichi Kangyo, Fuji, Industrial Bank of Japan, Mitsubishi, Sanwa, Sumitomo
United Kingdom	Barclays, Lloyds, Midland, National Westminster, Standard Chartered
United States	Bank of America, Bankers Trust, Chase Manhattan, Chemical, Citibank, Continental Illinois, First National Bank of Chicago, J. P. Morgan, Manufacturers Hanover
West Germany	Commerzbank, Deutsche, Dresdner

Source: Rieffel (2003).

A bank's function as an intermediary includes monitoring the creditworthiness of its borrowers, but that screening function broke down on this occasion. The bank lending to the developing economies had characteristics that would occur again in international credit flows in subsequent periods. First, the loans were based on very optimistic expectations of the borrowing countries' abilities to repay the debt (Guttentag and Herring 1985), often reflecting a boom in the prices of commodities. Second, private bankers in the advanced economies believed that their own governments would assist them in the event of a crisis (Dooley 1995, Folkerts-Landau 1985). In addition, the IFIs were willing to assist countries with financial difficulties. Consequently, the banks were unconcerned about risk; Walter Wriston, chair of Citibank, was widely quoted as saying that "a country does not go bankrupt."

From the viewpoint of the borrowing countries, private market loans carried an important advantage over credit from the IMF: no conditionality. Moreover, the benchmark LIBOR was relatively low during this period, providing an additional incentive to borrow. However, not all developing countries received significant amounts of private capital. The largest borrowers – Argentina, Brazil, Chile, Mexico, the Philippines, South Korea, and Venezuela – accounted for more than half of the bank loans to developing countries by the end of 1977 (Table 3.3).

Many of the remaining developing countries, such as Bangladesh and Sudan, were dependent on the IMF's facilities, as well as bilateral official assistance, to finance their current account deficits. Their ability to borrow in the Euromarkets was limited at best, and they certainly would have paid

Table 3.3. *Bank Loans to Developing Nations: 1977–1982*
(Billions of U.S. Dollars)

Country	1977	1980	1982
Developing Countries	127.7	279.6	362.7
Mexico	20.3	42.5	62.9
Brazil	25.0	45.7	60.5
Venezuela	9.1	24.3	27.5
Argentina	4.9	19.9	25.7
South Korea	5.2	16.7	23.2
Philippines	3.4	9.3	12.6
Chile	1.6	7.3	11.6

Source: Mattione (1985), table 3–3.

a steep rate. The Fund's lending operations, therefore, did provide it with a special role in international financial flows.

The second oil shock took place during the 1979–80 period in response to events in Iran, including its revolution against the shah and its war with Iraq. The price of oil doubled, and the economic magnitude of the transfer of resources was similar to that of the preceding transfer (Table 3.1). The OPEC nations again initially registered large surpluses, and the recycling process was repeated. Developing countries, including oil exporters such as Mexico, borrowed extensively from private banks; their bank debt totaled $279.6 billion by 1980 and $362.7 billion by the end of 1982 (Table 3.2).

The recycling of oil revenues was seen at the time as a successful accomplishment for the private financial markets and a vindication for the U.S. position on the use of private markets rather than the IMF for the recycling of oil revenues (Lissakers 1991). The oil shocks could be accommodated by the Eurodollar banks, which were eager to find new borrowers. The flows of money were larger relative to world GDP at that time than those recorded in the decade of the 2000s, when oil prices rose again (Table 3.1).

The legacies of this process, however, were a high exposure for the international banks to the developing economies and a sizable debt burden for the borrowing nations. Moreover, world interest rates had risen in response to increases in inflation, and by the end of the decade the cost of borrowing had increased significantly. Concerns raised by IMF officials, including Managing Director Witteveen, about the risks posed by the escalation of debt to developing nations were ignored (James 1996: 320).

3.4 New Organizations

The establishment of special committees to supervise the growth of international financial flows (Section 3.2) was part of a movement during the 1970s to create new committees and IGOs and to use existing ones to meet new purposes (Bakker 1996).[3] Universal organizations such as the IMF were bypassed by the new groups, which possessed several advantages as forums for dialogue and the formulation of common policies. First, their smaller size allowed more efficient communication and negotiation among the members. Second, they usually had homogeneous memberships that allowed member governments with similar views to agree on joint positions. A consequence of this division, however, was a separation of countries by income levels, with upper-income and lower-income nations forming their own groups.

The G7 had its genesis at meetings in 1973 of U.S. Treasury Secretary George Schultz with the finance ministers of France, the United Kingdom, and West Germany to discuss the breakdown of Bretton Woods. They were joined at a subsequent meeting by their Japanese counterpart. Summit meetings of the heads of the Group of Five (G5) nations began in 1975 in Rambouillet, France; subsequent meetings in the 1970s took place in Puerto Rico, London, Bonn, and Tokyo. Membership in the group broadened to include Canada and Italy in 1976, when it became known as the G7.[4]

The meetings of the G7 leaders provided a forum for them to discuss common challenges and initiatives in economic policy (De Menil and Solomon 1983, Hajnal 1999, Putnam and Bayne 1987). The discussions at Rambouillet, for example, provided the basis of the agreement reached at Jamaica on the new international monetary arrangements. Over time, the summits came to be used by the participants as a venue to issue instructions to the IMF on how to respond to financial crises. This use of the summit process contributed to the perception that the IMF was effectively controlled by the G7.

The Organization for Economic Co-operation and Development (OECD) began its existence in 1948 as the Organisation for European Economic Co-operation, established in Paris to administer the Marshall Plan for the reconstruction of Europe. In 1961 it was reorganized under its current name for the purpose of promoting cooperation on a range of economic matters, and Canada and the United States joined. Japan and Finland became

---

[3] The IMF provides *A Guide to Committees, Groups, and Clubs* on its Web site.
[4] The president of the European Commission also attends the meetings of heads of state.

members in the 1960s, as did Australia and New Zealand in the following decade. The organization's position on capital controls evolved during the 1970s in favor of liberalization (Abdelal 2007).

In 1962, ten members of the IMF agreed to lend to the Fund in the event that the IMF's existing financial resources were exhausted. The countries, known as the Group of Ten (G10), were Belgium, Canada, France, Italy, Japan, the Netherlands, Sweden, the United Kingdom, the United States, and West Germany. Switzerland joined the group in 1964, but the group retained its original name. The lending arrangement, known as the General Arrangements to Borrow (GAB), provided for up to $6 billion in the lenders' currencies to be available to the IMF and was renewable every five years. The GAB was activated several times during the 1960s and 1970s to finance drawings from the IMF by members of the group.

During the 1960s, the G10 was an important forum for its members, which had a predominant voice at the Fund, to discuss issues related to the international monetary system. The members of the G10 also belonged to the OECD's Working Party 3 of its Economic Policy Committee, which had the task of analyzing the impact of government policies on the balance of payments. In the 1970s the G10's influence waned, partly because the European Community emerged as a voice for its constituent governments.

Other bodies dealt specifically with financial issues. The BIS had been established in Basel in 1930 to deal with German reparation payments from World War I. The European central banks found that the organization served a useful role as a forum for cooperation, and the BIS as an institution survived the breakdown of the reparations agreement as well as a call at Bretton Woods for its abolition due to concerns over its activities during World War II. During the 1970s and 1980s, membership on the Board of Directors of the BIS was confined to the members of the G10.[5]

The BIS hosts monthly meetings for central bank governors to discuss financial globalization and exchange ideas. In addition, the BIS collects data on international financial flows, issues reports and research findings, and supplies credit on occasion to its members, drawing upon the foreign currency deposits of its member banks. It also provides administrative support for a number of committees with international memberships that deal with financial issues.

The growing number of committees and supervisory groups in Basel formed a "Basel Hub," which became a counterweight to the Washington

---

[5] The membership of the BIS was enlarged in the 1990s and now includes 55 central banks. The Board of Directors has also been expanded.

Hub (Chapter 2). The proliferation of these organizations can be viewed as a response to the increasing complexity of financial issues as international capital flows grew. The Basel agencies offered expertise on financial issues that was not available at the IMF or other "Washington Hub" IGOs. The BCBS, for example, has played an important role in standardizing bank regulations across countries (Chapter 4).[6] The possession of technical knowledge provides the basis for international organizations' claims to authority in constructivist analyses (Barnett and Finnemore 2004).

The developing nations created their own associations to act as a counterweight to the organizations set up by the advanced economies. The domination of the G7 nations within the IMF was particularly resented. The Group of 77 (G77) was formed in 1964 to represent the economic interests of developing nations in international forums.[7] In 1971, the Group of 24 (G24) was established to express the position of the developing countries in international monetary discussions. The membership of the G24 consists of finance ministers and other government officials from Asia, Africa, and Latin America. But these groups represented countries with much less economic weight than the upper-income countries possessed, and thus less influence in discussions of international monetary issues.

3.5 IMF and the Nonsystem: Appraisal

By the end of the 1970s, it was clear that the era of international monetary systems – common responses to the constraint of the "impossible trinity" – had ended. A variety of exchange rate regimes had emerged, ranging from floating to bilateral and regional fixed exchange rates. Flexible exchange rates were viewed by many as an appropriate mechanism for adjustments in the balance of payments. The oil shocks, however, demonstrated that flexible arrangements could not always provide the insulation from foreign shocks that policy makers sought (Kahler 1995).

Moreover, international capital flows had been reestablished in an uncoordinated fashion. The advanced economies led the way in dismantling the capital controls that had been erected to protect countries from destabilizing capital movements in the Bretton Woods era. The recycling of the oil revenues of the OPEC countries by private banks seemed to demonstrate the effectiveness of financial intermediaries and markets. The BCBS

---

[6] The membership of the BCBS currently includes the G20 plus Belgium, Hong Kong, Luxembourg, the Netherlands, Singapore, Spain, Sweden, and Switzerland.
[7] Membership has since expanded to include 130 nations.

provided a forum for governments to discuss rules that they could enact to govern financial flows. But there was no agreement among policy makers on how to prevent crises or how to deal with those that did take place.

These developments reflected the breakdown in the Bretton Woods consensus over the need to ensure international economic and financial stability explicitly. Williamson (1976: 54) was one of the first to use the term "nonsystem" to refer to the post–Bretton Woods period, when he wrote that "the world is to function on the basis of a set of conventions and practices that have evolved out of a mixture of custom and crisis." Corden (1994: 166) also referred to the existing set of practices as a nonsystem, due to "the absence of uniform, world-wide rules of real significance." He pointed out that "an international system that is not centrally planned or is not systematically coordinated … can nevertheless reach an equilibrium" (Corden 1994: 165). However, whether the outcome of such an arrangement was optimal was not clear.

Some analysts, such as Keohane (1984: 209), argued that cooperative agreements continued to govern international economic transactions, even though the rules were less explicit. But there remained areas of substantive disagreement and gaps in international governance. The disagreement between the United States and European nations over the efficacy of flexible exchange rates had not been resolved, and the Europeans consequently established their own exchange rate arrangement (Chapter 6). The ability of private capital flows to provide a stable source of financing of current account deficits was untested, and no institutional mechanisms for dealing with financial instability had been established.

What was the IMF's role in this decentralized world? The Fund had established a niche for itself in providing funds to those developing countries that were not able to access the international capital markets. The new Article IV listed a series of obligations for all the members and a process – surveillance – to enforce compliance. But defining compliance with the new duties was complicated by the changes in exchange rate and capital account practices. Moreover, charging a sovereign government with noncompliance with an Article IV obligation would be a difficult task for an agent of that government, even when the government had agreed to the Articles of Agreement.

Overall, the G7 governments showed little interest in utilizing the IMF to coordinate national policies in order to provide international stability.[8]

---

[8]   The G7 meetings were used as a vehicle for this purpose during the 1970s, but such planning exercises fell out of favor after the 1978 Bonn summit (Putnam and Bayne 1987).

After the agreement on the Second Amendment of the IMF's Articles of Agreements, Williamson (1976: 59) predicted:

The Jamaica Agreement is helpful in adapting the IMF Articles so as to enable the Fund legally to play its modest but useful role in organizing get-togethers where the international financial establishment can rub shoulders with one another and thereby wear down their nationalistic edges, and in serving in a fire-brigade role to keep the developing countries from disaster.

However, this evaluation of the usefulness of the IMF occurred at a time of relative euphoria in the private financial markets. As we shall see in Chapter 4, the debt crisis of the 1980s would demonstrate the crucial importance of a financial "fire-brigade." Moreover, this cycle of financial "boom" followed by a "bust" in the developing countries would become a recurring pattern during the 1990s (Chapters 6, 7).

4

The Debt Crisis

The recycling of oil revenues by banks seemed to relegate the IMF to a niche within the international financial system as a lender to those countries not yet able to attract flows of private capital. However, the emergence of the debt crisis of the 1980s revealed weaknesses in private financial intermediation and provided the IMF with an opportunity to play a critical role in the global markets as a "crisis manager." It also implicitly marked the group of developing nations that had borrowed extensively during the 1970s but now faced disruptions as the "weaker links" in the expanding international financial system.

This chapter deals with the IMF's actions during the debt crisis of the 1980s. The IMF's policies evolved during the decade, but it consistently sought to restore the debtor nations' access to the international financial markets. The advanced economies separately used the BCBS to develop new financial standards, thus establishing a two-tier organizational structure to deal with financial instability.

The first section presents the outbreak of the crisis in 1982, which differed from previous ones in several ways, including the extensive involvement of the IMF. The crisis was precipitated by increases in interest rates and slowdowns in economic activity in the advanced economies. The nations that had borrowed extensively, which were concentrated in Latin America, were unable to meet their scheduled payments and sought some form of relief. The international banks that had lent to them formed committees to negotiate with the governments of the debtor nations.

The IMF's involvement in these discussions is described in the following section. The Fund coordinated the negotiations between the banks and debtor governments over restructuring the debt. It also provided credit to the countries through its "concerted lending" with the banks, which agreed to provide new credit to the borrowers. Official creditors dealt with the debtor governments in a separate process.

The record of the IMF's programs during this period is analyzed in the third section. Their policy conditions were compatible with the "first generation" of currency crises that viewed the breakdown of currency pegs as the consequence of expansionary monetary policies. Many of these programs were not successfully completed as a result of incomplete implementation of their conditions. The stipulations to contract spending and the creation of credit were not popular with governments, and some of these sought to develop alternative policies.

The recognition that more active steps were needed to resolve the crisis led to new proposed solutions, and these are described in the fourth section. The IMF played a lesser but still crucial role in these stages of the crisis. Eventually, the debt crisis was resolved through the restructuring of the banks' loans, which resulted in an expansion of bond financing to the developing economies.

The IMF was not the only IFI involved in dealing with the impact of the debt crisis. The following section deals with the establishment of minimum capital standards for banks by the BCBS. The adoption of the proposals was voluntary, but they were widely accepted by countries not represented on the BCBS. The use of the BCBS for this purpose reveals that the advanced economies used the IFIs for specialized purposes: devising regulations to promote financial stability in the case of the BCBS and crisis management by the IMF.

The IMF's record in the debt crisis is assessed in the last section. The IMF emerged from the crisis with a new reputation as a crisis manager, although the Fund's activities were always limited by the governments of the advanced economies. The IMF provided an important service in coordinating the bargaining of the debtor governments and creditor banks. However, by working with the banks, the IMF implicitly acknowledged them as partners in the Fund's relations with its sovereign principals.

4.1 Crisis Emergence

The debt crisis erupted in 1982, when the Mexican finance minister informed the U.S. government and the IMF that his country could not make the next scheduled payment on its bank loans (Kraft 1984). He asked the banks for a postponement of repayment while new terms were arranged, and the United States and the IMF for financial assistance. Mexico's request was soon followed by appeals from other debtor nations, particularly in South America, unable to meet their debt obligations.

The rise in world interest rates in 1979 due to monetary tightening by the Federal Reserve in the United States had raised the cost of borrowing on the adjustable-rate loans. The subsequent downturn in economic activity in the upper-income countries and a decline in the terms of trade of the developing countries lowered the export revenues of the latter groups and their ability to make their scheduled payments. The ensuing crisis continued for the rest of the decade, which became known as the "lost decade" for the developing economies.[1] Many countries were involved, but seventeen were identified as the most heavily indebted: Argentina, Bolivia, Brazil, Chile, Colombia, Costa Rica, Côte d'Ivoire, Ecuador, Jamaica, Mexico, Morocco, Nigeria, Peru, Philippines, Uruguay, Venezuela, and Yugoslavia. The five largest debtors were Argentina, Brazil, Mexico, the Philippines, and Venezuela (Cline 1995). Several of the debtor countries were oil exporters that had borrowed to finance increased government expenditures in anticipation of continued oil revenues. Ironically, many of these countries would become the emerging markets of the next decade.

The banks engaged in the efforts to resolve the crisis included not only the major money center banks in Europe, Japan, and the United States, but also the smaller regional banks that had joined the larger banks in the syndicates that made the loans (Chapter 3). The lending banks formed representative committees – known as "Bank Advisory Committees" – to act in their interests in the negotiations with the debtor governments. The committees were collectively known as the London Club, but there was no organization associated with them and the meetings often took place in New York.

While there had been defaults on sovereign debt before, there were several distinguishing characteristics of this crisis.[2] First, the money had been borrowed in the form of bank loans rather than bonds, which had been the primary channel of international capital flows during the nineteenth century. Second, the IMF under Managing Director Jacques de Larosière, who had replaced Witteveen in 1978, and the governments of the home countries of the banks, particularly the U.S. government, became extensively involved in achieving a resolution. The home country governments were concerned about the impact on their financial systems if the debtor countries defaulted, while the IMF was apprehensive about the stability of the international financial system. Third, the remedy to the crisis involved

---

[1] Cline (1995) presents a thorough account of the debt crisis, while Cuddington (1989) reviewed its causes. Boughton (2001b) and James (1996) describe the IMF's activities during this period.

[2] Eichengreen (1991), Fishlow (1986), and Lindert and Morton (1989) provide historical surveys of international debt crises in earlier periods.

debt reschedulings and restructurings, rather than the outright defaults that had been more common in previous crises.

4.2 Crisis Manager

There were several stages in the progression of the debt crisis. During the initial phase, government officials and many analysts believed that it was a liquidity crisis, rather than one of insolvency. In such a situation, the debt can be repaid if the terms of the loan are restructured. Additional credit can give the borrower more time to make the adjustments needed to make the payments.

The IMF played a key role by coordinating the responses of the banks and borrowing governments.[3] It also extended credit to the debtor nations in conjunction with the banks, a process that became known as "concerted lending." The IMF's intervention provided a focal point for the negotiations, and its financial support provided an extra incentive to participate in the joint effort. This represented a shift from the IMF's lending to members with balance of payments deficits during the Bretton Woods era to "crisis management" with governments and private financial institutions.

This situation can be illustrated with a coordination game, the chicken game, as shown in Figure 4.1.[4] In the model, both the debtor government and the creditor banks wish to avert a default. The banks prefer that the government act to avoid the crisis, that is, "adjust," by implementing contractionary policies that result in a sufficient flow of foreign exchange to service the debt (upper right-hand cell), albeit at the cost of lost output and higher unemployment. The government would rather the banks reschedule and lend new funds (lower left-hand cell) at the cost of lower profits. These payoffs are both Nash equilibriums. But they are suboptimal from a collective viewpoint as compared to the upper-left hand cell, where both sides commit to measures to resolve the crisis and gain from the other party's activities as well as their own.

The IMF changed this bargaining situation by coordinating the actions of the two sides and providing a mechanism to monitor a country's adherence to an agreement over time. A Fund program with a debtor country

---

[3] See discussions of this aspect of the IMF's activities by Aggarwal (1987), Cline (1995), and Lipson (1986).

[4] Aggarwal (1996) identifies the bargaining between Mexico and its creditors during the September 1985–November 1987 period as a specific example of such a confrontation, as well as the situation between Argentina and the banks from April to December 1985.

Debtors and Lenders:
Chicken Game

Banks

		Adjust	Do Not Adjust
Government	Adjust	(3, 3)	(2, 4)*
	Do Not Adjust	(4, 2)*	(1, 1)

Figure 4.1. Debtors and Lenders: Chicken Game.
Note: Numbers in parentheses represent ordinal payoffs to (Government, Banks); 4 is the highest, 1 the lowest.
(x, y)* is a Nash equilibrium.

served as a "commitment device," signaling a country's acceptance of its responsibility to service its debt and its willingness to make the necessary adjustments. Aggarwal (1987: 37) noted that "debtor countries are usually more willing to submit to IMF scrutiny (they are, after all, members of that organization) than they are to give some 1,400 commercial banks access to privileged information." The Fund could serve as a neutral broker and facilitate a commitment that otherwise might not have been forthcoming (Diwan and Rodrik 1992).[5]

The main elements of the rescheduling process were (Sachs 1989: 24):

- The IMF made high-conditionality loans to the debtor governments, contingent on a rescheduling agreement between the country and the commercial bank creditors;
- The commercial banks rescheduled their claims on a debtor government, contingent on the country adopting an IMF program, by stretching out interest payments, but without reducing the contractual present value of repayments;

[5] In 1976, a group of U.S. banks entered into a loan agreement with the government of Peru without an accompanying IMF program. Disbursal of the loan was tied to the government's implementation of agreed-on policies. The banks found it impossible to enforce their lending conditions and resolved that they would not make any similar loans without the IMF's involvement (Cline 1981).

- The debtor countries agreed to maintain the servicing of interest payments on their bank loans;
- Official creditors rescheduled their claims on the debtor governments through the Paris Club, also contingent on an IMF agreement.

In the case of Mexico, for example, the IMF approved an EFF loan of $3.75 billion, while more than five hundred banks renewed existing credits and agreed to lend an additional $5 billion.[6] In return, Mexico agreed to cut its fiscal deficit by half. The credit from the banks was followed by another loan from the banks in 1983 for $3.8 billion with further easing of the terms of repayment. In 1984, the IMF proposed that a multiyear rescheduling agreement be signed by Mexico and the banks, which would provide the Mexican government with a longer time frame for planning purposes. The banks, however, insisted that the IMF continue monitoring Mexico's economic performance. After discussions among the Fund, the Mexican government, and the banks, an agreement was signed that delegated to the IMF the task of monitoring the country's progress in implementing the provisions of the agreement after the expiration of the EFF program.

The new system, called "enhanced surveillance," was based on the IMF's Article IV consultations with the Mexican government, supplemented by additional reviews. The IMF's actions as a de facto monitor for the banks had troubling implications for the IMF's position with the Mexican government, and more generally, its position as an agent for its sovereign members. Boughton (2001b: 411), for example, pointed out that "the challenge for the Fund (of the multiyear rescheduling agreement) was to develop a means of satisfying creditors enough to meet members' financing needs, while staying within and not weakening the institution's mandated role as advisor and financier to its members."

Declines in the price of oil, however, lowered Mexico's GDP growth and government revenues, and by 1985 the country was not complying with the original program's conditions. Disbursals were halted, although an emergency program was approved after an earthquake devastated parts of the country in September 1985. After protracted negotiations, a new stand-by arrangement for $1.7 billion, which was accompanied by $5 billion in further bank financing, was approved in November 1986.

---

[6] Boughton (2001b) and Copelovitch (2010) offer detailed accounts of the IMF's dealings with Mexico.

Concerted lending arrangements were also made with other debtors. Argentina, for example, arranged a loan for $1.95 billion from the IMF, while it negotiated with the banks for additional credit of $1.5 billion. Its program with the IMF specified reductions in the deficits of the public sector and the balance of payments. Difficulties emerged in the negotiations with the banks, however, and the program with the IMF was suspended in 1983 and eventually cancelled. A newly elected government negotiated another stand-by arrangement in December 1984 that included $1.4 billion in credit.

Similarly, Brazil and the IMF signed an agreement in 1983 for $5.4 billion, which also stipulated lower government borrowing. The country's private lenders were reluctant to commit themselves to extending further credit but eventually agreed to make additional loans to the country. However, Brazil's arrangement with the IMF collapsed in the face of mounting budget deficits and inflation.

4.3 Program Breakdowns

From 1982 through 1985, the IMF engaged in twenty-five lending arrangements with thirteen of the heavily indebted countries: Argentina, Brazil, Chile, Costa Rica, Ecuador, Jamaica, Mexico, Peru, and Uruguay in Central and South America, and Côte d'Ivoire, Morocco, the Philippines, and Yugoslavia. As a result of the increase in lending activities, the IMF drew upon the GAB (Chapter 3) for additional financial resources. The governments of the G10 countries agreed in 1983 to increase the amount of credit they were willing to extend to the IMF to $24 billion. In addition, the G10 funds could be used to finance programs in non-G10 countries, a reversal of previous practice.

In nearly every case, the arrangement with the Fund was a precondition for new agreements with private and other official lenders (Boughton 2001b: 414). In some cases, final agreements with the banks were concluded after the Fund program had begun. The conditions associated with these policies were mainly related to monetary, fiscal, and exchange rate policies, the traditional areas associated with IMF conditionality. Many of the conditions of these programs were not fully implemented, however, and the programs often broke down. Boughton (2001b: 405) observed that only eleven of the Fund arrangements were fully utilized, and several of these were modified before they were finished.

This incomplete implementation of the IMF's programs during this period was examined in a number of studies. Killick (1995) undertook an examination of the programs that took place between 1979 and 1993 and used the proportion of credit actually disbursed by the end of a program relative to the amount initially committed as a criterion to measure program completion. He selected an 80 percent disbursal rate as a threshold to indicate whether or not a program had been completed and reported that by this standard only 47 percent of all programs were successfully completed.

Mussa and Savastano (2000) provided a review of the IMF's lending arrangements over the period of 1973 through 1997. They pointed out that a country may not have received all of the originally planned credit for a number of reasons, including external shocks. In some cases, a program was cancelled early because of an unanticipated change in the external environment and a new arrangement was made. They characterized those programs where 75 percent or more of the planned credit was actually disbursed as situations where the governments generally completed the agreed-on policies. Such programs represented 46 percent of the total, which is almost identical to Killick's (1995) calculation of the proportion of successful completions.[7]

The interruptions of the stabilization policies were often accompanied by currency devaluations forced in part by speculative capital flows. The experiences of these countries were the basis of new academic models of currency crises (Flood and Garber 1984, Krugman 1979).[8] The "first-generation models" of currency crises, as they were called, were based on a few key macroeconomic relationships: the demand and supply of money, purchasing power parity for exchange rates, and uncovered interest rate parity (Box 4.1).[9] In these models, an initial expansion by a country's central bank of its holdings of domestic credit assets raises the supply of domestic money. If the new supply exceeds money demand, the country's residents will exchange the excess money for foreign currency to purchase foreign securities. A central bank committed to a fixed exchange rate must sell foreign exchange, which returns the money supply to its original level.

---

[7] Recent empirical studies of the implementation of IMF program include those of Dreher (2003), Ivanova *et al.* (2006), and Nsouli, Atoyan, and Mourmouras (2006). Joyce (2006) presented a model of program implementation based on a divergence between the IMF and a borrowing country in their assessments of the benefits of a program.

[8] Flood and Marion (1999) offer a review of this literature.

[9] There were a number of extensions of the model that relaxed some of these assumptions. Flood and Marion (2000), for example, introduced a risk premium.

Box 4.1. First-Generation Model of Currency Crises

All variables below except for interest rates are measured in logarithms.

The demand for money takes the form:

$$m_t - p_t = \phi y - \alpha i_t \qquad \phi, \alpha > 0 \qquad (4.1)$$

where m_t is the nominal supply of money, p_t is the price level, y_t the level of output, i_t the interest rate, and ϕ and α are the income elasticity and the semi-interest rate elasticity of the demand for money.

If the money multiplier is set equal to unity, then the supply of money can be expressed as:

$$m_t = \gamma D_t + (1 - \gamma)R_t \qquad 0 < \gamma < 1 \qquad (4.2)$$

where D_t is the domestic credit held by the central bank, R_t is the domestic currency value of the central bank's holdings of foreign exchange, and γ the initial share of domestic credit in the monetary base.

The growth rate of domestic credit is a constant, μ:

$$D_t = \mu \qquad \mu < 0 \qquad (4.3)$$

Purchasing power parity between domestic and foreign prices holds:

$$p_t = e_t + p_t^f \qquad (4.4)$$

where p_t is the domestic price level, e_t is the domestic value of foreign exchange, and p^f the foreign price level.

Uncovered interest rate parity also prevails:

$$i_t = i_t^f + E_t\, e_t \qquad (4.5)$$

where i^f is the foreign interest rate and E_t is the expectations operator. Under rational expectations, the expected change in the exchange rate is equal to the actual change.

In equilibrium, the demand for money equals its supply, and equations 4.1 and 4.2 can be set equal. We substitute equations 4.4 and 4.5 into 4.1, set domestic income equal to unity so that its natural logarithm is equal to zero, and simplify:

$$m_t = e_t - \alpha\, e_t \qquad (4.6)$$

With a fixed exchange rate, the right-hand term becomes zero.

The value of foreign exchange reserves under a fixed exchange rate, ($\bar{e}$), can be found by substituting equation 4.6 into equation 4.2:

$$R_t = \frac{\bar{e} - \gamma D_t}{1 - \gamma} \tag{4.7}$$

Then, by substituting equation 4.3 into equation 4.7, we obtain the rate by which the amount of reserves falls as domestic credit grows:

$$\dot{R}_t = \frac{-\mu}{\Theta} \quad \text{where} \quad \Theta = \frac{(1 - \gamma)}{\gamma} \tag{4.8}$$

If the central bank's holdings of foreign exchange are falling because of the constant expansion of domestic credit (μ), then speculators can anticipate the eventual devaluation of the currency.

The timing of the attack is based on the calculation of the "shadow exchange rate," which is the hypothetical exchange rate that would prevail if it were determined in the foreign exchange market. Speculators compare this value with the actual fixed rate. As long as the shadow value of the exchange rate is below the pegged rate, there is no incentive to sell the currency. But once the shadow rate matches the pegged rate, speculators strike in order to lock in their profits from the inevitable devaluation. This is the speculative attack, which moves forward in time the date when the central bank actually runs out of reserves and brings about the very crisis that the speculators anticipated.

The timing of the crisis, t_c, is:

$$t_c = \left(\frac{\Theta R_0}{\mu} \right) - \alpha \tag{4.9}$$

The collapse occurs more quickly the larger is the proportion of domestic credit in the money stock (which results in a smaller value of Θ), the lower is the initial stock of reserves, and the higher is the rate of credit expansion.

Sources: Agénor (2004), Agénor, Bhandari, and Flood (1992), Flood and Garber (1984), Hallwood and MacDonald (2000), Krugman (1979).

Moreover, the growth of domestic credit results in a wave of speculative selling in the exchange markets. Speculators who witness the expansion of the central bank's holdings of domestic credit will anticipate a continuing decline in foreign reserves and the eventual collapse of the bank's ability to fulfill its exchange rate commitment. They sell the domestic currency when the central bank's reserve holdings fall below the minimum level needed to maintain the exchange rate peg. This speculative attack brings about the collapse of the exchange rate peg sooner than would have occurred otherwise. But the actual cause of the collapse is the central bank's expansionary monetary policy, which may be the consequence of political pressure on the monetary authorities to finance a fiscal deficit.

These first-generation models were compatible with the IMF's policy prescriptions for countries with balance of payments disequilibria (Chapter 2). To prevent a collapse of a pegged exchange rate regime, a country needs to implement stable macroeconomic policies. These include limiting the expansion of the domestic money supply to match any increase in money demand due to economic growth, and an avoidance of fiscal deficits financed by the central bank.

However, these policy prescriptions were not popular with the debtor governments, which searched for other solutions to their economic situations. Argentina and Brazil attempted to remedy their difficulties through unusual, or heterodox, policies. Argentina introduced a new currency, the *austral*, in 1985 and implemented an antiinflationary plan that included a wage-price freeze and controls on interest rates. Continued fiscal expansion led to renewed inflation, and additional policy initiatives failed to stabilize the fiscal situation. Similarly, Brazil initiated a new currency, the *cruzado*, in 1986, which was also accompanied by price controls. However, wage increases led to further inflation and additional unsuccessful initiatives. Heterodox policies failed to deliver the increase in growth that governments desired.

4.4 Crisis Resolution

Despite the extensions of new credit and the reschedulings of the bank loans during the first half of the 1980s, it became clear over time that the debtor countries were not achieving a position where they could resume normal commercial relations with the private lenders. The total amount of outstanding debt was increasing, in both absolute and relative terms

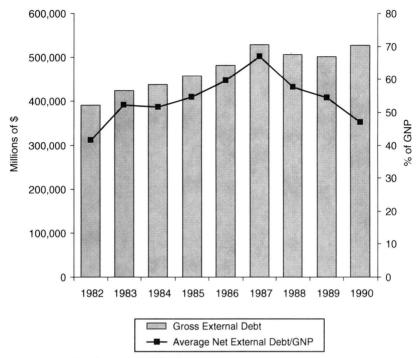

Figure 4.2. Debt of Heavily Indebted Countries: 1982–1990.
Note: Net External Debt = Gross Debt − Reserves.
Countries: Argentina, Bolivia, Brazil, Chile, Colombia, Costa Rica, Côte d'Ivoire, Ecuador, Jamaica, Mexico, Morocco, Nigeria, Peru, Philippines, Uruguay, Venezuela, and Yugoslavia.
Source: Cline (1995).

(Figure 4.2), and there was a net private capital outflow from the emerging markets and developing economies by 1984 (Figure 4.3). Economic growth in the most heavily indebted nations disappeared, while investment in new capital goods declined (Table 4.1). The burden of debt was clearly weighing down the developing countries, with little sign of any improvement as a consequence of IMF policies.

Many private analysts developed plans for a "global" solution to the debt crisis, such as the establishment of a new international agency that would buy up the debt of the developing nations. A group of Latin American countries met in Cartagena, Colombia, in 1984 to discuss a multilateral position on debt rescheduling. Some governments wanted to go further by considering default as a policy option.

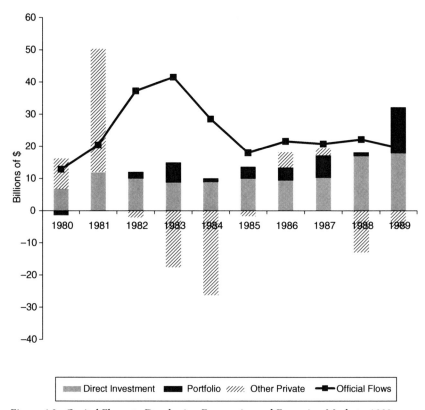

Figure 4.3. Capital Flows to Developing Economies and Emerging Markets: 1980s.
Source: IMF, *World Economic Outlook* Database, September 2011.

In 1985 U.S. Secretary of the Treasury James Baker proposed a new program of lending to the most indebted countries. The private banks would lend $20 billion over a three-year period to the debtors, and the multilateral development institutions, such as the World Bank and the Inter-American Development Bank, would provide another $10 billion. The program included structural changes in the indebted countries to facilitate growth and allow their debt to be repaid.

Among the policy initiatives that the debtor governments would enact were the liberalization of imports and foreign direct investment (FDI), and the privatization of state-owned firms. These were collectively known as "structural adjustment" policies and became more widely used over time. The World Bank had begun its structural adjustment loans in 1979, and the IMF instituted a new facility, the Structural Adjustment Facility (SAF), in 1986 to make loans to the poorest members over a longer period to allow

Table 4.1. *Economic Conditions in Heavily Indebted Countries*

	Per Capita GDP (% Change)	Inflation (%)	Gross Capital Formation/GDP (%)	Debt/Exports (%)
1969–78 (Average)	3.6	28.5	NA	NA
1979	3.6	40.8	24.9	182.3
1980	2.6	47.4	24.7	167.1
1981	−1.6	53.2	24.5	201.4
1982	−2.7	57.7	22.3	269.8
1983	−5.5	90.8	18.2	289.7
1984	−0.1	116.4	17.4	272.1
1985	0.9	126.9	16.5	284.2
1986	1.4	76.2	16.8	337.9

Note: The countries are those listed for Figure 4.2 without Jamaica and Morocco. Inflation is measured by changes in the Consumer Price Index
Source: Sachs (1989).

them to implement the structural reforms. The SAF in turn became the Enhanced Structural Adjustment Facility (ESAF) in 1989.[10]

The key role assigned to the multilateral development institutions rather than the IMF indicated a change in emphasis to growth rather than stabilization (Cline 1995). The IMF continued to be involved with the debtor countries, however, and the new bank loans were usually contingent on adoption of a Fund program. Programs were arranged for Bolivia, Chile, Colombia, and other debtors. Nevertheless, these new credits were not enough to offset the repayments of credit extended previously in the decade, and there continued to be a net transfer to the IMF.

The actual implementation of the Baker plan eventually fell short of its goals. New bank lending totaled $13 billion, about two-thirds of its target level, while multilateral lending was much smaller than its target. In several cases, private and multilateral lending to debtor governments was less than originally planned because IMF programs were not in place (Cline 1995).

By 1987 there was a realization that the debtor countries were not growing out of the crisis. This failure was due in part to the collapse of oil prices in 1986, which hindered the prospects for oil-exporting debtors such as Mexico, Venezuela, and Nigeria. Banks, reluctant to maintain the cycle

[10] In 1999 the ESAF was renamed the Poverty Reduction and Growth Facility (PRGF).

of continued negotiations, began to set aside reserves to cover the cost of writing down the loans on their balance sheets. A secondary international market in securitized debt emerged; it allowed the banks to take the loans off their balance sheets, although at a discount from their face value. Voluntary debt reduction also took place through debt-equity swaps and debt buybacks.

In 1989 the new U.S. Treasury secretary, Nicholas J. Brady, announced a plan to reduce the amount of outstanding debt through a combination of debt forgiveness and restructuring. The banks were offered a choice among several options: accepting bonds – which came to be called "Brady bonds" – from the debtor countries with a discounted value below a bank's claim but carrying a market-based return; a "par bond" equal in value to the principal but carrying a rate of return below the market's; or retention of a bank's original claim but with the provision of additional funds. The IMF and World Bank each earmarked $12 billion to be used to collateralize the new bonds. As a further incentive for the banks to come to an agreement with the debtors, the IMF announced that it would no longer refrain from lending to a country before it had reached a settlement with its private lenders, a practice known as "lending into arrears."

The Brady Plan became an effective solution to the impasse in the negotiations between the banks and the borrowing countries. The first countries to take advantage of the new strategy were Mexico, the Philippines, and Costa Rica. By 1994, eighteen countries, which accounted for $191 billion in eligible debt, had made arrangements with their bank lenders.[11] The secondary market value of their debt rose, indicating a revival of confidence. Even more striking was the resumption of capital flows to the developing countries in the 1990s (Chapter 5). The introduction of the Brady bonds was widely seen as contributing to the resumption of lending to emerging economies (Calvo 2002, Isard 2005). These new flows of money largely consisted of portfolio flows and foreign direct investment rather than bank lending.

The Brady Plan was praised for its flexibility and willingness to accommodate the needs of different lenders. Cline (1995: 254) attributed the Brady Plan's success to its "emphasis throughout on a cooperative, case-by-case, voluntary rather than mandatory and market-oriented solution to the problem." Rieffel (2003: 153) believed that the "commercial bank debt-reduction deals negotiated in the Brady Plan framework at the end of

---

[11] Mexico was the first country to retire its Brady bond debt in 2003 and was followed by several other borrowing nations.

the decade represented a major advance in the art of sovereign workouts." Volcker and Gyohten (1992: 319) claimed that the response to the crisis was a collective solution, "based on contributions from both creditor and debtor countries, private and official entities, and national and international institutions."

However, the Brady Plan did not deal with the official debt of the developing countries, which consisted of bilateral government debt as well as loans from the international financial institutions, including the IMF. Daseking and Powell (1999) estimate that there were eighty-one reschedulings of official debt on nonconcessional terms involving twenty-seven countries before 1988. Rescheduling these payments, however, did nothing to reduce the stock of outstanding debt.

The G7 leaders addressed this issue at their summit in Toronto in 1988, when they agreed to consider debt relief. Different proposals for structuring the new arrangements, collectively called the "Toronto terms," were offered: the United Kingdom suggested lower interest rates, France a reduction in payments, and the United States rescheduling with a longer grace period. All these modifications were permitted, and from 1988 to 1991 there were twenty-eight reschedulings with twenty lower-income countries on Toronto terms, with $6 million of debt consolidated. However, the debt stocks of these countries continued to rise. In 1991 the G7 countries agreed to revised guidelines terms, known as the "London terms," which increased the degree of concessionality on debt relief. These governed twenty-six reschedulings for twenty-three countries from 1991 through 1994, and $8.9 million of debt was rescheduled.

4.5 Basel I

The rescheduling and eventual reduction in the debt of the developing countries was one part of the response of the banks' home country governments to the debt crisis. Another component was an increased scrutiny of the banks' financial positions and the introduction of regulatory policy changes to strengthen them. These initiatives reflected a new level of coordination among the advanced economies, and the use of one of the Basel Hub agencies, the BCBS (Chapter 3), as a regulatory forum.

Bank capital is a measurement of a bank's net value, the difference between its assets and liabilities, and includes shareholders' equity and loan loss provisions. A higher capital base provides a bank a bigger buffer to offset losses in the value of its assets. Domestic bank regulators impose minimum capital requirements for commercial banks and other financial institutions, and these had traditionally been based on domestic considerations.

The adequacy of bank capital requirements across countries, however, became an area of concern during the debt crisis (Kapstein 1994, Singer 2007, Wood 2005). U.S. banking authorities wanted to increase capital standards on banks under their jurisdiction but realized that a unilateral move in this direction would leave these banks at a disadvantage in relation to foreign banks with lower requirements. The U.S. regulators, therefore, approached their counterparts in the United Kingdom about developing common guidelines. In 1987 the United Kingdom and U.S. authorities announced an agreement on common standards for capital adequacy, which they then took to the BCBS.

In 1988, the BCBS issued its proposals for minimum capital requirements for banks, known as Basel I. The new standard consisted of a minimum capital to risk-adjusted asset ratio of 8 percent. The assets of the banks were weighted by their degree of risk. Cash and OECD government securities were assigned a weight of zero; loans to OECD banks and securities firms carried higher weights, set by national authorities; mortgages were given a weight of 50 percent; loans to nonfinancial firms and long-term loans to banks outside the OECD were assigned a weight of 100 percent. Bank capital consisted of two tiers: Tier 1 included the value of the banks' equity and retained earnings; Tier 2 incorporated loan loss provisions and subordinated debt. A maximum of 50 percent of a bank's capital could be held in the form of Tier 2 reserves. To meet the new standards, banks had to raise new capital, or reduce or change the composition of its assets.

The accord initially applied only to BCBS members, and the committee could only issue recommendations to their governments.[12] However, the BCBS held discussions with bank regulators of countries that did not belong to the committee in order to minimize any discrepancy with the new standards. The standards represented an international club good, which could be extended at little or no cost to countries outside the BCBS "club." The accord was eventually adopted by regulators in more than one hundred countries.[13]

---

[12] In addition, the accord only applied to commercial banks. There was a discrepancy between the regulatory practices of Japan, the United Kingdom, and the United States, which distinguished between commercial and investment banks, and the European countries that did not.

[13] Pattison (2006) discussed the reasons for the wide adoption of Basel I, and Simmons (2001) offered a model of the international harmonization of financial regulations.

The new rules and their common application represented a major step in international financial regulation. Kapstein (1994: 118) claimed that "the Basel Accord represents the most significant step taken to date by bank supervisors in advancing policy convergence and creating an international banking regime." Similarly, Fratianni and Pattison (2001: 208) judged that the accord "made history in that a common capital requirement had been established internationally." This was a significant achievement for securing international financial stability, since, as Kapstein (1994: 126) pointed out, a "smoothly running international payments system has something of the quality of a public good."

However, there were unintended consequences of the wide-scale adoption of the Basel I guidelines. While non-OECD bank debt with a maturity of less than one year was assigned a weight of .20, longer-term non-OECD debt was weighted at 1. This created an incentive for banks in the non-OECD countries to issue short-term obligations, since foreign banks would be more willing to hold this form of debt. Consequently, the balance sheets of the non-OECD banks showed both currency and maturity mismatches, with short-term foreign currency-denominated liabilities financing long-term lending denominated in the domestic currency. This left the domestic banks vulnerable to a withdrawal of funds by their foreign creditors (Chapters 6, 7).

The Basel Accord revealed a two-track approach to international economic governance. Since the membership of the BCBS at the time consisted solely of the G10 countries, they were able to devise bank policies without consulting other nations. The IMF, on the other hand, with its broad membership was assigned the task of dealing with those developing economies that faced crises. This two-tier approach continued to be utilized over time (Chapter 9), even though it became a source of resentment in the developing economies that were excluded from the process of developing the financial standards.

4.6 IMF and the Debt Crisis: Appraisal

The debt crisis itself can be viewed as a market failure, reflecting a "combination of myopia and free-rider barriers to collective lending and forgiveness" (Bowe and Dean 1997: 17). It led to a "lost decade" for the debtor countries, with lower per-capita income in several Latin American countries (Pilbeam 2006). On the other hand, a collapse of the global financial markets was prevented, and the debtor countries were able to access the capital markets by the end of the decade. An assessment of the IMF's activities, therefore, must take all these outcomes into account.

The IMF played an important role in the early stages of the debt crisis by coordinating the response of the banks that had made loans to the debtor countries. However, the IMF's activities were based on an assumption that debtor governments both could and should repay their contractual obligations in full (Fischer 1987). This reflected the initial view that the debt crisis was a liquidity crisis, rather than an issue of solvency. The IMF sought to facilitate the repayment of the countries' obligations at the cost of what some saw as overly strict conditions that led to continuing economic stagnation. The incomplete implementation of many of the IMF's programs demonstrates that the governments of the borrowing nations found conditionality burdensome.

Some believed that the IMF served the interests of the banks and their governments more than those of the debtors. Lissakers (1991: 201), for example, claimed that "the IMF was in a sense ... the credit community's enforcer." Similarly, Dornbusch (1986: 140) wrote that that there was "little doubt that the strategy protected bank shareholders at the expense of the LDCs." The IMF replied that avoiding a default by debtor governments was its primary goal, and a breakdown in financial flows would have been a catastrophe. But its focus during the early stages of the crisis on concerted lending may have delayed the inevitable restructuring of the debt that finally occurred at the end of the decade.

One consequence of the IMF's actions in the debt crisis was an expansion of its target audience. Traditionally the IMF had dealt exclusively with the representatives of the member governments. However, during the crisis the Fund negotiated with the private bankers, and its lending became a complement to private capital flows. Gould (2003) has claimed that the dependence of the IMF on supplementary credit from private institutions gave the financiers influence over the design of the Fund's programs. Boughton (2001b: 406) admitted that the IMF's concerted lending "gave the banks a virtual veto over the approval and financing of adjustment programs."

The IMF (2004a: 13) later acknowledged that a substantive change had occurred during this period:

The Mexican standstill of 1982 and the debt crisis that followed marked the beginning of a new relationship between the Fund and private creditors. The success of Fund-supported programs now depended, more than ever before, on the reactions of the banks. While the banks needed the Fund's expertise and its ability to obtain credible policy commitments from the member, the Fund needed the banks to contribute resources to cover financing gaps, and assurance that potential Fund lending would not just lead to a commensurate reduction in bank exposures.

The IMF was also criticized for exceeding its original mandate by lending for purposes other than short-term balance of payments financing. In public choice analysis, crises provide international agencies with an excuse to expand their operations. Vaubel (1994: 44), for example, claimed that "the international debt crisis of 1982 provided the IMF officials with an opportunity to secure the survival and growth of their organization." Similarly, Schwartz (1989: 13) claimed that the multilateral agencies, including the IMF, "seized the opportunity afforded by the debt crisis in the 1980s to enlarge the scope of their involvement in the economies of the problem countries."

However, it can be argued that the debt crisis actually showed the limitations on the IMF's range of operations. The G7 governments oversaw the IMF's actions and placed constraints on how far the Fund could go at each stage. When the initial strategy of concerted lending was exhausted, the U.S. Treasury secretary, after consultation with the other members of the G7, announced a change in the handling of the crisis, and the Fund adjusted its operations. The G7 also showed that it would use other IFIs, such as the BCBS with its restricted membership, to develop financial standards. The IMF's ability as an agent to perform its job as a crisis manager, therefore, was constrained by the preferences of its chief principals, as well as its own commitment to support the workings of the international financial markets.

The IMF's handling of the debt crisis had important implications for its response to future crises. Boughton (2000: 284) viewed the crisis as the "major turning point for the international financial system and for the crisis-management role of the IMF." He cited the speed of the IMF's response and the size of its loans as groundbreaking. But Boughton (2000: 287) also admitted that concerted lending left the IMF open to the charge that it operated in the interests of the banks, and that the financial arrangements provided a "temporary patch, not a lasting solution." Thirty years later in Europe, the IMF's actions in the European debt crisis would receive similar criticisms (Chapter 11).

There were also more immediate repercussions for the Fund. The resumption of financial flows to the developing countries was part of the process of financial globalization. The IMF was an active participant in this process, as shown in the next chapter.

5

Global Finance Redux

The debt crisis slowed but did not stop the expansion of global financial markets after the end of the Bretton Woods era. The growth of capital flows, which had begun in the 1960s and 1970s, accelerated in the 1980s and 1990s. This chapter deals with the IMF's response to the widening scope of international capital. The record demonstrates that the IMF saw no conflict during this period between encouraging capital account liberalization and its mandate to promote economic stability.

The first section provides an overview of the reemergence of global finance. The trend was more pronounced in the upper-income countries but was also a part of the increased economic openness of some emerging market nations. The movement to the integration of financial markets was driven by many forces, including advances in communications and financial instruments, the growing acceptance of market-based resource allocations, and the promotion of deregulation by those who stood to benefit from this trend.

The IMF has been criticized for fostering premature capital deregulation, and the evidence on this charge is presented in the second section. The evidence confirms that the IMF encouraged its members, including those that borrowed from it, to decontrol capital movements. While the IMF did not compel governments to remove capital account restrictions, it did underestimate the risks associated with increased financial flows. There was ample evidence of the instability associated with financial deregulation in the experiences of several South American countries.

The IMF sought to tie its lending to increased flows of private capital, and the third section deals with the record of this "catalytic" effect. The majority of empirical studies have found little evidence of an impact of IMF programs on the quantity or cost of capital. An IMF program must be supplemented by credible government policies before foreign investors channel funds to a country.

The IMF's activities in support of capital decontrol crested during the middle 1990s. The fourth section explains how the IMF sought to amend its Articles of Agreement to establish capital account liberalization as a goal for its members and to give the Fund jurisdiction in this area. The IMF was able to use the divisions among its members on this issue to promote its agenda. But the onset of the Asian crisis (Chapter 7) slowed the movement toward adoption of the amendment, and the opposition of the U.S. Congress effectively ended the initiative.

The final section provides an overview of the IMF's advocacy of financial globalization during this period. Its position lacked empirical justification, and there were theoretical analyses that raised doubts about the supposed positive impact of capital flows on growth. The upper-income members supported the general movement toward increased financial integration, but the IMF needed little guidance by its principals to move in this direction. The IMF saw a stronger role in international financial markets as an extension of its mandate to promote stability and growth. The expansion also justified an expansion of the organization to support its new duties.

5.1 Resurgence of Capital Flows

The course of capital movements in modern history has been U-shaped, falling after the end of the Gold Standard and during the interwar period and then rising, slowly after 1945 and more rapidly after the 1970s (Bordo, Eichengreen, and Kim 1998, Obstfeld and Taylor 2004). Financial flows increased during the 1980s and 1990s after a wave of capital account deregulation, and international finance became integrated with domestic financial markets in the upper-income countries (Frieden 2006, Goodman and Pauly 1993). The increase in capital mobility was often accompanied by more flexible exchange rates, which satisfied the constraint of the "impossible trinity," although there were also countries such as those in the Eurozone that sacrificed monetary autonomy in order to preserve fixed exchange rates.

Many developing countries, particularly in Asia and Latin America, also increased their openness to foreign finance. By the early 1990s, a large proportion of these countries could be described as "financially open" (Montiel 1994: 342). Many of them were the nations that became characterized as "emerging markets" because of their rapid economic growth, and these countries attracted the interest of foreign investors. African and Middle Eastern countries, however, did not move as far in opening their capital accounts (Quinn 2003).

These trends appear in the data provided by Lane and Milesi-Ferretti (2007), who calculated the stocks of foreign assets and liabilities for a broad sample of countries. They reported that the sum of foreign assets and liabilities scaled by GDP, which serves as a measure of financial market integration, rose for a group of upper-income countries from about 45 percent in 1970 to more than 300 percent in 2004, a sevenfold increase. The same measure for a group of emerging market and developing economies rose from a similar ratio in 1970 to about 150 percent in 2004.

A great deal of the capital flows in the upper-income countries consisted of asset diversification among these countries. Obstfeld and Taylor (2004: 232) reported that gross assets and liabilities in a group of OECD countries relative to the area's GDP rose from about 0.25 to 1 during the last two decades of the twentieth century, but their net position changed very little. For developing countries, the increase in gross position was much smaller, and the rise in their net debtor position larger. During the early 1990s, portfolio flows dominated the flow of capital to this group of nations, but over time FDI came to account for the largest proportion (Figure 5.1).

The reasons for the reemergence of global capital markets can broadly be summarized by three sets of determinants: innovations, ideas, and interests.[1] First, technological advances in information systems and communications increased the ability of investors to track global developments and direct their funds to achieve the highest (risk-adjusted) returns. The deregulation of financial markets also encouraged the development of new instruments and techniques. Financial enhancements, such as securitization, were intended to provide new means of diversifying portfolios and minimizing risk.[2]

Second, the benefits of cross-border capital flows, such as a more efficient allocation of savings and more opportunities to diversify portfolios and smooth consumption expenditures, were incorporated into the intellectual movement known as "neoliberalism."[3] These policies were designed to advance the distribution of resources by markets, including the allocation of credit, by eliminating government regulations that interfered with market allocations. Many of the policy reforms for developing economies

[1]   Bhagwati (1988) used a similar classification scheme (ideas, interests, and institutions) in explaining the determinants of trade policy.

[2]   The global financial crisis of 2008 demonstrated, however, the limitations of these financial instruments in managing risk.

[3]   Blyth (2002) provides an account of the main economic and political trends of this period.

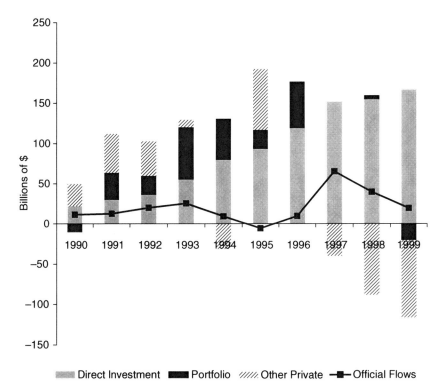

Figure 5.1. Capital Flows to Developing Economies and Emerging Markets: 1990s. *Source:* IMF, *World Economic Outlook* Database, September 2011.

that were advanced during this period appeared in Williamson's (1990) "Washington Consensus," a summary of measures recommended by analysts based in the "Washington Hub" agencies.[4]

In addition, the European nations made the integration of their financial markets with foreign markets as well as each other part of the transformation of the European Community (EC) into the European Union (EU). They carried this perspective over to the OECD (Abdelal 2007), where new members such as Mexico and South Korea had to comply with the organization's position on capital account openness. Johnson and Kwak (2010) have compared the belief in the positive properties of free capital movements that increased during this period to the support for the efficient

---

[4] Williamson (1990), however, included the liberalization of only FDI flows in his list of policies.

market hypothesis and the move toward domestic regulatory decontrol in the United States and other upper-income countries.[5]

Finally, borrowers and lenders who stood to benefit from the relaxation of restrictions on international capital flows served as its advocates. Private borrowers in capital-scarce countries who were not able to obtain credit from domestic sources, for example, promoted the opening of domestic financial markets and increased access to foreign finance (Rajan and Zingales 2003). Governments also realized that they could finance fiscal deficits by borrowing in the international markets. Financial services firms based in upper-income nations that sought to expand their markets encouraged their own governments to advocate decontrol in other countries (Frieden 1991). The government of the United Kingdom supported capital liberalization in part to confirm the position of London as an international financial center (Chapter 3).

5.2 IMF Programs and Capital Decontrol

The broadening of global finance coincided with an increase in the membership of the IMF, which rose from 125 countries in 1973 to 140 in 1980 and 151 in 1990. These were developing countries, many of them former colonies (Table 5.1). There was a further expansion in membership after the dissolution of the Soviet Union and the emergence of the transition economies. These countries looked to the IMF for guidance on financial matters, and in many cases the IMF played a key role in their decisions to eliminate capital controls.

There are many types of regulations and controls designed to affect the amount or composition of international capital flows (Dooley 1996, Magud and Reinhart 2007). These regulations can take the form of legal restrictions on the various categories of capital transactions, special taxes, or requirements that funds be deposited in special accounts. Controls on short-term capital inflows are designed to regulate the amount and/or composition of short-term capital. The rationale for controlling capital outflows is that such outflows occur during a crisis when a government may need to "buy time" to stabilize the economy.

The determinants of capital controls and their removal have been widely studied (Eichengreen 2001). The results vary, but a number of empirical relationships appear consistently. Richer countries are less likely to maintain controls, as are countries with independent central banks. Countries with larger

---

[5] Simon Johnson served as head of the IMF's Research Department in 2007–8.

Table 5.1. *New Members Post-1973*

Year	New Members
1973	Bahamas
1975	Grenada, Papua New Guinea
1976	Comoros
1977	Guinea-Bissau, São Tomé and Príncipe, Seychelles
1978	Cape Verde, Djibouti, Dominica, Maldives, Solomon Islands, Suriname
1979	St. Lucia, St. Vincent, and Grenadines
1980	Zimbabwe
1981	Bhutan, Vanuatu
1982	Antigua and Barbuda, Belize, Hungary
1984	Mozambique, St. Kitts and Nevis
1985	Tonga
1986	Kiribati, Poland (readmitted)
1989	Angola
1990	Bulgaria, Czechoslovakia (readmitted), Namibia, Republic of Yemen
1991	Albania, Mongolia
1992	Armenia, Azerbaijan, Belarus, Bosnia and Herzegovina, Estonia, Georgia, Kazakhstan, Croatia, Kyrgyz Republic, Latvia, Lithuania, Macedonia, Marshall Islands, Moldova, Russian Federation, San Marino, Slovenia, Switzerland, Turkmenistan, Ukraine, Uzbekistan, Yugoslavia
1993	Czech Republic, Micronesia, Slovak Republic, Tajikistan
1994	Eritrea
1995	Brunei Darussalam
1997	Palau
2002	Timor Leste
2007	Montenegro
2009	Kosovo
2010	Tuvalu
2012	South Sudan

Source: IMF, External Relations Department.

trade sectors are more likely to liberalize capital flows. Some of the earlier studies reported that left-wing governments were more inclined to maintain controls, as were governments with large consumption shares of GDP. A government's policy stance may also be influenced by the position taken by its competitors for global capital flows (Simmons and Elkins 2004).

A change in the policies governing capital flows may occur in response to a discrete event, such as a crisis in the balance of payments.[6] The direction of the change in these circumstances, however, is ambiguous. On the one

---

[6] See Drazen (2000) for a review of the literature on economic crises and reform.

hand, a government may impose controls in order to stem capital outflows; on the other hand, capital account liberalization could serve as a signaling device for government officials who seek to establish their reliability with global capital markets. Convertibility signals the government's intention to undertake reforms and constrains its ability to engage in budget deficit financing (Bartolini and Drazen 1997, Haggard and Maxfield 1993, 1996).

Capital account liberalization has also occurred within the context of IMF programs. The Fund has been blamed for promoting the deregulation of capital to countries that did not have the necessary institutions and regulations to cope with capital movements. Stiglitz (2002: 15), for example, wrote that "many of the policies that the IMF pushed, in particular, premature capital market liberalization, have contributed to global instability." Similarly, Desai (2003: 217) claimed that "the IMF encouraged a disaster-prone policy gamble of capital account liberalization in these economies before they had put their 'structural house' in order."

The two hypotheses – decontrol takes place in the context of an IMF program *or* decontrol is a form of signaling during a crisis – are not mutually exclusive. Governments may adopt IMF programs in response to crises in the external sector, and the programs themselves serve as a type of commitment device. On the other hand, not all countries facing crises adopt Fund programs, and not all IMF programs are introduced in response to currency crises.

Capital decontrol was not included in the purposes of the IMF in its Articles of Agreement and therefore could not be part of the conditions associated with Fund programs. However, the IMF often advocated movement toward liberalization during the 1990s. A study by an IMF staff team (Quirk and Evans 1995: 6), for example, reported in a discussion of the Fund's position that "the institution has in some cases encouraged developing countries to open their economies to foreign capital inflows and to liberalize restrictions on capital account transactions."

There have been few empirical studies of the impact of the IMF on the process of capital decontrol. Simmons and Elkins (2004) found that the use of IMF credit was associated with capital account restrictions, which they attribute to the existence of capital flight at the time of the adoption of a Fund program. Abiad and Mody (2005) reported that IMF programs have a strong impact on financial reform in countries that are highly repressed, but this effect declines as repression is diminished.

Joyce and Noy (2008) undertook an empirical analysis of the impact of Fund programs on capital decontrol and found that countries that participated in IMF programs during the 1990s were more likely to decontrol their capital accounts than other countries in similar circumstances. The countries enrolled in IMF programs had experienced larger current account deficits and possessed fewer reserves than countries that removed capital restrictions independently. However, they found little evidence to support the charge that IMF-related liberalization was more likely to occur in countries experiencing a financial crisis, and the economic differences between the two groups of countries were not significant after the enactment of Fund programs.

There is no evidence in these studies to suggest that countries liberalized their capital accounts against their will. While the IMF did not have the ability to require countries that entered Fund lending programs to eliminate capital restrictions, governments could voluntarily include their removal in their Letters of Intent. Edwards (2003) points out that the initial push for economic opening in the 1980s often originated with national policy makers, many of them from Latin America, and governments in these cases voluntarily decontrolled capital flows during this period without pressure from the IMF.

The IMF's Independent Evaluation Office (IMF IEO) (2005: 94), in its examination of the IMF's policy stance on this issue, reached a similar evaluation:[7]

In summary, the IMF undoubtedly encouraged countries that wanted to move ahead with capital account liberalization, and even acted as a cheerleader when it wished to do so, especially before the East Asian crisis, but there is no evidence that it exerted significant leverage to push countries to move faster than they were willing to go.

The advocacy of capital account liberalization may have been part of the consensus of the time that the IMF adopted. However, the absence of evidence that the IMF "drove" countries into decontrolling capital does not absolve the Fund of the charge of irresponsibility in this particular area. The IMF's advocacy of capital liberalization implied that there were few, if any, downside risks of decontrol. But capital controls were often part of a larger set of restrictions and requirements that governments in developing countries had imposed on their banks, which were collectively called "financial repression" (Montiel 2003a). These policies allowed the fiscal authorities to finance their deficit expenditures through increased bank holdings of government securities at lower costs than would otherwise prevail. They also gave governments the ability to direct credit to sectors of the economy that

---

[7] See also Williamson's (2004) conclusion regarding the IMF's activities in this area.

they wanted to promote. Interest rate ceilings allowed favored firms to borrow at lower rates than unrestricted financial institutions or markets would have charged.

Removing capital controls without the reform of a repressed financial sector could be a recipe for disaster. The correct sequence and timing of reforms depend in part on the circumstances of the country and should begin with macroeconomic stabilization, including fiscal consolidation. The preconditions also include the creation of a financial regulatory structure to monitor bank conduct, the adoption of accounting standards, and the protection of investors' rights. Once these changes have been made, the removal of the controls on long-term capital flows such as FDI should be undertaken before short-term capital is liberalized.

It may be reasonable to ask whether it was possible at the time for the IMF to foresee any of the risks associated with deregulation. But the dangers of ignoring these steps had become evident in the Southern Cone countries of Argentina, Chile, and Uruguay in the late 1970s and early 1980s (Diaz-Alejandro 1985, Frenkel 2003). These countries had liberalized their financial systems, including decontrolling their capital accounts, without adequate regulatory reform and supervision. They all suffered subsequent financial crises that demonstrated that financial reform was a complex affair and that capital decontrol had to be preceded by a range of measures if it were to contribute to economic growth without threatening financial stability.

Capital account liberalization need not be destabilizing, and there are examples of successful deregulation in developing economies (Montiel 2003a). However, the IMF during the 1980s and early 1990s did not provide the newly emerging markets with templates of successful decontrol. In response to concerns about the need for macroeconomic stability before liberalization took place, Guitián (1995: 85), one of the IMF's strongest advocates for decontrol (Section 5.4), claimed that capital account liberalization itself would "constrain domestic policies to the extent necessary to bring about balance and stability to the economy." But there was no evidence that decontrol would create the necessary preconditions.

Indeed, the historical record demonstrates that increased capital mobility has often led to a higher incidence of crises (Reinhart and Rogoff 2009). Capital inflows can be followed by increases in the prices of domestic assets, such as housing, which encourage risky lending by banks. These problems are exacerbated if capital inflows are accompanied by procyclical macroeconomic policies, as they often are in developing economies (Kaminsky, Reinhart, and Végh 2005). The subsequent support of domestic financial intermediaries by the central bank may conflict with its exchange rate management and lead to a currency crisis followed by a financial crisis (Kaminsky and Reinhart 1999). The situation can be further exacerbated by capital flight by foreign and domestic investors, which may result in a sudden stop. But the IMF seemed little prepared for the instability that followed the deregulation of capital it promoted in the 1980s and most of the 1990s.

5.3 Catalysis

The IMF's involvement with private banks during the debt crisis of the 1980s gave it experience in linking Fund credit to private capital flows. As capital movements increased in size during the 1990s, the IMF realized that they offered a means of financing external sector deficits that could supplement the Fund's own efforts. Guitián (1982: 91) specifically pointed to the "complementarity between the resources from the Fund and those from the private international capital markets." This linkage between official and private capital became known as catalytic finance and was predicated on the assumption that the existence of an IMF lending program would increase the willingness of private investors to lend to a country. If the catalytic effect prevailed, the country could finance a larger deficit than it could if it only had access to credit provided by the IMF.

Several factors could be responsible for the occurrence of such an effect (Cottarelli and Giannini 2003). First, the policies implemented under an IMF program can improve a country's economy, thus making it more attractive to foreign investors. Second, the IMF may have better information regarding a country's circumstances than do private investors, who would follow the IMF's lead.[8] Third, a Fund program can serve as a commitment device for a government to implement policies favored by investors. Fourth, an IMF program can serve to differentiate countries with viable policies from those without. Finally, an IMF program could be viewed by private investors as a type of insurance in case of mishap, thus reducing the risks of investing there.

Hovaguimian (2003) reviewed the basis of a catalytic effect of IMF lending and distinguished between the "lending channel" and the "policy

---

[8] Copelovitch (2010) claims that the IMF sought to promote catalytic financing through the size and terms of its loans. The IMF's loans to countries that relied on bond financing received more credit but carried more extensive conditionality than did loans to countries with bank credit. The differences in the amounts and associated conditionality were designed to appeal to the relatively larger number of bondholders than banks, thereby exacerbating collective action problems.

channel." The former emphasizes IMF credit to governments with liquidity difficulties, which can induce private inflows if confidence is restored. The latter channel is a response to the IMF's program and could be due to the Fund's informational advantage or the commitment effect.

A large number of studies have sought to determine whether there is a catalytic effect of IMF programs on private finance. Rodrik (1996) and Bird and Rowlands (1997, 2000), using different measurements of private capital flows, found no evidence that IMF lending to a country was followed by an increase in private credit flows and concluded that there was no general catalytic effect. Bird (2007: 720), in a summary of the econometric literature on this topic, wrote that the results of these studies "are not generally supportive of a catalytic role for the Fund."[9]

These findings indicate that the mere existence of a Fund program does not serve as a sufficient condition to bring about an increase in private capital flows. This result is not surprising in view of the record on program completion, which shows that many programs are not successfully implemented (Chapter 4). However, private markets may be able to differentiate between successful and unsuccessful programs. Edwards (2005) addressed this issue and found evidence of capital outflows in those countries where an IMF program had been suspended. The impact of successful implementation on private inflows was less clear, suggesting that the IMF program operated as a "one-way signal." In another study, Bordo, Mody, and Oomes (2004) found that IMF programs are associated with increased capital flows in the case of a country recovering from bad, but not very bad, "fundamentals," that is, economic factors such as foreign exchange reserves. They hypothesized that the IMF program serves as a commitment mechanism for a government that is changing its macroeconomic policies.

Researchers have investigated the impact of Fund programs on the cost of private capital as well as the quantity of credit. Mody and Saravia (2006) reported that the presence of an IMF program is associated with both an increased issuance of bonds and lower spreads when a country's fundamentals are in "intermediate" range. They interpret these results as an indication of an increase in demand for the bonds of a country in an IMF program when there is evidence that the program will be effective. Similarly, Eichengreen, Kletzer, and Mody (2006) found that the cost of borrowing in the bond markets was lower for countries that were engaged

---

[9]   Rowlands (2001) did find evidence, however, of an increase in lending from other public sources, which is consistent with the Fund's lead role in coordinating multilateral assistance.

in IMF programs and interpreted this as evidence that the existence of a program has a positive impact on bondholders' evaluations of a country's creditworthiness.

The catalytic financing of the debt crisis of the 1980s was the product of a unique set of circumstances that are unlikely to be replicated. In the early stages of the crisis, the IMF could stipulate the specific amounts of new credit it wanted the banks to contribute to the overall package of loans extended to the borrowing countries. The banks complied with the IMF's stipulations as long as they sought to prevent defaults by the sovereign borrowers. However, they became less willing to do so as time passed without any change in the economic status of the debtor countries, and eventually they decided to accept the restructuring of the debt (Chapter 4). The financial crises that took place during the 1990s would transpire more quickly and would generally not allow the IMF sufficient time to engage in similar negotiations with foreign bondholders (Chapters 6, 7). Catalytic financing would not prove to be a reliable tool of crisis resolution.[10]

5.4 New Amendment

The Fund's increased involvement with the private capital markets in the 1980s and early 1990s crested in a proposal for a new amendment to the Fund's Articles of Agreement that would have established capital account liberalization as a goal for the IMF's members.[11] The amendment also gave the IMF jurisdiction over capital flows. The proposed amendment would have been a reversal of Article VI in the original Articles of Agreement, which had endorsed the use of controls to regulate international capital movements. It would have treated the capital account in a similar fashion to the current account by prohibiting restrictions on capital account transactions, but allowing transitional arrangements.

Bhagwati (1998) blamed what he called the "Wall Street–Treasury complex" for the initiative to liberalize capital accounts in the developing nations, effectively casting the IMF as an agent responding to the interests of its most powerful principal. However, research by Abdelal (2007) and Chwieroth (2010) indicates that impetus for the initiative actually originated within the Fund. Abdelal (2007: 129), for example, states: "The effort to amend

---

[10] One exception is South Korea, where the IMF and G7 governments were able to convince reluctant banks to roll over the debt of Korean banks (Chapter 7).

[11] Abdelal (2007) provides a detailed account of the evolution of the proposed amendment. See also Leiteritz (2005).

the Fund's Articles had been conceived and pushed forward by the management of the Fund itself, and most emphatically by (Managing Director Michel) Camdessus." Camdessus, who had taken over as managing director from Jacques de Larosière in 1987, had been active in France's endorsement of financial liberalization as part of the move toward European integration. In addition to Camdessus, Manuel Guitián, the head of the Fund's Legal, Monetary and Exchange Affairs Department, and Jack Boorman, head of the Policy Development and Review Department, were strong supporters of the amendment (Abdelal 2007).

The positions of the IMF administrative officials reflected several factors. First, the Fund sought to establish an institutional and legal basis for its involvement in the expanding capital markets. The IMF's ability to monitor its members' policies was limited by the lack of a specific grant of authority in this field. Second, private capital flows were seen as necessary to provide the financial resources needed to resume growth after the "lost decade" of the 1980s. Polak (1991: 58), for example, stated, "There can be no doubt that one of the conditions for successful growth-oriented adjustment … is an adequate and assured supply of foreign capital." Third, there was a desire for symmetry in the treatment of the current and capital accounts. Guitián (1995: 78) argued that capital transactions should not be seen as different from transactions in goods: "The analysis of the costs and benefits of capital account liberalization does not differ from the traditional tenets derived from the conventional examination of the advantages and disadvantages of free trade, in general."[12]

This view of capital movements represented a major departure from the views of White and Keynes (Chapter 2). Chwieroth (2010) has traced the evolution of views on capital controls within the IMF over time. During the years of the Bretton Woods system and immediately thereafter, the IMF's staff shared concerns about the disruptive effects of capital flows due to their training in Keynesian-based economics and their familiarity with the experiences of the 1930s. Beginning in the 1980s, however, there was a shift within the IMF as this generation of economists retired and a new cohort was recruited. Their graduate school training emphasized the benefits of market-based resource allocations. Chwieroth (2010) points out that there was not a monolithic view of the correct pace of capital decontrol, but there was a consensus that treated capital account liberalization as a long-term goal.

---

[12] Edwards (2003), who organized the conference where Guitián delivered these comments, wrote that his paper was one of the first documents that reflected the change in the IMF's views on capital account convertibility.

The position of the U.S. Treasury Department regarding the proposal was mixed. On the one hand, the United States was an advocate of open markets, and the move toward capital decontrol was consistent with this ideology. On the other hand, the United States was less willing to grant the IMF jurisdiction over global capital. The U.S. executive director to the IMF at the time, Karin Lissakers, was in favor of the proposed amendment, but the Treasury secretary, Lawrence Summers, was ambivalent. Summers told Abdelal (2007: 139) that the proposal "was not a priority for the Treasury." Similarly, the Institute of International Finance, a research organization in Washington, D.C., funded by private financial institutions, generally supported liberalization but did not endorse a grant of authority to the IMF over private capital flows.

During the first half of the 1990s, Camdessus and the Fund's staff prepared the case for amending the Articles of Agreement. Stanley Fischer became the Fund's first deputy managing director in 1994, after the movement had begun. Fischer was a well-known and highly respected economist before joining the IMF, and his support for the proposal carried much weight. In making the case for the amendment, Fischer (1997) pointed out that most advanced economies had open capital accounts, thus establishing the experience of those countries as an exemplar for other countries to follow.

In 1995 the G7 governments announced their support for extending the obligations of Fund membership to include capital account liberalization. The IMF's Executive Board was split on this issue, and not all directors accepted the case for removing restrictions on capital flows or the need for amending the Articles of Agreement.[13] By 1997, however, Camdessus thought he had sufficient support on the Executive Board to proceed, and in September the IMF's Interim Committee announced its approval of the amendment.

However, as Fischer (2004: 115) later admitted, "The timing could hardly have been worse." The Asian financial crisis that had begun that summer traveled across East Asia and continued to ensnare countries (Chapter 7). Support for the amendment collapsed in the face of the economic disruptions linked to capital outflows. After members of the U.S. Congress expressed their opposition to the proposed amendment, the Treasury Department withdrew its support. The amendment was shelved after the Russian crisis of August 1998.

The rise and fall of the proposed amendment provides an insight into the relationship of the IMF with its principals. The Fund exploited the split

---

[13] Thomas Bernes, an executive director from Canada, was opposed to the amendment, even though his government supported it.

among its members over capital decontrol to pursue its own agenda. The proposed amendment extended the scope of the IMF's oversight and would have given the organization a broad mandate on matters related to global finance. A number of governments with substantial voting power backed the proposal, but other countries were strongly opposed. Nonetheless, the IMF's management was able to push the new amendment forward as long as it had the backing of its largest member, the United States.

However, once the risks associated with capital decontrol became evident, support for the amendment collapsed. The IMF's ability to maneuver among their principals ended once there were no longer diverse views. The IMF would not be able to claim regulatory authority over financial flows until its members granted it some form of administrative powers in this area, and they were unlikely to do so since financial regulation was still considered a domestic matter. Any changes in that area would occur in the specialized Basel Hub agencies (Chapter 9).

5.5 IMF and Financial Liberalization: Appraisal

The IMF's advocacy of capital account decontrol during the late 1980s and the 1990s occurred during a time when its membership of low- and middle-income countries was expanding, and its guidance in this area was particularly important. The IMF was subsequently blamed for contributing to the financial instability that occurred later in the 1990s (Chapters 6, 7, 8). The IMF damaged its reputation for impartiality and confirmed the impression given during the debt crisis that the organization served the interests of private finance.

Among the specific charges levied against the IMF was a lack of theoretical underpinning for its policy guidance (Stiglitz 2000, 2008). The analogy to trade liberalization by Guitían and others ignores fundamental differences between the markets for goods and financial assets. Financial markets assess the profitability of proposed investments in order to allocate funds to their highest returns, adjusted for risk. But informational asymmetries between borrowers and lenders can distort the distribution of funds and lead to increased volatility in financial flows. The theory of the "second-best" indicates that the existence of market failures may justify the retention of some form of government intervention.

Moreover, there was scarce empirical support for the proposition that capital decontrol promoted growth or lessened consumption volatility. Fischer (2003: 14) admitted that the empirical evidence on the benefits of capital account liberalization was "weak and disputed." A review by Prasad *et al.* (2003) of fourteen research papers that dealt with the impact of financial integration upon economic growth reported that the majority of the papers found no effect or a mixed effect for developing countries. Similarly, Kose, Prasad, and Terrones (2003) found that financial openness was associated with increased consumption volatility.

Why, then, did the IMF promote financial globalization? The upper-income members who dominated the governance of the IMF were deregulating their own financial sectors during this period, and those who had not previously removed restrictions on foreign capital were doing so. Moreover, the increases in capital flows to emerging markets were welcomed by most of those nations. Therefore, the IMF was responding to the change in the views of many members on the benefits of financial flows.

But a social constructivist view points out that capital decontrol was also compatible with the views of the IMF's staff regarding the purpose of the organization. Monitoring financial developments was a logical extension of the IMF's surveillance of macroeconomic policies, and establishing capital account liberalization as a goal for its membership would allow the Fund to formulate a consistent position in its interactions with its members. Moreover, norms were needed to govern the expansion of financial globalization. The IMF sought to establish its institutional position as an agent with authority over its members' policies in this area.

The IMF's advocacy of decontrol can also be viewed from a public choice perspective. The extension of its authority would have increased the duties and powers of the IMF's staff. More resources would have been needed to monitor the compliance of member governments with their new obligations. The Fund would have been able to play a more central role in articulating international financial norms, which had been the responsibility of the BCBS and other Basel agencies. Paradoxically, while the IMF was not able to establish capital market deregulation as a goal for its members, it did receive new responsibilities and powers in the financial sphere in the aftermath of the Mexican crisis (Chapter 6).

But while endorsing the integration of financial markets may have served the IMF's interests, it did not contribute to financial stability. The IMF ignored the lessons of the 1930s that had been the impetus for the restrictions on capital flows in the Bretton Woods system. Moreover, the debt crisis had revealed that private financial markets did not function as efficiently as their promoters claimed, and their imperfections had severe economic consequences for the countries involved. The European and Mexican crises, which we examine in the next chapter, would further demonstrate the risks associated with financial globalization.

6

Currency Crises

Future historians may, in fact, dub this the Age of Currency Crises: never before, not even in the interwar period, have currency crises played such a central role in world affairs....Currency crises – both crises that actually do happen and the sometimes desperate efforts of national governments and international agencies to head them off – have become a defining force for economic policy in much of the world.

Krugman (2000:1)

The wave of financial globalization during the early and mid-1990s was accompanied by crises that demonstrated the volatility of capital flows. This chapter describes the European currency crisis of 1992–3 and the Mexican crisis of 1994–5. These events revealed that capital inflows could be quickly reversed and pose a threat to financial stability by undermining exchange rate commitments.

The background and outbreak of the European crisis are presented in the first section. European governments had formed a fixed exchange rate pact in the 1980s as part of a move toward deeper economic integration within the EC and strengthened their ties in the 1990s. But increases in German interest rates put pressure on the exchange rate pegs and demonstrated how fixed rates and unregulated capital could constrain national policies. Most of the governments subsequently proceeded with the introduction of the euro, although the United Kingdom withdrew from the arrangement.

The next section examines several implications of the crisis. The European governments dealt with the crisis without the involvement of the IMF, thus reinforcing the division between the upper-income countries and other members of the Fund. The events in Europe also raised questions about the IMF's crisis response policies, as the collapse of the fixed rates was not due to expansionary domestic policies. A new class of currency crisis models, which demonstrated that the expectations of a crisis could be self-fulfilling under some circumstances, was developed.

A very different crisis occurred in Mexico in 1994–5, and these events are summarized in the third section. A period of current account deficits financed by capital inflows was followed by one of capital flight in response to deteriorating economic and political conditions. The Mexican government was forced to abandon its exchange rate commitment and faced the possibility of defaulting on its debt. The IMF collaborated with the United States in managing a response to the crisis, which included a relatively large amount of credit from the Fund. The Mexican economy subsequently made a relatively rapid recovery.

A number of institutional initiatives that were undertaken in response to the Mexican crisis are reviewed in the fourth section. The IMF established a new arrangement to obtain additional financial resources from its members. The G7 called for the development of banking standards by the BCBS, while the IMF created data dissemination guidelines and oversaw the adoption of the new codes by the emerging markets and developing countries. The IMF's responsibilities in crisis prevention were enhanced, but the Fund shared these new duties with the World Bank and other agencies.

The last section appraises the IMF's response to the crisis in Mexico. The IMF moved quickly in coordination with the United States to deal with Mexico's deteriorating financial position. But some G7 governments criticized the IMF's program, claiming that it had been designed to assist bondholders and other lenders in the United States. Others were concerned about the moral hazard implications of the IMF's crisis management. In addition, some of the conditions attached to the IMF's program with Mexico were seen as unnecessarily austere. Many of these charges were to be raised again during the East Asian crisis.

6.1 ERM

The first major international financial crisis of the 1990s differed from its successors in several aspects.[1] First, it involved only European nations, unlike the subsequent crises, which occurred in emerging markets. Second, the IMF played no role in its resolution. The European governments dealt with the collapse of their fixed exchange rates without outside assistance, emphasizing the split between the advanced countries and the other

---

[1] Eichengreen (2008) and Gandolfo (2002) provide overviews of the ERM crises of 1992–3.

members of the IMF. Third, the volatility was confined to the currency markets and did not lead to instability in the financial sectors of the European countries. The situation would be different in the emerging markets.

After the collapse of Bretton Woods, the member nations of the European Community (EC) sought to establish exchange rate stability on a regional basis by tying their currencies to each other through an arrangement known as the "snake in the tunnel." The central banks of these countries had difficulties in maintaining their commitments, and the pact broke down. In 1979, however, the EC members agreed to form the European Monetary System (EMS), and eight of these countries participated in the Exchange Rate Mechanism (ERM), a fixed exchange rate arrangement. Bilateral parity exchange rates that could fluctuate within bands of ±2¼ percent were established.[2] While the central banks of the ERM members were obliged to intervene in the exchange rate markets to maintain the parity rates, the rates could be adjusted if there was common agreement.

After 1989, there were several changes in the ERM. First, the member governments agreed to maintain the fixed currency values through the use of domestic monetary policy. Second, the EC agreed to replace the EMS with a full monetary union and a single currency, to be known as the *euro*. Third, controls on capital flows within the *euro* area were removed. In addition, Spain joined the ERM in 1989, followed by the United Kingdom in 1990 and Portugal in 1992. Several countries outside the European Community – Austria, Norway, and Sweden – became de facto participants in the exchange rate arrangement by pegging their currencies to the West German *deutsche mark*, the predominant currency in the exchange rate bloc.

In 1991, the member governments of the EC met in Maastricht, the Netherlands, to plan the transition to a monetary union. They established guidelines for national economic policies, including limits on budget deficits, government debt, national inflation, long-term interest rates, and exchange rate volatility. The EC members also agreed to establish a European Central Bank (ECB) to administer the new currency and renamed their organization the European Union.

However, a series of shocks soon threatened the stability of the ERM. After the fall of the Berlin Wall and the reunification of Germany, the German government sought to foster economic welfare in the former East Germany through expenditures on social programs and infrastructure. The country's central bank, anxious about the impact on inflation of the expansionary fiscal policy, raised German interest rates in the summer of 1992.

---

[2]   Larger bands of ±6% were allowed in special circumstances.

This move put pressure on the other central banks in the ERM to match the German interest rate hike with similar increases in order to preserve their fixed currency values. In addition, a Danish referendum in June 1992 on the Maastricht Treaty resulted in a rejection of the treaty by the Danes and raised doubts about the future of the EMS.[3]

Speculative activity in the currency markets began to mount, reflecting skepticism about the willingness of the central banks to maintain their currency values. Currency sellers concentrated on Italy and the United Kingdom, and George Soros achieved fame (or notoriety) for selling short $10 billion of pounds. The Bank of England, concerned by that country's high unemployment rate, initially sought to defend the pound by raising interest rates, but continuing reserve losses forced it to exit from the ERM in September 1992. Italy followed and abandoned its support of the *lira*.

Speculative pressure then mounted against the currencies of other members of the ERM. Despite a (narrow) vote by the French public in favor of the Maastricht agreements, the French central bank was forced to support the *franc* in the face of massive sales in the exchange markets. Other countries, including Spain, Portugal, and Ireland, responded to pressure on their currencies through devaluations. By the summer of 1993, finance ministers of the EMS countries agreed to widen the bands around the parity rates substantially, from ±2¼ percent to ±15 percent, a tacit suspension of the system.

The ERM crisis of 1992–3 demonstrated the force of the constraint of the "impossible trinity." Once capital controls had been removed, the central banks of the EMS no longer could set their interest rates in response to domestic conditions. The decision by the German central bank to raise its interest rates required a matching increase (or some other measure) by the other countries if the exchange parity rates were to be maintained. But higher interest rates could be accompanied by rising unemployment, which was not politically acceptable. Each country had to choose which aspect of macroeconomic policy – fixed exchange rates or monetary autonomy – it was willing to sacrifice.

The United Kingdom rejected the constraint of the fixed exchange rate and left the ERM. The countries that remained in the arrangement proceeded with their plans to adopt the *euro*, and the values of eleven national currencies were fixed against the *euro* at the end of 1998. The transition to the Eurozone (the area that adopted the *euro*) began the following year under the direction of the ECB, and notes and coins were introduced in

---

[3] The Danes eventually accepted the Maastricht Treaty in a second referendum.

2001. Other European countries subsequently sought to adopt the euro, including East European countries that joined the EU after the disintegration of the Soviet Union.

The Europeans, therefore, responded to the breakdown of the Bretton Woods system by supporting economic and financial stability on a regional basis. This model would be studied by countries in other parts of the world that also sought to create regional alternatives to the IMF. However, while new users of the *euro* had to meet guidelines on their macroeconomic policies, these rules were not binding once a country entered the Eurozone. Subsequent events demonstrated that national policies could threaten the viability of the currency arrangements (Chapter 11).

6.2 IMF and the ERM Crisis: Appraisal

The Western European governments in the ERM saw no need to involve the IMF in resolving the crisis. The number of countries that were involved was small, and their governments could negotiate directly without the need of an intergovernmental organization. Moreover, by the 1980s these countries no longer borrowed from the IMF.[4]

The European countries were not the only advanced economies with crises that did not turn to the IMF for assistance. In the United States there were widespread failures of savings and loans associations, financial intermediaries that had specialized in extending mortgages before being deregulated in the early 1980s, and the sector was reorganized in 1989. A deterioration in the balance sheets of Japanese banks during the 1990s followed asset booms in housing and the stock market that required government intervention to stabilize the system. Several Nordic countries also suffered crises in their banking sectors. Moreover, the continuing appreciation of the U.S. dollar against the Japanese yen during the early 1980s was countered by exchange market intervention in 1985 after a meeting of the G5 finance ministers. National policy makers dealt with all these emergencies, collaborating with their peers when necessary, but not involving the IMF in their efforts.

One consequence of these developments was that the IMF no longer functioned as a credit union, lending to all members. The membership of the IMF became split between those countries that did not borrow from the IMF and those that did. This stratification of the IMF membership exacerbated the existing division between the richer and poorer nations and

---

[4] Portugal borrowed from the IMF during the period of 1982–4, before its membership in the EU and while it was classified as a developing economy (Boughton 2001b).

would be a factor in future disagreements over the programs and policies of the Fund.

Even if the IMF had been asked to help resolve the 1992–3 EMS crisis, it is not clear what measures it would have recommended. The crisis was not due to expansionary macroeconomic policies, as the IMF's models (Chapter 2) and the first-generation currency crisis models (Chapter 4) assumed. While the German government had increased its expenditures, its central bank implemented a relatively contractionary monetary policy and kept inflation under control. Similarly, the other European countries had not engaged in expansionary policies before the crisis took place. Consequently, the IMF's policy models could not explain the root causes of the crises or offer policies to resolve them.

The EMS crisis also resurrected the issue of speculation, which was frequently blamed by politicians as the cause of the crisis. Speculators appeared to have played a more active part in bringing about the collapse of the EMS than the first-generation models indicated they could. Moreover, their activities seem to have been motivated more by doubts regarding future policy actions than by current and recent monetary policy.

Obstfeld (1994, 1996) pointed out that a speculative attack usually followed deterioration in the economic fundamentals of a country with a pegged exchange rate, while crises are not likely to occur when economic fundamentals are strong. However, he also raised the possibility of a third range of circumstances where a crisis is possible but not inevitable. Obstfeld (1994, 1996) and others offered models to analyze the properties of multiple equilibria in the exchange rate markets, and these have become known as the "second-generation" models of currency crises.[5]

Krugman (1996) offered a reduced form version of the second-generation models (Box 6.1). In the model, the government seeks to minimize a social welfare function that includes the deviation between the fixed rate and that desired by the government given the economic fundamentals, the change in the exchange rate expected by speculators, and a political cost that would be borne if the government broke its exchange rate commitment. If the fixed rate is close to that consistent with the desired rate given the current state of the economy and speculators do not expect a devaluation, then the fixed cost of a change in the exchange rate exceeds any benefit and the government maintains the peg. If, on the other hand, the economy deteriorates and a change from the current level of the exchange rate would benefit the economy, then the central bank will devalue.

---

[5] Jeanne (2000) offers a review of this class of models, which he refers to as "escape clause" models.

Box 6.1. Second-Generation Model of Currency Crises

The government has a loss function (L) that it seeks to minimize:

$$L = [a(e^*(\theta) - \tilde{e}) + b\, E(\Delta e)]^2 + C \qquad a, b > 0 \qquad (6.1)$$

where e^* is the exchange rate, the domestic value of foreign currency, preferred by the government given fundamental economic conditions as measured by θ; $\tilde{e}$ is the fixed exchange rate; $E(\Delta e)$ is the change in the exchange rate expected by speculators; and C is the political cost to the government's credibility of abandoning the peg.

The determination of e^* depends on the state of economy. A high value of θ signals a strong economy, so the government prefers a low exchange rate to minimize inflation. Conversely, a low value of θ represents unfavorable fundamental economic conditions, and the government favors a high exchange rate value to raise exports and output. The larger the gap between the exchange rate that the government would prefer and the pegged exchange rate, the larger the social cost. The speculators' expected change also enters the loss function: the greater the expectation that the exchange rate will be changed, the more difficult it is to maintain the exchange rate at the pegged level.

There are costs to the government of maintaining the exchange rate peg at its current level, but there are also costs to abandoning the peg. If the cost is greater than the circumstances that favor a devaluation, then the government maintains it. This happens if:

$$[a(e^*(\theta) - \tilde{e}) + b\, E(\Delta e)]^2 < C \qquad (6.2)$$

If no devaluation is expected by speculators, then it will be optimal for the government to maintain the peg as long as the gap between the fixed value and the value desired by the government is not too great, that is, the exchange rate the government would like is close to the pegged exchange rate. This happens if:

$$[a(e^*(\theta) - \tilde{e})]^2 < C \qquad (6.3)$$

However, the government would abandon the peg if the economy deteriorated and the gap between the desired exchange rate and the pegged value grew:

$$[a(e^*(\theta) - \tilde{e})]^2 > C \qquad (6.4)$$

Therefore, there are two possible situations: either the government favors the existing arrangement or it does not. But with speculative activity, the situation changes. Domestic conditions may themselves not require a devaluation, but if speculators expect one, the inequality could turn:

$$[a(e^*(\theta) - \tilde{e}) + b\, E(\Delta e)]^2 > C \qquad (6.5)$$

If speculators expect the government to devalue the exchange rate to the desired level, then this reduces to:

$$[(a + b)(e^*(\theta) - \tilde{e})]^2 > C \qquad (6.6)$$

When economic fundamentals are strong, therefore, there is no reason to expect the government to abandon the exchange rate peg. On the other hand, if economic conditions are weak, then the government has an incentive to abandon the fixed exchange rate regardless of what the speculators do. The speculators' expectations reinforce the case for a devaluation since it raises the cost to the government of further maintaining the peg.

There may also be an intermediate zone:

$$[a(e^*(\theta) - \tilde{e})]^2 < C < [(a + b)(e^*(\theta) - \tilde{e}]^2 \qquad (6.7)$$

In this case, the government maintains the peg as long as speculators do not expect a devaluation. But if the speculators do expect a change, then the additional weight of the expected devaluation will bring about the devaluation, and expectations become self-fulfilling.

Source: Krugman (1996).

There is a third possible case, where the economy is weak but not weak enough to justify a devaluation. However, if speculators expect a devaluation to be imminent, their selling can force the government's hand. The specific causes of a change in the speculators' expectations, however, are not specified, and consequently the timing of a crisis in these models is indeterminate.[6]

Subsequent empirical research sought to determine whether there had been currency crises with the characteristics outlined in the second-generation models. Eichengreen, Rose, and Wyplosz (1995: 294) examined the record of exchange rate crises in twenty upper-income countries after 1959 and found evidence that governments had brought about currency crises through "the reckless pursuit of excessively expansionary

---

[6] Morris and Shin (1998) have shown that there exists a unique equilibrium in a currency crisis model if there is private information about the fundamental state of the economy.

policies." However, there were also occasions where transitions from fixed exchange rates were not preceded by expansionary monetary or fiscal policies, and they concluded that "speculative attacks can be a symptom of self-fulfilling attacks, in the sense that markets may believe that the government will not resist pressure and will shift to more expansionary policies as it abandons its exchange rate commitment in response to the attack itself" (Eichengreen, Rose and Wyplosz 1995: 294).

These models demonstrate the need for a country to maintain strong fundamentals if it wishes to prevent a crisis. In future years, the governments of many developing economies would seek to deter speculators by accumulating stocks of foreign exchange reserves (Chapter 9). The implications of the second-generation models for the IMF's role in preventing currency crises were not as clear-cut. The IMF's surveillance activities could serve to signal that a government has implemented stable policies and that its economy possesses strong fundamentals. On the other hand, any discussions of a government with the Fund outside the usual surveillance framework may send the opposite message, even if a government is only pursuing options in the event of a future external shock.

6.3 Mexico: Crisis

Mexico had emerged from the debt crisis of the 1980s with a commitment to economic stability and reform.[7] An agreement among the government, private firms, and the labor unions – the *Pacto* – controlled price and wage increases as well as changes in the exchange rate. The government controlled movements in the *peso* through an adjustable band that allowed a nominal depreciation. During the early 1990s, the government enacted stable monetary and fiscal policies, and subsequently inflation fell below 10 percent by 1993 (Table 6.1).

The government also sought to liberalize the economy, particularly the financial sector, with the active encouragement of the IMF and the World Bank (Edwards 1998, Woods 2006). Controls on lending rates were removed, and banks that had been nationalized in 1982 during the debt crisis were privatized. Relatively loose capital requirements and weak regulatory supervision resulted in a rapid expansion of bank credit, which

---

[7] For accounts of the Mexican crisis of 1994–5 see Edwards (1998), Edwards and Naím (1998), Loser and Williams (1997), Sachs, Tornell, and Velasco (1996a, b), and the United States General Accountability Office (1996), as well as the relevant chapters in Copelovitch (2010), De Beaufort Wijnholds (2011), Isard (2005), Lamfalussy (2000), and Montiel (2003a).

Table 6.1. *Mexico: 1991–1996*

	1991	1992	1993	1994	1995	1996
GDP growth (%)	4.22	3.63	1.95	4.46	−6.22	5.14
CPI growth (%)	22.66	15.51	9.75	6.97	35.00	34.38
Fiscal surplus/deficit (% of GDP)	0.00	0.98	0.23	0.00	−0.62	−0.13
Money and quasi-money growth (%)	49.21	23.57	16.90	20.11	31.86	27.01
Domestic credit of banks (% of GDP)	37.82	40.42	41.11	48.97	49.55	37.35
Current account (% of GDP)	−4.73	−6.72	−5.80	−7.03	−0.55	−0.75
Short-term debt (% of total reserves)	121.08	127.98	143.32	610.47	218.83	152.81

Source: World Development Indicators, March 2012.

grew at an average rate of 40 percent a year during the period of 1991 through 1993.

In addition, restrictions on capital flows were removed. Private capital inflows rose from $5.8 billion in 1990 to $19.9 billion in 1991, $23.5 billion in 1992, and $30.3 billion in 1993. About half of this amount took the form of portfolio flows. Foreign investors were encouraged by the government's liberalization of governmental regulations as well as the passage of the North American Free Trade Agreement with Canada and the United States, which opened the prospect of expanded export markets. The government sterilized the monetary impact of the inflows, which contributed to the increase in credit, by issuing *peso*-denominated debt, *Cetes*.

These private capital flows were large enough to finance a current account deficit that reached 8 percent of GDP by 1994. This deficit did not reflect excessive government spending, however, as the government's budget registered a small surplus. Instead, a decline in private savings and an appreciation of the real exchange rate led to a surge in imports, while the anticipated rapid increase in exports did not materialize.

Mexican officials pointed to the inflow of foreign funds as evidence of foreign confidence in the government's policies and the economy's long-run prospects. However, not everyone shared this assessment. Dornbusch and Werner (1994) pointed to the low growth rate of GDP, which had fallen below 2 percent in 1993, and the current account deficits as signs that the real exchange rate was overvalued, despite the nominal depreciation of the currency. They called for the government to abandon its procedure for controlling the exchange rate and to devalue the currency by at least 20 percent. But their appeal occurred during the year before a presidential election, which was not a propitious time for the government to make macroeconomic adjustments.

An uprising in the southern state of Chiapas in January 1994 raised doubts about the stability of the political situation, and these concerns were reinforced by the assassination in March of the presidential candidate of the ruling political party. Capital inflows slowed, and the Banco de México responded to a wave of selling of the *peso* by drawing upon its reserves of dollars. The interest rate on the government's debt, the *Cetes*, rose, and the government moved to limit the rise and reassure investor fears of a devaluation by issuing another type of debt, *Tesobonos*, which were linked to the value of the dollar. The outstanding stock of short-term debt tied to exchange values grew rapidly vis-à-vis the central bank's reserves.

The election of a new president in August did not resolve the uncertainties, and further negative shocks, including a second political assassination in September, added to the unease. Increases in interest rates in the United States encouraged capital flight out of the country. Reserves continued to decline throughout the fall, but the government did not announce any new policies to stop the deterioration in its external position. By late December, however, central bank reserves had fallen to about $11 billion. The authorities responded by enlarging the band of permissible exchange rate fluctuations, but the *peso* immediately reached the limit of the band, and foreign reserve holdings fell further. On December 22, the Banco de México, the country's central bank, announced it would no longer support its currency in the foreign exchange markets, and the *peso* collapsed.

The rapid depreciation of the *peso* alarmed foreign investors, who feared that the country would not be able to fulfill its debt obligations (Sachs, Tornell, and Velasco 1996b). Unlike the situation in 1982, when the government could directly negotiate with the banks that had lent to it, the country's creditors were now the many foreign holders of Mexican securities. The differential between the rate of return paid on U.S. Treasury bills and the *Tesobonos* rose from 1.4 percent in November to 5 percent at the end of December, 7 percent in January 1995, and 19 percent the following month. Moreover, fears about debt repayment by other Latin American borrowers began to spread, and these negative reappraisals led to reductions in capital inflows throughout the region. The extension of the crisis beyond Mexico was named the "tequila effect." [8]

The U.S. government initially took the lead in responding to the collapse of the *peso*, in part because of Mexican concerns that an arrangement with

---

[8] Argentina suffered a decline in output in 1995 in response to the higher interest rates that were a consequence of the "tequila effect," although domestic conditions including an overvalued exchange rate were also responsible.

the IMF would be construed as a sign of weakness (Lustig 1997).[9] The U.S. Treasury Department arranged a financial rescue arrangement with Canada and other G10 countries. However, the continuing decline of the *peso* led to the realization that additional financial assistance was needed. Mounting political opposition within the United States to the support extended to Mexico drove the Clinton administration to turn to the IMF for further assistance.

After further negotiations, new arrangements with the United States and the IMF were formulated. The final financial rescue package totaled $48.8 billion, with $20 billion committed by the United States, an eighteen-month IMF SBA arrangement of $17.8 billion, $10 billion from the BIS, and a Canadian contribution of $1 billion.[10] Not only was the IMF credit the largest absolute amount ever lent, but it was equal to almost seven times Mexico's quota, thus exceeding the usual borrowing access limits of 100 percent of quota in a year and a cumulative limit of 300 percent. In addition, the IMF disbursed $7.8 billion when the program was signed, an unusually large amount to be "front-loaded" at the beginning of the program.

The IMF's financial support was tied to the establishment of a fiscal surplus, a wage policy that included limits on nominal wage hikes, limits on credit expansion by the central bank, and continuance of the floating exchange rate regime. The program included structural measures as well, including the privatization of infrastructure such as railways and ports. The government also enacted a series of measures to stabilize the banking sector, including dollar loans to banks with foreign currency liabilities, measures to increase banks' capital, and the removal of restrictions to allow greater foreign ownership. The measures to reform the financial sector were costly, and their fiscal cost reached 14.4 percent of GDP for 1997 (Ortiz Martinez 1998).

The additional financial support and the announcement of the government's revised economic program finally stabilized the situation in March, although there was a decline in GDP of 6.2 percent in 1995. The current account deficit narrowed to less than 1 percent of GDP, private capital flows resumed, and the economy grew by 5.1 percent in 1996 and 6.8 percent in 1997. The Mexican government drew only $12.5 billion from the financial arrangement it had made with the United States and about three-quarters

---

[9] See Ghosh *et al.* (2002) and Lustig (1997) on the details of the response of the IMF and the United States.

[10] The U.S. Congress did not support the earlier arrangements the Treasury Department had made with the Mexican government. President William J. Clinton used his executive authority to provide the funds through the Exchange Stabilization Fund.

of the amount that the IMF made available. The government repaid its obligations to the United States and the IMF in advance of the original schedule.

6.4 Mexico: Aftermath

The Mexican crisis was on the agenda when the G7 leaders met at Halifax in 1995 (Bayne 2005). While the United States had pushed for international support in its rescue efforts, many European nations believed that Mexico's financial crisis was a problem for the U.S. government to resolve. The G7 leaders, however, concurred on the need for new measures to forestall additional crises and to deal with those that did occur. They called for stronger surveillance by the IMF; the establishment of a new emergency financing mechanism at the Fund with faster access, supported with additional financial resources for the IMF; improved cooperation between financial regulators; and the investigation of procedures for the resolution of debt insolvency.

The IMF followed up the call to secure more financing by arranging a new credit arrangement, the New Arrangements to Borrow (NAB), to supplement the GAB (Chapter 3). The membership of the NAB, which was established in November 1998, reflected the growth of the global financial markets to include the emerging markets, and the participants include the G10 countries, Australia, Austria, Denmark, Finland, Hong Kong, Korea, Kuwait, Malaysia, Norway, Saudi Arabia, Singapore, Spain, Sweden, and Thailand. They pledged to provide credit of up to $24 billion that could be used to finance programs to non-NAB countries.

At the 1997 summit meeting in Lyons, the G7 heads of government renewed their calls for increased cooperation among the regulators of internationally active financial institutions. They also encouraged the adoption of strong prudential standards in emerging markets. Once again, the G7 followed a dual track in their treatment of financial regulations. The responsibility for devising the new regulations was assigned to the BCSB, while the IMF and the World Bank were delegated the task of monitoring the compliance of their members with the requirements.

In 1997, the BCBS issued its "Core Principles on Banking Supervision," and a methodology for implementing them was published in 1999.[11] The principles deal with different aspects of banking supervision, including the

---

[11] Both the principles and the methodology were revised and reissued in 2006.

objectives of supervision, the determination of capital adequacy, the assessment of the different kinds of risk, and relations with supervisors in other countries. Implementation was voluntary, but there were incentives to follow the guidelines in the form of international market access, as with the Basel I capital requirements.

In addition, the IMF took the initiative to create the *Special Data Dissemination Standard* and the *General Data Dissemination Standard* after the Mexican crisis. The former provided guidelines for countries in providing economic and financial data to the international capital markets, while the latter provided guidance for national statistical systems. Participation is voluntary, and the IMF provides technical assistance to countries in meeting the standards.

Implicit in the call for new regulations and standards was the belief that providing more timely data would contribute to stability in the international financial markets. The lack of transparency regarding Mexico's foreign exchange holdings had been blamed for contributing to a loss of confidence among investors. The standards, therefore, were intermediate public goods, and implementing them would contribute to the IPG of financial stability. However, the appropriateness of the standards for the emerging markets was questioned (Scott 2007). Moreover, a study later undertaken at the IMF found no relationship between bank risk and compliance with the Basel Core Principles (Demirgüç-Kunt and Detragiache 2010).

The assignment to the IMF to monitor adherence to the financial benchmarks represented an expansion of the IMF's duties. The efforts by the IMF to participate in the task of crisis prevention had been implicit in the charge in the revised Article IV to undertake surveillance (Chapter 3), but the enforcement of the new standards represented a more concrete responsibility. The Fund was willing to undertake this work as it represented a logical extension of the IMF's technical expertise, and it expanded its mission.

While the IMF did not receive the wide-ranging mandate it desired to oversee global finance markets (Chapter 5), the new standards did provide a rationale for monitoring domestic financial developments. However, the IMF shared this responsibility with other IGOs, including the World Bank and the Basel Hub agencies that set the standards. International financial governance continued to be split, therefore, between the upper-income governments that established the financial regulations and emerging market nations that needed to accept them to participate in the global financial markets.

6.5 IMF and Mexico: Appraisal

The crisis in Mexico was called by Camdessus (1995) the "first financial crisis of the twenty-first century." While the country's current account deficit had been a source of concern, the IMF (like many others) was caught by surprise by the collapse of the *peso* and the volatility in the market for the country's sovereign debt. The crisis was the product of an overvalued exchange rate and rapid credit expansion by a banking sector that had been rapidly liberalized without establishing adequate supervision and regulatory reform. When the exchange rate came under speculative pressure, the central bank faced the difficult choice of tightening monetary policy to support the currency at the cost of undermining the financial system, or supporting the banks through credit creation that would weaken its ability to maintain the exchange rate (Calvo and Mendoza 1996).

Was the IMF's program an appropriate response to the threat to international stability? Mexico's debt crisis was viewed as one of illiquidity, not insolvency (DeLong, DeLong, and Robinson 1996, Montiel 2003a). Under such circumstances, a lender of last resort needs to provide sufficient credit against good collateral to stem a panic. The IMF moved relatively rapidly and the amount provided was large and timely. The "collateral" consisted of the country's good economic fundamentals, which allowed it to recover quickly and restore its reputation in the international credit markets.

But some of the conditions attached to the IMF's program were suitable for a country that had engaged in expansionary government policies, and these circumstances were not relevant in the case of Mexico. Similarly, the privatization of public sector enterprises and other structural conditions, while perhaps useful for promoting long-term growth, were not necessary to resolve the financial crisis facing the country. The imposition of relatively austere macroeconomic policies and the improper use of structural conditionality would also become issues in the Asian crisis (Chapter 7).

The subsequent recovery in Mexican GDP and the resumption of private capital inflows were seen as indications that the IMF's intervention had been successful. There were, however, concerns about beneficiaries of the rescue plan. While foreign holders of equity in Mexico, both portfolio and direct, suffered sharp losses, the foreign holders of debt recovered the full value of their investments (Lamfalussy 2000). Schwartz (1998: 254) posed the question "Is there any doubt that the loan package (for Mexico) was designed to pay dollars to Americans and other nationals who invested in *Tesobonos* and *Cetes* and dollar-denominated loans to Mexican nonfinancial firms?"

Opposition to the rescue plan reflected other concerns as well. Within the United States there was political resistance to what was viewed as a bailout of domestic financial interests.[12] The disagreement was based in part on the mistaken belief that support of Mexico was at a cost to taxpayers in the United States, whereas in reality the U.S. Treasury profited from the repayment of loans with interest. The antagonism to the efforts to assist Mexico was also mixed in with opposition to the passage of the North American Free Trade Agreement.

International discord and a split within the G7 governments arose over the use of the IMF by the United States to protect its interests in a neighboring country (Copelovitch 2010). The United States had moved rapidly to obtain the IMF's assistance to Mexico without consulting the other G7 nations, and the executive directors of Germany and the United Kingdom subsequently abstained from the vote on the program with Mexico. In this case, the chief principals were split over how to proceed, and the IMF's intervention placed it on the side of the major power.

In addition, there were European concerns regarding the moral hazard aspect of the program (Blustein 2001). A perception among private investors that the IMF would protect them from any loss could distort their assessment of risk and the provision of credit by lenders. Alternatively, governments could discount the risks involved in borrowing for risky purposes if they thought the IMF would bail them out. The IMF's support of Mexico was later cited as a contributing factor to the Asian crises (Chapter 7).[13]

It is not clear, however, what policy options the IMF had once the Mexican situation deteriorated as far as it did. A default by the Mexican government on its debt obligations would have exacerbated that country's economic situation and worsened the "tequila crisis" among its neighbors. The IMF may have been pressured by the United States in responding quickly, but its actions were consistent with its obligations under the Articles of Agreement to help nations avoid "measures destructive of national or international prosperity." The commitment of substantial funds by the IMF was a sign of the Fund's awareness of the magnitude of the challenge it faced in Mexico.

---

[12] Similar opposition arose in the wake of the passage of the Troubled Asset Relief Program within the United States in 2008.

[13] Kamin (2004) sought to test whether the financial rescue of Mexico lowered investors' concerns by comparing the spread between the rate of return on emerging market bonds and U.S. Treasury bonds before and after the crisis. If lenders believed after the crisis that the obligations of emerging markets were relatively safer because of the response by the IMF, then the spread should have been lower in the post–1995 period than that predicted by fundamental factors. He found, however, little evidence that spreads were lower than they would otherwise have been.

Another question that was raised at the time was whether the IMF should have foreseen the coming crisis. The IMF had not seen a need for reconsideration of Mexico's exchange rate policy in its Article IV consultations with Mexico in early 1994, although it did urge the country to reduce its current account deficit. After the meetings with the Mexican authorities, the IMF received limited data on a lagged basis from them. Since Mexico was not engaged in a program, the IMF had limited leverage over the government's policies. There was also a reluctance to interfere with a member's policies when they were seen as successful, as they had been viewed before 1994.

The IMF drew several lessons for its operations from the crisis in Mexico (Loser and Williams 1997). The Fund called for more timely and complete disclosure of information by members and promised more scrutiny of financial flows. Camdessus (1995) called for more "pointed and candid surveillance" of members' policies. However, the issue of what the IMF could do if a member implemented policies that could lead to instability was unresolved. Camdessus also cited the need for "sound and credible" macroeconomic measures to provide stable expectations for the exchange rate but did not address the question of how to reconcile exchange rate stability with unregulated capital flows.

There was no reason to believe that the conditions that led to the crisis in Mexico were unique to that country. However, the rapid recovery of the Mexican economy contributed to a lack of concern about a repetition of the events that occurred there. The financial markets seemed to regard Mexico's crisis as a transient event due to unique circumstances. But the consequences of the combination of fixed exchange rates and short-term capital flows would be faced again on an even greater scale in Asia, as the next chapter will demonstrate.

7

The Widening Gyre

The Mexican crisis of 1994–5 proved to be the first of a wave of financial catastrophes in emerging market countries that took place during the rest of the decade and continued into the next. Their occurrence effectively marked the emerging markets as the "weaker links" in the global financial markets. This chapter provides an account of the East Asian crisis of 1997–8 and an appraisal of the IMF's response, which was tested by the collapses of currency pegs and domestic financial systems.

The East Asian crisis had several distinguishing characteristics. First, it was a crisis of the private sector, not sovereign borrowing. Private capital flows, which contributed to asset booms across the region, left domestic financial sectors with large foreign exposures. Second, the crisis spread rapidly across the region, allowing it to be characterized as one "crisis" rather than a series of "crises," although the details differed from country to country. Third, there were substantial capital outflows from the crisis countries, and the IMF had to rewrite its own rules on access limits in order to lend very large amounts to the countries that accepted assistance.

The first section offers a précis of the background and outbreak of the crisis. The East Asian countries had enjoyed rapid growth in the years preceding the crises, in part because of stable macroeconomic policies. But inflows of short-term capital coupled with fixed exchange rate regimes had left them vulnerable to reversals of capital movements. The crisis originated in Thailand, where capital outflows overwhelmed the efforts of the central bank to maintain the pegged exchange rate. Similar flows of capital took place in other East Asian countries, reflecting a pattern of contagion. The IMF extended financial support to Thailand, Indonesia, and South Korea, and other multilateral institutions and national governments gave additional assistance.

But the Fund's programs were criticized on a number of grounds, which are summarized in the second section. The initial conditions called for contractionary policies that were inappropriate for countries that faced collapses in private expenditures. The IMF revised its fiscal projections as the extent of the downturn became evident, although it maintained its stance on the need for higher interest rates. The extensive structural conditionality included in the programs was also seen as unsuitable for dealing with financial emergencies. In addition, the IMF's advocacy of capital account deregulation was also blamed for precipitating the crises. Consequently, the IMF's reputation in East Asia was damaged by its position on capital decontrol as well as its responses to the crises.

7.1 East Asia

The crisis in East Asia was preceded by a period of rapid growth that lifted incomes and lowered poverty rates.[1] Real GDP increased an annual average of 5–10 percent during the three years before the outbreak of the crisis in Indonesia, Korea, Malaysia, the Philippines, and Thailand, the countries in the area most affected by the financial turbulence, while annual inflation averaged 4–9 percent. The World Bank called the combination of growth with an equitable distribution of its benefits the "East Asian Miracle" and issued a report (World Bank 1993) that attributed the growth to high levels of investment and domestic savings, education policies that increased human capital, sound macroeconomic management, and in some instances government policies designed to foster the development of specific industries.[2]

The deregulation of capital flows in many of these countries was also seen as conducive to economic growth and supportive of the IMF's policy stance on this issue (Chapter 5). The rapid economic expansion of these countries attracted foreign capital. Net private capital flows to the largest Asian countries (excluding China)[3] averaged $32 billion a year between 1991 and 1993, fell to $24 billion in 1994 in the wake of the Mexican crisis, before rising to $38 billion in 1995 and $77 billion the following year

---

[1] There is a wide literature devoted to the East Asian financial crisis. The overview of the main events given here is based on the accounts provided by the Bank for International Settlements (1998, 1999), Berg (1999), Blustein (2001), Browne, Hellerstein and Little (1998), Corsetti, Pesenti, and Roubini (1999a, 1999b), De Beaufort Wijnholds (2011), Ghosh *et al.* (2002), Goldstein (1998), Grenville (2004), Hahm and Mishkin (2000), Isard (2005), Montiel (2003a), and Radelet and Sachs (1998, 2000).

[2] Krugman (1994) and others, however, attributed Asian growth to the increased use of resources such as labor rather than technical progress, and therefore unlikely to continue at the same rate.

[3] India, Indonesia, Republic of Korea, Malaysia, the Philippines, Singapore, Taiwan, and Thailand.

(Bank for International Settlements 1998). Much of this money consisted of bonds denominated in foreign currencies with short-term maturities, but there were also loans from international banks. The rise in inflows was attributed to high economic growth, financial deregulation accompanied by lax supervision, pegged exchange rates that reduced risk for investors, and government incentives to encourage foreign borrowing (Radelet and Sachs 2000).

One effect of the inflows of financial capital was a rapid expansion of bank credit in the recipient countries, which contributed to their economic growth. The average annual increase in bank credit to the private sector during the period of 1990 through 1997 ranged from 12 percent in Korea to 16 percent in Malaysia and 18 percent in Indonesia, the Philippines, and Thailand (Bank for International Settlements 1998). The short-term loans the domestic banks received were used to finance long-term credits to their borrowers, thus producing maturity mismatches on the banks' balance sheets. In addition, the banks often lent in their domestic currencies, thus exposing their balance sheets to currency mismatches as well. Moreover, the domestic financial institutions were often "undercapitalized and poorly regulated" (Berg 1999: 9). As a result, the expansion of credit left the banks and other financial institutions highly vulnerable to economic downturns or reversals of foreign capital. But there were no political incentives to slow the boom in private spending, and the events in Mexico were disregarded as the governments of the Asian countries had not incurred large amounts of debt.

The first signs of economic and financial distress appeared in Thailand (Table 7.1). The government had encouraged capital inflows to establish the country as a regional financial center. Much of this borrowing was short-term, and the amount of short-term debt exceeded the country's foreign exchange reserves by 1995. The domestic financial sector rapidly expanded its lending activities, particularly the finance companies, which provided funds for real estate development. The increase in financial activity led to run-ups in stock prices and property values.

The central bank had tied the value of the domestic currency, the *baht*, to the dollar. When the dollar began to rise against the Japanese *yen* in 1995, the accompanying increase in the value of the *baht* contributed to a slowdown in Thailand's exports. Economic growth fell from 9.3 percent in 1995 to 5.9 percent in 1996, while the current account deficit grew to 8.1 percent of GDP. Stock and property prices declined, weakening the position of firms in the financial sector. The Bank of Thailand initially sought to stabilize the financial sector by lending to the distressed institutions, but

Table 7.1. *Thailand: 1994–1999*

	1994	1995	1996	1997	1998	1999
GDP growth (%)	8.99	9.24	5.90	−1.37	−10.51	4.45
CPI growth (%)	5.05	5.82	5.81	5.63	7.99	0.28
Cash surplus/deficit (% of GDP)	NA	NA	NA	NA	NA	NA
Money and quasi-money growth (%)	10.69	17.74	10.62	19.55	10.07	3.80
Domestic credit of banks (% of GDP)	130.68	141.32	146.36	177.58	176.75	155.78
Current account (% of GDP)	−5.58	−8.08	−8.07	−2.00	12.73	10.16
Short-term debt (% of total reserves)	96.36	119.37	123.47	140.67	100.42	67.33

Source: World Development Indicators, March 2012.

increasing losses compelled the authorities to take over or arrange the private takeover of failing banks and financial firms.

The weakening position of the Thai economy was not unnoticed. After the crises in Europe and Mexico, foreign investors were aware of the fragility of exchange rate defenses. Sales of the *baht* in the foreign exchange markets escalated, and the Bank of Thailand was forced to support the domestic currency. The central bank's intervention included unpublicized transactions in the forward market, which effectively lowered the amount of foreign exchange reserves available to the central bank.

The IMF was also aware of the deterioration in Thailand's financial position. It had been criticized for not anticipating the Mexican crisis of 1994–5 and in response had improved its abilities to monitor global markets (Blustein 2001). The IMF was also more willing to draw the attention of national authorities to increases in potential financial instability. In January 1997, Managing Director Camdessus wrote a letter to the Thai finance minister expressing the Fund's concern and urging adoption of a more flexible exchange rate regime to allow a controlled depreciation of the currency. The IMF mission that went to Thailand in March for an Article IV consultation reiterated that message, as did First Deputy Managing Director Fischer during a visit in May. But the Fund could not compel the government to revise its policies, and there was no domestic constituency to advocate changes in practices that had seemingly served the country well.

In June, however, the pace of selling of the *baht* accelerated. The central bank abandoned its support of the currency in July, and the government turned to the IMF for assistance. In August the IMF approved an SBA of $4 billion, which represented 505 percent of Thailand's quota at the Fund, with additional financing of $13 billion from Japan as well as the World Bank and the Asian Development Bank. The program's conditions included

Table 7.2. *Indonesia: 1994–1999*

	1994	1995	1996	1997	1998	1999
GDP growth (%)	7.54	8.40	7.64	4.70	−13.13	0.79
CPI growth (%)	8.52	9.43	7.97	6.23	58.39	20.49
Cash surplus/deficit (% of GDP)	2.83	1.72	1.98	1.32	−1.84	−3.68
Money and quasi-money growth (%)	20.20	27.52	27.08	25.25	62.76	12.23
Domestic credit of banks (% of GDP)	50.58	51.82	54.02	59.55	59.93	62.07
Current account (% of GDP)	−1.58	−3.18	−3.37	−2.27	4.29	4.13
Short-term debt (% of total reserves)	146.06	174.18	166.17	187.94	85.20	73.25

Source: World Development Indicators, March 2012.

the restructuring of the financial sector through the closure of insolvent institutions, fiscal measures to produce a budget surplus, and higher interest rates.

The announcement of the IMF program did not stop the decline in the value of the *baht*, and this drop was reinforced by the disclosure of the central bank's activities in the forward currency market that drained reserves. The continuing fall of the currency led to adjustments in the IMF's program in November, although the program continued to include projections of a fiscal surplus. But declines in output during the last quarter of 1997 and the beginning of the following year forced a major modification of the program in the first half of 1998 to allow a fiscal deficit of 2 percent of GDP (subsequently raised to 3 percent), lower interest rates, and a strengthening of the social safety net.

After the Thai devaluation in July 1997, the currencies of other East Asian economies came under pressure, particularly the Indonesian *rupiah*, the Philippine *peso*, and the Malaysian *ringgit*. Indonesia had established a strong economic record, with economic growth averaging 8 percent in the period of 1994–6 (Table 7.2). The country had also been the recipient of capital inflows, which were often allocated directly to domestic borrowers rather than being intermediated by domestic banks. Many of the concerns that had been raised about Thailand before the crisis were absent in the case of Indonesia, in part because of its budget position and small (but growing) current account deficit. However, the ratio of its short-term debt to foreign exchange reserves exceeded Thailand's.

The government initially raised interest rates to prop up the currency but lowered them because of fears of a financial collapse and allowed the *rupiah* to float in August. Speculative pressures grew in October, in part due to uncertainty about whether President Suharto, who had been in office since 1967, would seek another term in office. The president's family and his friends had used their positions to establish extensive business enterprises with government support, and these could be threatened by a successor's reforms.

A three-year SBA was announced in November, with the Fund providing $10 billion, equal in value to 490 percent of the country's quota, and other governments and multilateral agencies contributing an additional $26 billion. The program's policy measures included a fiscal surplus and tight monetary policy to defend the *rupiah*. The Indonesian government also agreed to restructure the financial sector and subsequently closed sixteen banks in an attempt to improve the viability of the banking sector. However, nervous depositors withdrew their deposits from all private banks, and domestic firms defaulted on their obligations to foreign and domestic lenders. The central bank sought to support the financial system by providing additional credit, which only contributed to the pressure on the *rupiah*.

After further negotiations, a revised Letter of Intent was signed in January. The new agreement included a restructuring program for the banks, and it extended the provisions of the previous agreement to incorporate a wide range of structural conditions, including the termination of government support for businesses owned by Suharto's family and associates, and the abolition of subsidies on consumer goods. A widely circulated photograph of IMF Director Camdessus standing with arms folded while President Suharto signed the new agreement contributed to a perception that the IMF was imposing its policies of austerity on the country.

But President Suharto, who was reelected in March, showed little willingness to implement the conditions of the program. For a time the president showed an interest in a proposal to adopt a currency board, which would tie the quantity of *rupiah* in circulation to the amount of foreign exchange reserves held by the central bank. He backed away from the new currency arrangement in the face of opposition by the IMF and foreign leaders.

The increases in food and fuel prices that followed the removal of subsidies led to civil unrest and demonstrations. A revision in the agreement with the IMF in April contained some concessions in the timing of the cessation of subsidies, but President Suharto was not able to retain power and resigned from office in May. The continuing social and political unrest was accompanied by a severe economic contraction. In August, the SBA with the IMF was replaced by an EFF.

The Philippines lagged behind its neighbors in economic performance during the 1990s (Table 7.3). But while the country had experienced current account deficits in the period before the crisis, its short-term debt to

Table 7.3. *Philippines: 1994–1999*

	1994	1995	1996	1997	1998	1999
GDP growth (%)	4.39	4.68	5.85	5.19	−0.58	3.08
CPI growth (%)	8.36	6.71	7.51	5.59	9.27	5.95
Cash surplus/deficit (% of GDP)	NA	NA	NA	NA	NA	NA
Money and quasi-money growth (%)	26.73	23.87	23.73	23.11	8.57	16.88
Domestic credit of banks (% of GDP)	48.05	55.74	67.92	78.54	63.28	58.93
Current account (% of GDP)	−4.60	−2.67	−4.77	−5.28	2.14	−3.46
Short-term debt (% of total reserves)	79.98	67.85	67.68	134.87	54.04	32.84

Source: World Development Indicators, March 2012.

reserves coverage had not exceeded 100 percent. Moreover, asset prices had not escalated as sharply as they had in other countries, and the major banks were in a relatively stronger financial position.

When its currency came under pressure after the devaluation of the Thai *baht*, the central bank initially tightened monetary policy but soon abandoned its de facto peg to the dollar. The IMF agreed to an extension of an existing program in July with credit of $1 billion, which represented 119 percent of its quota, with an additional $450 million from other sources. The program included macroeconomic and structural policies designed to stabilize the currency. In this case, the *peso*'s decline eased after the announcement of the program. The central bank was able to lower interest rates while fiscal policy was eased to allow a deficit. The installation of a new president in June 1998 did not throw the program off course, and the almost-zero growth the economy recorded for that year was substantially better than the substantial declines recorded in the other crisis countries.

Korea was another country with a record of strong growth with moderate inflation and small fiscal surpluses (Table 7.4). Much of the export growth was due to the *chaebols*, conglomerates that were financed by domestic banks that themselves had borrowed extensively from foreign banks. The government had used the financial sector to promote economic development and blocked FDI to encourage domestic industrialization. A slowdown in exports in the mid-1990s led to a growing current account deficit and contributed to weak corporate performance. Several of the *chaebols* failed during the first half of 1997, exposing the fragility of the financial sector.

Korea was at first relatively untouched by the financial turbulence that had erupted in Southeast Asia. However, a devaluation of the Taiwanese currency, the New Taiwan dollar, and a speculative attack on the Hong Kong

Table 7.4. *South Korea: 1994–1999*

	1994	1995	1996	1997	1998	1999
GDP growth (%)	8.54	9.17	7.00	4.65	−6.85	9.49
CPI growth (%)	6.26	4.48	4.92	4.45	7.51	0.81
Cash surplus/deficit (% of GDP)	2.12	2.45	2.60	2.64	1.25	1.33
Money and quasi-money growth (%)	18.68	15.59	15.83	14.14	27.03	27.38
Domestic credit of banks (% of GDP)	51.58	50.19	53.59	59.33	67.03	72.18
Current account (% of GDP)	−0.83	−1.55	−4.12	−1.58	12.35	5.50
Short-term debt (% of foreign exchange reserves)	227.48	240.58	279.75	309.82	59.24	NA

Sources: World Development Indicators, March 2012; Hahm and Mishkin (2000).

dollar in October raised doubts about Korea's ability to maintain the value of its currency, the *won*. The failure of the government to win passage of a bill to deal with the debt of the banks further shook foreign confidence, and the Bank of Korea's foreign exchange reserves rapidly declined. The central bank's situation was more precarious than perceived at the time, since it had committed some of its reserves to the foreign branches of Korean banks to be used to meet demands for payment by foreign creditors (Berg 1999).

In November the Bank of Korea abandoned its support of the *won* and the government applied for an SBA from the IMF. The agreement with the IMF for $21 billion represented 1,939 percent of the country's quota, with another $37 billion from other sources, and was the largest amount the IMF had ever committed to one country. The IMF could disburse the exceptionally large amount through a provision in its guidelines that accounted for exceptional circumstances, but it was understood that the drawings would subsequently be converted to a new program, the Supplemental Reserve Facility (SRF).

The program's conditions included a tightening of monetary and fiscal policies, liberalization of trade and capital flows, and permission for foreign financial institutions to enter domestic markets. However, the agreement did not ease the concerns about the renewal of short-term loans that were due at the end of the month. The election of a new president, Kim Dae Jung, also raised fears about the implementation of the program. In response, the Korean government agreed to speed up reform measures, including the lifting of capital account restrictions, and the IMF approved the immediate disbursal of $2 billion of the credit that had been committed in the original agreement. Moreover, the IMF and the U.S. government urged private international banks to roll over their loans to Korea. After intense

Table 7.5. *Malaysia: 1994–1999*

	1994	1995	1996	1997	1998	1999
GDP growth (%)	9.21	9.83	10.00	7.32	−7.36	6.14
CPI growth (%)	3.72	3.45	3.49	2.66	5.27	2.74
Cash surplus/deficit (% of GDP)	NA	NA	1.45	2.92	−0.82	−3.83
Money and quasi-money growth (%)	11.51	18.53	18.48	16.04	0.23	12.10
Domestic credit of banks (% of GDP)	112.22	126.71	142.42	163.35	162.13	150.11
Current account (% of GDP)	−6.07	−9.73	−4.42	−5.93	13.20	15.92
Short-term debt (% of total reserves)	23.50	29.45	39.68	69.58	32.28	19.44

Source: World Development Indicators, March 2012.

negotiations, the banks agreed in early January to a voluntary rescheduling of short-term loans equal to $22 billion (Ghosh *et al.* 2002), and the pressure on the *won* eased.

The sharp fall in Korean output and widespread corporate bankruptcies resulted in a new program with the IMF in February. The fiscal target was lowered from a surplus of 0.2 percent of GDP to a deficit of 0.8 percent, and further financial liberalization measures were stipulated. Monetary policy was left unchanged, however, as a result of concerns about the *won*.

The government of Malaysia chose a different course in addressing its crisis, which came to a head later than those of the other East Asian countries. Its average annual growth rate had been an impressive 9.7 percent during the three years before the crisis (Table 7.5). Prices increased at an average rate of 3.6 percent during this period, and the government's budgets had been in surplus. While the current account had registered deficits averaging 6.8 percent of GDP, the country's ratio of short-term debt to reserves was substantially lower than those of the other crisis countries.

The Malaysians initially sought to counter the downward pressure on their currency, the *ringgit*, after the Thai devaluation but subsequently allowed the currency to float. The Malaysian prime minister, Mahathir Mohamad, publicly blamed speculators such as George Soros for the financial turbulence in the region. However, the government enacted policies, including high interest rates, that were consistent with IMF remedies and were characterized as "an IMF package without the IMF" (Haggard 2000: 61). The government also adopted regulatory measures to strengthen the financial sector.

In September 1998, the authorities adopted a new approach. The government imposed controls on capital outflows, reestablished a pegged exchange rate, and limited offshore currency transactions. By controlling capital flows it regained its ability to use macroeconomic policies for domestic stabilization. The central bank lowered interest rates, and the government enacted expansionary fiscal policies in order to arrest the economic decline.

The government was severely criticized for placing restrictions on capital outflows, and there were predictions that foreign firms and investors would never return to the country. But once the controls were removed in response to the improving economic conditions, capital inflows resumed. Malaysia's experience was subsequently cited by some as evidence that capital controls could be an effective crisis emergency measure, and an example of a heterodox alternative to the IMF's policies.

The financial and economic turmoil that began in the summer of 1997 continued through the following year. The rate of currency depreciation as measured by the domestic currency value of the U.S. dollar by February was more than 50 percent for the Korean and Thai currencies, and more than 200 percent for the Indonesian *ringgit* (Bank for International Settlements 1998). Net private capital flows to Asian emerging markets became outflows of $45 billion in 1997 and $69 billion the following year (Bank for International Settlements 1999). Output fell in the crisis countries, particularly Indonesia and Thailand. Current account deficits swung into surpluses, in part because of the drop in the demand for imports as incomes collapsed. One positive note was the subdued response of inflation to the currency depreciations, with the exception of an escalation in price rises in Indonesia. The restraint reflected the collapse in private demand and falling wages throughout the region.

The economic contraction bottomed out in the second half of 1998, and growth resumed in 1999 in all the countries except Indonesia, where political uncertainty continued to slow recovery. The economic revival reflected increasing exports and a pickup in domestic demand. However, the decline in private investment expenditures that occurred during the crisis was never fully recovered, resulting in a permanent loss of output (Cerra and Saxena 2005). The cumulative output loss five years after the crisis was estimated at 23 percent for the Philippines, 40 percent for Korea, 67 percent for Malaysia, 90 percent for Thailand, and 109 percent for Indonesia (Mussa *et al.* 2000).

The G7 leaders met in Denver in June 1997 before the scope of the crisis was clear, and their final communiqué made no mention of it. But at their next meeting in Birmingham in June 1998 they endorsed a series of reform measures proposed by their finance ministers. These included increasing transparency, using an orderly approach to capital account liberalization, strengthening national regulatory systems, developing measures to ensure the resolution of financial crises with the involvement of the private sector, and enhancing the role of the IFIs and their cooperation with the international regulatory groups (Bayne 2005). Many of these proposals, however, were overtaken by the outbreak of new crises (Chapter 8).

7.2 IMF and East Asia: Appraisal

The IMF faced immediate opposition to its policies in the East Asian crisis. The criticisms were not only from the governments of the countries with Fund programs but also from economists outside Asia. Their objections were leveled at the Fund's analysis of the nature of the crisis, its macroeconomic policy conditions, and its use of structural conditionality. In addition, the IMF's policy stance regarding the decontrol of capital flows in the period leading up to the outbreak of the crisis was faulted (Chapter 6).

The crisis was widely attributed to misaligned exchange rates and balance sheet problems due to nonperforming loans and mismatched maturity and currency exposures (Dornbusch 2001). The current accounts of the countries most affected had recorded small surpluses, with the exception of Thailand. However, they had accumulated short-run debt that left them susceptible to rapid outflows of capital – sudden stops – that overwhelmed the ability of their central banks to defend their exchange rate values and triggered currency crises.

The withdrawal of foreign funds also disrupted the domestic banking sector. The experience of the East Asian countries demonstrated that the occurrence of a banking crisis with a currency crisis – a twin crisis – exacerbates the impact of the currency crisis on the economy (Kaminsky and Reinhart 1999). These crises often take place after a shock to the financial sector due to financial liberalization or increased access to international capital markets. The banking crisis usually precedes the currency crisis, but the latter deepens the impact of the former, creating a "vicious cycle."[4]

The conditions that led to the outbreak of twin crises were explored in what were called "third-generation" models. The third-generation models differed from the first- and second-generation models in their incorporation of the domestic financial sectors in the transmission of instability. The increase in the liabilities of banks and firms poses a source of potential fragility, particularly when they are denominated in foreign currencies. Capital outflows and currency depreciations left domestic borrowers unable to meet their obligations and resulted in a breakdown of the financial system.

---

[4] See also Glick and Hutchison (2001) and Hutchison and Noy (2005) on twin crises.

The government plays a smaller and more passive role in the events leading up to the eruption of a crisis than it does in the first- and second-generation models. These circumstances were particularly likely to occur in the emerging market economies, since their financial sectors often lacked institutional mechanisms to deal with excessive volatility.

In some of these models (Corsetti, Pesenti, and Roubini 1999a), moral hazard is the root cause of the crisis. Domestic firms borrow in the international markets to finance risky projects because they believe their governments will bail them out if their ventures fail. When foreign creditors cut off the supply of credit, the domestic borrowers turn to the government to be bailed out. Private liabilities become public debt, and expectations of central bank intervention trigger a currency crisis. In the case of the Asian crisis, capital inflows had fueled asset bubbles (Sarno and Taylor 1999). Once the bubbles burst, financial intermediaries failed and private capital fled, further depressing asset prices.

Other third-generation models treat the crises as coordination failures, similar to bank runs (Chang and Velasco 2000). Foreign creditors and domestic depositors deposit funds at domestic banks, which invest money in long-term illiquid assets. If all the depositors seek to withdraw their funds, the bank will not be able to satisfy the demands of the foreign lenders for foreign currency and the institution will close if it does not receive outside assistance. The run is self-fulfilling, and illiquidity results in insolvency.

Under these circumstances, the policies of governmental austerity initially urged by the IMF in the Asian crisis only deepened the adverse economic impact of the initial shock. While reductions in government expenditures and credit creation were consistent with the first- and second-generation models, the East Asian countries had records of budget surpluses, and contractionary fiscal policies would have aggravated the impact of the collapse in the private sector (Radelet and Sachs 2000). Similarly, some claimed that higher interest rates brought about increased bankruptcy rates among borrowers and increased the incidence of bank failures (Furman and Stiglitz 1998).

The IMF later defended its policy recommendations in the crisis countries (Boorman *et al.* 2000). The staff pointed out that their original fiscal targets were based on the need to raise public savings to offset private capital outflows. But the IMF admitted that these targets were based on overly optimistic projections of output growth, and the Fund changed its fiscal policy projections during the crisis in response to changing conditions. With respect to contractionary monetary policies, the IMF (Ghosh *et al.* 2002) claimed that there was little evidence to substantiate the assertion that tighter monetary policy was responsible for the declines in income. On the other hand, the IMF asserted, monetary policy was relatively successful in containing inflation and stemming capital outflows.[5]

The inclusion of multiple structural conditions in the programs for the Asian countries was also challenged. The number of policy conditions in the Asian programs was very large, particularly in the Indonesian program, which had 140 structural policy conditions (Goldstein 2003). The inclusion of a broad range of structural conditions in the IMF's programs was attributed to the influence of the IMF's principal members, particularly the United States (Corden 2001, Goldstein 2003). This perception damaged the reputation of the IMF in the Asian countries and contributed to the perception that the IMF was used by the United States and other upper-income nations to promote their commercial and financial interests.

There were several objections to the use of structural conditionality. First, many of the conditions included in the programs were in areas outside the IMF's expertise in macroeconomics. Second, in many cases there was limited domestic political support for structural conditions, which were viewed as an infringement of national sovereignty. Consequently, there was a lack of country "ownership" of the policies. Third, there was a lack of evidence connecting many of the structural conditions to increased growth. Countries that had established strong records of growth in the past, such as Taiwan and Korea, had allowed domestic firms to develop before opening up their economies to foreign competition, thus raising doubts regarding the need for rapid trade liberalization. Boughton (2001b: 590) admitted that "there was no generally accepted model or paradigm linking specific structural policies either to macroeconomic performance or to external viability."

The IMF defended its use of structural conditions to resolve the crisis. Fischer (1998: 105), for example, claimed that "financial sector and other structural reforms are vital to the reform programs of Thailand, Indonesia, and Korea.... IMF lending to these counties would serve no purpose if these problems were not addressed." Similarly, Boorman *et al.* (2000) suggested that postponing the restructuring of the financial sector would have led to a deepening of the crisis. However, these arguments did not rebut the proposition that many conditions were not directly related to the origins or the resolution of the crisis.[6]

---

[5] Corden (2001: 56), who reviewed the use of interest rates to defend currency values, concluded that the expected exchange rate response occurred in Thailand and Korea, but not in Indonesia. Montiel (2003b) examined the empirical literature on the effect of tight money on exchange rates and concluded that there is no evidence of a systemic impact.

[6] See Chapter 9 on changes in the Fund's use of structural conditionality.

Some of the harshest criticisms of the IMF were from those, such as Desai (2003) and Stiglitz (2002), who held the IMF responsible for the outbreak of the crisis in its encouragement of the liberalization of capital accounts (Chapter 5). The IMF was blamed for advocating capital account decontrol before countries possessed adequate regulatory structures (Wade 1998). The push for liberalization was attributed to the influence of what Bhagwati (1998) termed the "Wall Street–Treasury" complex and contributed to the perception that the United States determined IMF policies.

Another line of criticism was advanced by those who thought that the IMF's actions contributed to the occurrence of financial crises through moral hazard (Calomiris 1998, Meltzer 1998). These critics claimed that the Fund's support of the Mexican government in 1995 set the stage for the East Asian crisis, as foreign investors came to believe that the IMF would rescue them from the consequences of risky lending (Chapter 6). Moreover, the IMF's lending programs delayed the implementation of necessary domestic reform measures.

The crisis had one institutional consequence for the IMF: the establishment of the SRF. The IMF realized that the scale of capital outflows during a crisis and the resulting need for emergency assistance dwarfed the IMF's usual access limits. The new facility allowed it to provide significantly larger amounts of credit to countries with volatile capital accounts. The activation of the SRF was tied to the existence of an SBA or EFF, but its amount was not bound by the usual access limits on the SBAs and EFFs. However, the creation of the SRF was also a tacit admission that the catalytic effect of traditional IMF programs on private capital flows was insufficient to provide adequate financing to countries with balance of payments disequilibria.

Another initiative was less successful. An attempt to establish an Asian alternative to the IMF was made during the East Asian crisis, when Japanese financial officials proposed the creation of an Asian Monetary Fund (Blustein 2001, Lipsey 2003). The Japanese proposal was based in part on the perception that the United States was not willing to take as active a role in addressing that crisis, including endorsement of IMF assistance to the crisis nations, as it had in the case of Mexico. The plan called for the establishment of a $100 billion fund with contributions from ten East Asian countries. The plan was opposed by the United States because of moral hazard concerns and fears that the new body would duplicate the IMF's activities (Lipsey 2003). The Japanese subsequently withdrew their plan, but the idea of a regional organization would be resurrected in the future.

The IMF paid a high price for its actions in East Asia. The countries that adopted Fund programs believed that the attached conditions were harsher than circumstances justified and inappropriate given the nature of the crisis. The structural conditions were seen as unnecessary and driven by U.S. firms and investors who sought to take advantage of the crisis to obtain Asian assets at "fire sale" prices. The imposition of these conditions was taken as additional evidence that the IMF's policies favored the interests of foreign investors.

The fact that China and India, each with extensive capital control policies, were not affected by the crisis was widely noted, as was Malaysia's experience with controls on outflows. The events in East Asia led to a reassessment of the arguments in favor of capital account decontrol and brought about the withdrawal of the proposed amendment to the Articles of Agreement (Chapter 5). The lessons drawn by the East Asian nations from the events of 1997–8 would determine many of their policy choices in future years (Chapter 9). Moreover, the next chapter shows how the volatility in the Asian financial markets contributed to further crises in other emerging market nations.

8

Fiscal Follies

The impact of the East Asian crisis rippled across other emerging market nations that had borrowed in the international capital markets. Unlike the Asian crisis, these crises primarily involved the public sector. Lenders reassessed the ability of governments to meet their obligations and maintain their exchange rate commitments. Capital outflows led to more crises as sovereign borrowers defaulted on their debt and currency crises led to large devaluations. The IMF was active in managing the response to the emergencies but was hampered in some cases during the precrisis periods by the political aims of its principal members. This chapter provides an overview of the events leading up to the crises in Russia, Brazil, and Argentina, and how the IMF responded.

The first section summarizes the record of the Russian economy before its crisis in 1998 and its deterioration. The G7 leaders had supported Russia's movement to a market economy and given the IMF and the World Bank the task of facilitating the transition. The Russian government successfully completed several programs with the IMF during the early 1990s. However, continuing fiscal deficits financed by capital inflows were a source of financial weakness. In 1998 another program was arranged with the IMF that included measures to improve the state's finances, but the new policies were not approved by the Russian parliament. Capital flight from the country drained the country's foreign exchange reserves, forcing the government to abandon the exchange rate peg and restructure its debt.

The IMF's actions in the period leading up to the outbreak of the crisis are evaluated in the second section. The IMF was hampered in its dealings with the Russian government by the desire of the G7 governments to shore up the Russians. Consequently, the IMF was not able to push effectively for the necessary fiscal reforms and could only stop its lending when the G7 leaders realized that Russia's economic and financial situation was no longer viable.

The Brazilian government was also challenged by fiscal deficits that resulted in a currency crisis in 1999, but this emergency was resolved relatively quickly. These events and the IMF's response are summarized in the third section. The IMF endorsed the government's measures to deal with capital flight and enact fiscal reforms, but the central bank was unable to maintain its defense of the currency. The response to the resulting depreciation was not as severe as had occurred during other crises, in part because the banks were not exposed to currency mismatches. Consequently, the financial system recovered and the IMF and the Brazilian government were able to devise a new and viable arrangement.

The IMF's dealings with Argentina were much less successful, and the fourth section reviews these events. Argentina's rapid economic growth during the 1990s was seen as the product of economic and financial reforms, including establishing an anchor for its currency. But the country's mounting government debt position was a source of vulnerability, and in 2000 the government turned to the IMF for assistance. A series of policy initiatives were unable to reverse the escalation in the debt. In 2001 the government defaulted on its obligations and the currency system was abandoned.

The last section evaluates the IMF's policies in Argentina. The IMF was constrained by the government's resolve to maintain its exchange rate regime, and the initial desire of the G7 nations to support Argentina. Consequently, the IMF maintained its support for Argentina despite its worsening position over an extended period. But the IMF was held responsible within Argentine for the harsh consequences of the termination of its currency arrangement and default on its debt. The ending of a similar crisis in Turkey demonstrated that another outcome might have been achieved in Argentina under different circumstances.

8.1 Russia

The Russian crisis of 1998 followed a period of sustained involvement of the IMF with the Russian government.[1] The G7 leaders had delegated the task of assisting the Russian government and the countries that emerged from the collapse of the Soviet Union to the IMF and the World Bank. In the first half of the decade, the IMF made a series of loans to the Russian

---

[1] This account draws upon Arpac and Bird (2009), Åslund (2000), BIS (1998, 1999), Blustein (2001), De Beaufort Wijnholds (2011), Fischer (2001), Isard (2005), the IMF (1998), Kharas, Pinto, and Ulatov (2001), Mussa (2006), Odling-Smee (2006), Pinto, Gurvich, and Ulatov (2005), and Woods (2006).

Table 8.1. *Russia: 1995–2000*

	1995	1996	1997	1998	1999	2000
GDP growth (%)	−4.14	−3.60	1.40	−5.30	6.40	10.00
CPI growth (%)	197.47	47.74	14.77	27.67	85.74	20.78
Cash surplus/deficit (% of GDP)	NA	NA	NA	NA	NA	NA
Money and quasi-money growth (%)	112.58	29.56	28.85	37.64	56.75	58.46
Domestic credit of banks (% of GDP)	25.46	27.84	29.49	44.93	33.33	24.93
Current account (% of GDP)	1.76	2.77	−0.02	0.08	12.57	18.04
Short-term debt (% of total reserves)	56.60	73.51	33.49	122.28	127.75	56.52

Source: World Development Indicators, March 2012.

government. It also introduced a new facility, the Systemic Transformation Facility, which was established in 1993 to aid countries making the transition from centrally planned to market economies.

A collapse in the value of the *ruble* in 1994 was followed by an SBA the next year with strict macroeconomic policy goals. Monetary policy was tightened, inflation fell from almost 200 percent in 1995 to 15 percent in 1997, and the *ruble* recovered (Table 8.1). However, the implementation of stricter tax collection policies was not as successful. Government revenues fell below their projected levels, in part because firms with political support were able to reduce their tax liabilities (Odling-Smee 2006). Nonetheless, the program was judged to be a success and all the funds disbursed.

The IMF and the Russian government agreed on an EFF loan in 1996. The program included measures to lower budget deficits, but the fiscal situation actually deteriorated in 1996. President Boris Yeltsin's election campaign was accompanied by increases in spending, while the oligarchs who supported the government were able to negotiate lower tax payments. The government covered the shortfall by issuing short-term bills, known as "GKOs". The IMF and other multilateral agencies had advocated the liberalization of the country's capital account, and foreign investors responded by purchasing the GKOs (Woods 2006). Foreign portfolio inflows surged from $8.9 billion in 1996 to $45.6 billion in 1997, about 10 percent of the country's GDP (Åslund 2000). The support of the G7 leaders for the Yeltsin government may have encouraged foreign investors to believe that they or the IMF would intervene in the event of a default (Mussa 2006).

The Asian crisis, however, raised concerns about the riskiness of emerging markets, and foreign investors began to exit the GKO market. The situation was exacerbated by declines in the prices of oil and other exported commodities that further lowered government revenues. In an attempt to bolster confidence, the Russian authorities fixed the value of the *ruble* within a band of ±15 percent. However, yields on the GKOs rose as the demand for them weakened, and the fiscal situation worsened. Russian banks continued to hold government debt because of its high returns rather than extend loans to the private sector (BIS 1999: 53).

The IMF, the World Bank, and the Yeltsin government agreed to a new lending arrangement in July 1998. The program contained fiscal measures to achieve a surplus on the primary government budget, structural reforms to promote long-run fiscal sustainability and private sector development, and a swap arrangement to exchange short-term *ruble*-denominated GKOs for long-term dollar-denominated Eurobonds. The IMF pledged credit of $11.2 billion through a combination of an augmentation of the existing EFF, the SRF, and the Compensatory and Contingency Financing Facility, with another $5.9 billion to be provided by the World Bank and Japan (Woods 2006). The Fund offered an immediate disbursement of $4.8 billion, although much of that was lost to capital flight.

However, the Russian parliament – the *Duma* – would not approve the government's plan to deal with the country's emergency conditions. Foreign investors sold their Russian securities and converted the proceeds to dollars, draining reserves from the central bank. The government approached the G7 for assistance but was turned down (Blustein 2001). On August 17, the Russian government announced a series of measures designed to meet the financial crisis. It widened and then abandoned the exchange rate band, placed a ninety-day moratorium on the repayment of corporate and bank debt, and announced a compulsory restructuring of government debt.

In the aftermath of the emergency measures, the *ruble* plummeted in value, output fell, and inflation rose. The debt and currency crises were followed by a banking crisis, with failures of half of Russia's banks that had large exposures in the government debt market (Åslund 2000). Output subsequently recovered as a result of increases in oil prices and the depreciation of the currency. But an SBA arranged in 1999 was not fully disbursed because of disagreements over reserve management and other issues (Fischer 2001).

Outside Russia, its de facto default and Malaysia's imposition of controls on capital outflows heightened concerns about the ability of other emerging markets to meet their obligations. Liquidity in the international financial markets dried up, the spread on emerging markets bonds soared, and the issuance of new securities by emerging market borrowers ceased (IMF 1998). In the United States, the Federal Reserve orchestrated the takeover by creditors of the hedge fund Long-Term Capital Markets, which faced collapse after taking a large position on the spread between Russian and U.S. bond rates. The Federal Reserve also lowered its key policy rate in September in response to the volatility in the financial markets. It followed up with more cuts in October and November, when the turbulence in the global financial markets finally eased.

8.2 IMF and Russia: Appraisal

The Russian crisis was the result of fiscal imbalances and a fixed exchange rate, a profile consistent with the first-generation model of currency crises (Kharas, Pinto, and Ulatov 2001). Russia's fiscal deficit was a fundamental weakness that was never adequately addressed by its government despite the IMF's continuing efforts. In retrospect, resolving the fiscal situation required fundamental changes in tax administration and spending policies that were beyond the scope of the government at that time.

Some of the IMF's policy prescriptions may have exacerbated the situation. Deregulating the capital account allowed the Russian government to maintain its lax fiscal policies and left the country vulnerable to capital flight. Russia did not yet possess the institutional framework needed to handle volatile financial flows.

The ability of the IMF to obtain compliance with its programs' conditions was hampered by the support the Russians received from the G7 governments, and in particular the United States, during the 1990s. The Russian authorities came to believe that the G7 and the IMF would not let the country fail, and the resulting moral hazard distorted the decisions of both foreign investors and Russian policy makers. A senior member of the IMF team working with Russia later claimed that the Russians often viewed their negotiations with the Fund as a "charade, since they believed that the G7 would ultimately insist that the IMF go ahead with the loans" (Odling-Smee 2006: 163). However, by the summer of 1998 the G7 national leaders had reached the end of their patience with the delays in Russian reforms and were no longer willing to commit the IMF's resources or their own to support the Yeltsin government.

The IMF as an agent could not challenge the policies of its main principals, and it had little latitude in negotiating with the Russian government. It only ceased lending when Russia's situation was no longer viable and the G7 governments withdrew their backing. The use of the IMF by the G7 governments to pursue their political goals tainted the credibility of the Fund, already damaged by the events in East Asia.

8.3 Brazil

Brazil's currency crisis in January 1999 was the product of domestic developments and the rise in risk aversion among foreign investors after the Asian and Russian crises.[2] The government had introduced a plan to stabilize the economy, known as the *Real* Plan, in 1994. The plan established a new currency, the *real*, which was linked in value to the U.S. dollar. The following year a "crawling peg" exchange rate regime was instituted to offset the impact of high inflation on the real exchange rate. Some restrictions on capital inflows were introduced, but these were subsequently relaxed, and the country gained access to the global financial markets (Goldfajn and Minella 2007).

The new currency was accompanied by high interest rates, and the plan was successful in lowering inflation from more than 2,000 percent in 1994 to 66 percent in 1995 and 16 percent the following year (Table 8.2). But the government's fiscal position was not stabilized, in part because of expenditures by state authorities financed by the federal government. The fiscal deficits, combined with some appreciation of the real exchange rate, contributed to the country's escalating current account imbalances and required interest rates high enough to attract foreign funds.

In the fall of 1998 capital began to flow out of Brazil in the wake of the Russian crisis. The government raised interest rates to more than 40 percent in response and turned to the IMF for support before a crisis actually took place. In December the Fund approved credit of $18.3 billion, which was 600 percent of the country's quota, with $9 billion made available immediately.[3] Part of this amount – $12.6 billion – was provided through an SRF, and the remainder through an SBA. An additional $14.5 billion was pledged by the World Bank and other institutions for a total financing package of $41.8 billion. Capital outflows fell in response to the announcement and the accompanying set of reforms.

However, the fiscal reform measures faced opposition in the Brazilian Congress, and the state governors announced their intention to continue their expenditures. Renewed capital flows led to mounting losses in foreign exchange reserves that were unsustainable. The government sought to replace the existing crawling peg with another but by mid-January was forced to abandon its defense of the *real* and allow the currency to float. The

[2] Sources include relevant material from the BIS (1999), Blustein (2001), De Beaufort Wijnholds (2011), Goldfajn (2003), Goldfajn and Minella (2007), Isard (2005), IMF (1999b), and IMF IEO (2003).
[3] The IMF activated the NAB to lend to Brazil.

Table 8.2. *Brazil: 1995–2000*

	1995	1996	1997	1998	1999	2000
GDP growth (%)	4.42	2.15	3.37	0.04	0.25	4.31
CPI growth (%)	66.01	15.76	6.93	3.20	4.86	7.04
Cash surplus/deficit (% of GDP)	NA	NA	−0.01	−3.67	−2.53	−1.83
Money and quasi-money growth (%)	44.30	31.03	17.24	12.02	18.12	19.70
Domestic credit of banks (% of GDP)	56.12	57.13	59.44	66.79	70.88	71.86
Current account (% of GDP)	−2.36	−2.77	−3.50	−4.01	−4.33	−3.76
Short-term debt (% of total reserves)	60.68	60.19	67.41	68.09	80.43	93.81

Source: World Development Indicators, March 2012.

currency depreciated by 40 percent in the two months following the adoption of a floating rate (BIS 1999).

The response to the decline in the value of the *real* was not as severe as had occurred after devaluations in East Asia or Russia. In part this reflected the anticipation of the need for a devaluation, which had allowed domestic firms and residents to prepare for it through the use of currency futures and other instruments. Moreover, the domestic banks had relatively little exposure to foreign exchange risk, and therefore their balance sheets were not particularly exposed to the effects of the depreciation.

The government and the IMF reached an agreement on a revised program by the end of March. The new measures included the adoption of an inflation rate target by the central bank in place of the nominal exchange rate target. Foreign banks agreed to maintain their credit lines with the Brazilian banks. Economic growth was slow for the year but recovered from its initial decline while the rate of inflation remained below double digits. The central bank was able to lower interest rates below the punishing levels it had set during the defense of the *real*.

The Brazilian crisis of 1999 was relatively benign when compared to its predecessors, and the IMF received credit for its quick response to the government's call for assistance. The IMF was later criticized by its IEO (2003) for not pushing more strongly for an exit to the crawling peg, but the government had invested its prestige in the Plan *Real* and was reluctant to abandon it. Once again, the IMF's options were constrained by what the government was willing to accept. In this case, the IMF's early support was rewarded by Brazil's subsequent economic performance and the absence of a financial meltdown.

Brazil turned to the IMF again in 2002, when fears about the outcome of the presidential election as well as the impact of Argentina's crisis resulted in capital outflows. The IMF lent the country $30 billion, and the newly elected government of Luis Inácio Lula da Silva raised its target for a fiscal policy surplus while the central bank increased interest rates to keep inflation under control. After an initial reversal, capital flows and the country recorded a current account surplus in 2003.

8.4 Argentina

Argentina's experience before its crisis resembled Brazil's in several aspects. Both countries had established exchange rate regimes in the 1990s that were designed to lower extremely high inflation rates, and these were successful. Both countries had fiscal imbalances, current account deficits, and mounting public debt. But when the crises occurred, the experiences of the two countries and their outcomes were quite different.[4]

Inflation had long been a chronic problem in Argentina, and it exploded in the 1980s, reaching an annual rate of 3,000 percent by the end of the decade. President Carlos Menem and Economy Minister Domingo Cavallo established a new exchange regime for the Argentine *peso*, the Convertibility Plan, which fixed the value of the *peso* to the U.S. dollar and limited the central bank's ability to create new money by requiring it to back the monetary base with foreign exchange reserves.[5] Consequently, the money supply could only grow as the central bank accumulated more dollars through the balance of payments. In addition, the government liberalized foreign trade and capital and privatized a number of public enterprises.

The rate of inflation fell to 25 percent in 1992, 11 percent in 1993, and single digits the following years while GDP, which had fallen during the era of hyperinflation, rose in the early 1990s. In 1995 the country suffered the impact of Mexico's "tequila crisis" (Chapter 6) and GDP contracted. However, the government maintained its commitment to the monetary arrangement, and economic growth resumed by 1997 (Table 8.3).

During this period the Fund was actively engaged with Argentina. An SBA in 1991 was followed by an EFF in 1992, another SBA in 1996, and another EFF loan in 1998. The IMF had initially been skeptical about the Convertibility Plan, but the country's stable growth in the first half of the decade and quick

---

[4] For accounts and analysis of the Argentine crisis, see BIS (2002), Blustein (2005), Daseking *et al.* (2004), De Beaufort Wijnholds (2011), Feldstein (2002), Hausmann and Velasco (2002), Helleiner (2005), IMF IEO (2004), Mussa (2002), Powell (2002), Servén and Perry (2005), and Setser and Gelpern (2006).

[5] The new arrangement resembled the procedures established under a currency board but differed from such an institution in several aspects.

Table 8.3. *Argentina: 1997–2002*

	1997	1998	1999	2000	2001	2002
GDP growth (%)	8.11	3.85	−3.39	−0.79	−4.41	−10.89
CPI growth (%)	0.53	0.92	−1.17	−0.94	−1.07	25.87
Cash surplus/deficit (% of GDP)	NA	NA	NA	NA	NA	−5.71
Money and quasi-money growth (%)	25.53	10.49	4.09	1.53	−19.44	19.71
Domestic credit of banks (% of GDP)	30.38	32.50	35.50	34.45	37.24	62.42
Current account (% of GDP)	−4.14	−4.84	−4.21	−3.16	−1.41	8.59
Short-term debt (% of total reserves)	142.65	124.54	111.63	112.58	137.43	140.75

Source: World Development Indicators, March 2012.

recovery after the Mexican crisis were seen as proof of successful policies. The IMF praised the government for its promarket positions, and President Menem addressed the IMF–World Bank annual meeting in 1998.

However, the economy's growth masked weaknesses in the fiscal sector. Continuing deficits in the central government's budget required foreign capital inflows as private savings were not sufficient to finance them. But the increase in the debt of the public sector reflected more than the central government's fiscal deficits. Powell (2002) pointed out that between 1995 and 2001 the difference between the change in debt and the accumulated fiscal deficit was $30 billion, which he attributes in part to provincial deficits. Hausmann and Velasco (2002) also include the growing deficit of the country's Social Security system as contributing to the country's mounting debt.

By the end of 2000, the debt/GDP ratio stood at more than 40 percent. While this number was higher in countries without crises, Mussa (2002) claimed that it posed problems for Argentina because of that country's restricted tax revenues, the denomination of its debt in dollars, the increasing level of the debt ratio over time, the country's vulnerability to external shocks such as the Brazilian crisis, and its exposure to changes in financial market sentiment. Servicing the debt would require a large proportion of the foreign exchange earnings of the country's relatively small export sector.

Market conditions began to move against Argentina in the aftermath of the East Asian crisis. Russia's default raised concerns regarding emerging market debt, while the depreciation of the Brazilian *real* threatened to worsen Argentina's current account deficits. The latter development was reinforced by a rise in the value of the dollar, which appreciated the *peso*. The government ruled out a change in the exchange rate regime that would have allowed a depreciation to rectify the current account deficits. The continuing slowdown in economic activity lowered tax revenues and the fiscal situation deteriorated.

In March 2000, the government under newly elected President Fernando de la Rúa negotiated an SBA with the IMF to replace the 1998 EFF, which had never been disbursed. The new arrangement provided credit of $7.2 billion and emphasized fiscal measures. The authorities announced that they intended to treat the program as precautionary and not draw upon it. However, the continuing stagnation in economic activity reduced tax payments and the country's debt position worsened.

By the end of the year, the weak economy prompted the government to negotiate a new support program from the IMF, other multilateral organizations, and the Spanish government. The total package included $40 billion in funds, with the IMF contributing $14 billion in part through an SRF. The program's conditions included a series of measures designed to address the country's fiscal situation, including an increase in its primary budget surplus. The government and the IMF hoped that the new program, known as the *blindaje*, the Spanish word for armor, would increase foreign investors' confidence in the country's ability to meet its debt obligations.

However, the resignation of two economy ministers in the spring of 2001 revealed divisions within the government over how to address the fiscal imbalance. Cavallo was restored to office and sought to turn around the country's position through a series of initiatives, including a financial transactions tax to raise revenue. But a change in the Convertibility Plan to peg the currency to both the dollar and the *euro* only reduced confidence in the government, as did the removal of the head of the central bank. The IMF approved a disbursement of $1.2 billion in May despite slippage in the country's compliance with the program's conditions. Several members of the Executive Board voiced strong reservations about the country's situation and the sustainability of the program but voted to proceed with the disbursement in order to express support for Argentina (IMF IEO 2004).

The government sought to stabilize its debt situation in June through a swap of $30 billion of outstanding government bonds for debt with a longer maturity, but the impact on bond spreads was short-lived. In July, the government proposed a "zero deficits" plan that would restrict the level of fiscal expenditures to the amount of collected taxes, but there was considerable doubt as to whether the required cuts in expenditures were politically feasible (IMF IEO 2004). The government pressed the IMF for another disbursement of credit, and the IMF approved another payment of $8 billion in September. But in a rare show of disunity, the executive directors from the Netherlands and Switzerland, who represented constituencies on the board, abstained from the vote to disburse the credit (Blustein 2005).

During the fall domestic depositors increased their withdrawals from the Argentine banks and bond spreads soared as capital flight accelerated. The country's fiscal positions fell below the projections in the IMF program, and the debt/GDP ratio rose above 60 percent (IMF 2004). On December 1, the government imposed restrictions on the amounts of money that depositors could withdraw from their accounts, thus effectively abandoning the currency arrangement. The IMF announced that a review of the country's compliance with the program's conditions could not be completed, and no more funds would be disbursed. A wave of civil unrest led to the resignations of President de la Rúa and Minister Cavallo.

The new president announced the suspension of debt repayments, and in January the Convertibility Plan was abandoned. Argentina's default on its sovereign debt of $132 billion was the largest in history. The *peso* fell by 70 percent against the dollar after the collapse of the exchange rate peg, and economic activity collapsed. Moreover, in February the government established a mechanism to set the exchange rate for converting dollar-denominated bank loans to *pesos* at the rate of one *peso* per dollar, but a conversion rate for dollar-denominated deposits of 1.4 *pesos* per dollar. This asymmetric conversion worsened the situation of the banks, which required government assistance.

Argentina's GDP fell by more than 4 percent in 2001 and a further 11 percent in 2002. The IMF became a subject of opprobrium within Argentina and was widely blamed for the crisis and ensuing economic contraction. The instability in Argentina carried over to Uruguay, where Argentine citizens had maintained bank deposits. Capital flight in the form of deposit outflows forced Uruguay to turn to the IMF for assistance through an SBA that eventually made $2 billion available.

In 2003 the IMF entered into a new agreement with the government of Argentina for $13.5 billion and allowed it to postpone repayment of the money it had previously borrowed. The Argentine economy began to grow again through rising prices for the country's exports and the depreciated *peso* while fiscal expenditures were kept under control. In 2005, the government reached an agreement with the majority of its private debtors under which they received new bonds worth about a third of the value of the debt that had been in default. At the end of that year the government repaid the $9.8 billion it owed the IMF.[6] However, the government continued to castigate the IMF publicly for the 2001 crisis.

---

[6]   Brazil repaid the IMF its outstanding credit at the same time.

Table 8.4. *Turkey: 1997–2002*

	1997	1998	1999	2000	2001	2002
GDP growth (%)	7.58	2.31	−3.37	6.77	−5.70	6.16
CPI growth (%)	85.73	84.64	64.87	54.92	54.40	44.96
Cash surplus/deficit (% of GDP)	NA	NA	NA	NA	NA	NA
Money and quasi-money growth (%)	97.80	89.32	101.99	40.66	90.28	27.87
Domestic credit of banks (% of GDP)	34.56	27.46	36.76	37.91	52.92	47.47
Current account (% of GDP)	−1.39	0.74	−0.37	−3.72	1.92	−0.27
Short-term debt (% of total reserves)	91.13	103.16	96.07	122.95	82.09	57.94

Source: World Development Indicators, March 2012.

The Argentine crisis largely overshadowed financial turbulence in another emerging market, Turkey.[7] While the crisis in Turkey shared many characteristics with that in Argentina (Table 8.4), the eventual outcomes differed (Eichengreen 2002). Both countries enjoyed stabilization booms after the adoption of new exchange rate arrangements. Capital inflows financed current account deficits, but concerns about competitiveness due to appreciating real exchange rates made foreign investors nervous. Both the Argentine and Turkish authorities were reluctant to abandon their exchange rate commitments, but their delays only postponed the needed adjustments.

The Turkish government turned to the IMF for assistance in 2000, and the Fund made $10 billion available (more than 900 percent of Turkey's quota), including $7.5 billion through an SRF, while the World Bank contributed another $5 billion. This program only lasted two months. The government was forced to abandon the exchange rate peg and allow the currency to float in February 2001, and the Turkish *lira* depreciated by more than 45 percent despite record interest rates. The results of all this volatility were a banking crisis and economic contraction.

A new SBA was negotiated in May 2001 with additional credit of $8 billion, which raised the IMF's total support to $19 billion, and there were also funds from the World Bank. The program's conditions included a primary surplus target of 6½ percent of GDP and a new banking law. The government subsequently closed down a number of weak banks and transformed the regulatory structure of the banking system. Moreover, the Central Bank

---

[7] This section on the Turkish crisis draws upon Akyüz and Boratav (2003), BIS (2002), De Beaufort Wijnholds (2011), Eichengreen (2002), Miller (2006), and Özatay and Sak (2002).

of the Republic of Turkey was made independent and assigned the task of price stability.

Inflation and interest rates continued at high levels and the economy did not turn around. The IMF continued its support of the government, however, which did attain its fiscal and monetary targets, including the primary budget surplus. After the events of September 11, 2001, the IMF agreed to a new SBA with credit of $10 billion. This program helped to stabilize the currency market and inflation, and interest rates finally fell as economic growth resumed.

8.5　IMF and Argentina: Appraisal

The IMF's involvement with Argentina was widely studied and criticized. Many thought that the IMF waited too long before terminating its financial support of the government (Feldstein 2002). This inaction was attributed by some to a desire by the IMF both to support the country and to avoid any blame for Argentina's collapse (Setser and Gelpern 2006). The government had been praised for its implementation of polices consistent with the Washington Consensus (Chapter 6), and the IMF was reluctant to abandon it, particularly in the wake of the breakdown in the program with Russia.

A subsequent self-review at the IMF (Daesking *et al.* 2004) raised the question of whether the Fund should have pushed Argentina to reconsider its currency arrangement at an earlier stage. However, the government was resolute in its support of its monetary system. The IMF continued to provide credit through 2001 despite its concerns about the government's policies in part because the alternative – default – was seen as very costly. The Argentine government, realizing this, unsuccessfully "gambled for redemption." The authors of the IMF's self-review concluded that the Argentine experience demonstrated that "ownership" of policies by a country is not sufficient to sustain their viability when the policies are not consistent.

However, the IMF's actions also reflected the positions of its most influential principals (IMF IEO 2004). During the 1990s, the G7 governments supported Argentina's economic liberalization. The country's deteriorating fiscal situation and a reassessment of the possibility of a crisis caused the government of the United Kingdom in 2000 to urge the other G7 members to consider the possibility of a failed program (Blustein 2005). The G7 members subsequently supported the new program, but the subsequent abstentions of the Dutch and Swiss executive directors (mentioned previously) demonstrated that this unease was shared by other upper-income countries. In the United States, Treasury Secretary Paul O'Neill and the

Treasury Undersecretary for International Affairs John Taylor shared a skeptical view of the effectiveness of IMF programs. They promoted a plan to allocate $3 billion to Argentina to support a restructuring of its debt, but the proposal failed to win support within the G7 or Argentina.

The IMF, therefore, was caught between the demands of Argentina, on the one hand, and the unwillingness of the G7 to support additional extensions of credit, on the other. Moreover, the financial community no longer had confidence in Argentina's ability to meet its debt obligations. Consequently, the IMF had little latitude when it ceased lending. While it can be faulted for not halting its support for the country at an earlier date (IMF IEO 2004: 64), such a move would have been difficult at best given the initial position of the United States.

There were significant differences between Argentina and Turkey that explain why one country was successful in avoiding a crisis and the other not. Eichengreen (2002) points out that Turkey had a larger trade sector to service its external debt and a more centralized fiscal system than did Argentina. But the two outcomes also demonstrate that the IMF's abilities to prevent instability depend on the actions of the countries at risk as well as their external circumstances.

By the time the Argentine and Turkish crises ended, emerging markets in South America and Asia had experienced almost six years of serial crises. In addition to the crises described in this and previous chapters, debt restructurings took place in Ecuador, Pakistan, the Ukraine, and other emerging market and developing countries (Sturzenegger and Zettelmeyer 2006). In retrospect, their governments had been unprepared for the volatility that capital account deregulation introduced to their economies. The upper-income countries exacerbated the situation by pressing the emerging markets to liberalize and to be more accessible to the global financial markets. Similarly, the IMF was not ready for the instability that followed financial deregulation and fell into a pattern of responding to the latest emergency with measures to restore the status quo. The next chapter shows how the IMF, the G7 governments, and the emerging markets drew very different lessons from the events of the late 1990s and early 2000s.

9

Lessons Learned

The crises in Argentina and Turkey proved to be the last of the wave of financial crises in emerging market economies that had begun in Mexico in 1994. The postcrisis period was used by the IMF and its members to engage in investigations of the causes of the crises and evaluations of the IMF's responses. This chapter presents on overview of the different lessons that the Fund and its members drew on how to counter the excessive volatility in financial flows and markets.

The IMF reassessed its crisis prevention and management policies and implemented a series of changes that are summarized in the first section. The Fund became more cautious in its approach to capital account deregulation and urged its members to implement regulatory and supervisory reforms before removing the barriers to capital inflows. But it continued to present an open capital account as the goal that middle- and low-income countries should pursue. Similarly, the IMF announced that it would apply conditions to its loans more sparingly, although the evidence on whether it adhered to this new policy is ambiguous. The Fund also attempted to develop new mechanisms for its own governance and to deal with sovereign defaults, but these initiatives were not accepted by its members.

Another aspect of the IMF's activities that came under examination was its ability to serve as an effective lender of last resort during an international panic, and this topic is reviewed in the second section. While there were important distinctions between the resources of a domestic central bank and an IFI such as the IMF, the IMF could effectively provide large amounts of credit during an international crisis. The IMF experimented with new lending facilities to enhance its abilitiy to respond to the outbreak of a crisis.

The response of the G7 and other advanced economies to the crises is summarized in the third section. Their governments viewed the crises as the result of weak domestic financial regulations in the countries where they occurred.

They established a new agency, the Financial Stability Forum, to coordinate the creation of new standards. The IMF and World Bank were assigned the responsibility of overseeing the adoption of the new measures. New capital requirement guidelines, known as the Basel II standards, were also devised.

The emerging economy nations moved to shed their "weaker link" status, and their efforts are reviewed in the fourth section. Many of them, particularly in East Asia, accumulated foreign exchange reserves to deter speculative attacks. They also established regional associations, such as the Chiang Mai Initiative, that allowed participants to form bilateral swap arrangements in the event of an incipient currency crisis.

9.1 Reforms

The IMF emerged from the financial crises of the late 1990s and early 2000s with its reputation badly battered. The Fund was criticized for not preventing (or even indirectly fostering) the crises that occurred and mishandling their resolution (Chapters 7, 8). Some of the criticism was unjustified, but much of it reflected the IMF's failure to keep pace with the rapid growth of the international financial markets. The IMF had not anticipated most of the crises and often functioned in a reactive mode, devising policy responses in response to the latest eruption of financial instability.

Under Managing Director Horst Köhler, who had taken office in 2000, the IMF underwent a process of self-review and study that led to adjustments in many of its policies and programs The new strategies sought to enhance its crisis prevention capabilities and to make its crisis management more effective and less intrusive. Among the areas under evaluation were capital account decontrol, the use of conditions in IMF programs, and the integration of the financial sector into the IMF's surveillance activities. The IMF also sought to develop new institutional mechanisms for improving its governance and its capabilities for handling cases of sovereign default, but these did not receive the support of all its members.

The contribution of capital outflows to financial instability prompted the IMF to revisit its stance on capital account liberalization. The IMF's economists and others who reviewed the evidence of the effects of financial globalization found limited support for the assertions that financial integration improved the growth performance of the emerging markets or reduced their macroeconomic volatility (Edison *et al.* 2004, Prasad *et al.* 2003).[1]

---

[1] Cline (2010) offers a survey of the literature on financial globalization and economic growth.

One of the factors that undermined the expected positive impact was the occurrence of excessive volatility in currency markets and domestic financial sectors.

The IMF did not retreat from its position that full capital decontrol was a suitable long-term goal, but it now emphasized the need to adopt sound macroeconomic and regulatory policies in advance of deregulation (Ishii, Habermeier *et al.* 2002). The latter included the development of financial markets and institutions; the strengthening of regulatory systems; the implementation of accounting, auditing, and disclosure standards; and the establishment of financial safety nets. The IMF also stressed the proper sequencing of the liberalization of the capital account, beginning with the opening of the economy to FDI and progressively allowing other types of capital flows as the necessary infrastructure was developed. Nonetheless, Fischer (2003) continued to advocate capital account liberalization as a proper objective for the governments of emerging market and developing economies to pursue, in part because the advanced economies had open capital accounts.

Kose *et al.* (2009) sought to link the establishment of sound institutions to capital account liberalization. They claimed that financial integration would provide "collateral benefits" that include the development of a country's financial sector and improved macroeconomic policies. The result would be an increase in total factor productivity, an important determinant of long-term growth. But such claims are reminiscent of Guitián's (1995) assertion that capital account openness would constrain domestic policies to achieve stability (Chapter 5). There is little support for this linkage in the experience of the emerging countries. Obstfeld (2009a: 91), who examined the evidence for this argument, found it to be "meager."

The IMF also reviewed its own practices regarding conditionality. An IMF (2001) study of the use of structural conditionality found that about two-thirds of these conditions were related to the fiscal and financial sectors, the exchange rate, trade, and economic statistics. But structural conditions also included provisions unrelated to the IMF's traditional areas of concern, such as the reform and privatization of state-owned enterprises and civil service reform. Moreover, structural conditions had become increasingly prevalent in SBAs and EFFs as well as the IMF's concessional programs. While only 14.4 percent of the SBAs in 1987 contained structural conditions, this share had risen to 100 percent by 1994 (IMF 2001).

In 2002 the IMF issued new guidelines for conditionality (IMF 2002a). The Fund pledged to restrict its conditions to the core areas of macroeconomic stabilization, that is, monetary, fiscal, and exchange rate policies, and financial system issues. It also invoked the principle of parsimony, that is, the principle that "program-related conditions should be limited to the minimum necessary to achieve the goals of the Fund-supported program or to monitor its implementation" (IMF 2002a: 9). In a subsequent review of the implementation of these new guidelines, the IMF (2005d) claimed that during the period of 2001–4 there had been a shift in the coverage of its program conditionality to a focus on fewer and more critical areas. However, it also found that the number of structural conditions had been stable overall, with a decline in the conditions in the concessionary programs but a rise in such conditions in the nonconcessionary programs. The report cited a decrease in the number of programs with permanent interruptions as evidence of an improvement in program implementation.

The IMF's IEO (2007b) conducted its own study of structural conditionality. The authors of the report confirmed the change in the sectoral composition of structural conditions toward the IMF's core areas. But they found no evidence of an overall reduction in the number of conditions and claimed that the lending arrangements it studied included conditions that were not critical to the objectives of the programs.

The continuing use of these conditions in IMF programs may have reflected disagreements among its principals, as well as the ability of IMF staff members to exploit these divisions (Martin 2006). The upper-income countries that were not borrowing from the IMF during this period supported the broad use and scope of conditions, while the middle- and lower-income countries that drew credit from the IMF were more critical of their use. Since the former group of members was relatively more influential within the Fund, the staff was able to maintain the degree of conditionality it thought was necessary.[2] The large number of conditions also made it difficult for outside observers to determine whether a country was fulfilling its program commitments, in effect increasing the autonomy of the staff in making these assessments (Vaubel 1991).

If the IMF was to monitor developments in the financial sectors of its members, it needed to expand its expertise and coverage in these areas. The IMF established the International Capital Markets Department in 2001 to focus on financial developments. In 2006 that department was merged with the Monetary and Financial Systems Department to create the Monetary and Capital Markets Department, which sought to integrate the work done

---

[2] Some of the expansion in conditionality reflected pressure on the IMF by its members to enlarge the scope of its overview. Polak (1991) pointed out, for example, that governments and NGOs insisted that the IMF incorporate environmental concerns in its policies.

at the Fund on international and domestic financial institutions and markets (IMF IEO 2011).

In 2005, Managing Director Rodrigo de Rato, who had succeeded Köhler in 2004, proposed a broad plan of changes for the IMF, called the "Medium-Term Strategy." The accompanying report (IMF 2005c) drew attention to the challenges that globalization posed for the IMF's members, including the size, speed, and reach of financial shocks. This initial report was followed by *The Managing Director's Report on Implementing the Fund's Medium-Term Strategy* (IMF 2006c), which included proposals related to the growth of financial flows. The proposed alterations in surveillance, for example, included the integration of macroeconomic and financial market analyses in the Fund's two main publications, the *World Economic Outlook (WEO)* and the *Global Financial Stability Report (GFSR)*, and more emphasis on the financial sector in the Article IV consultations.

The IMF also reviewed its own governance. The Independent Evaluation Office itself was established in 2001 in response to criticisms that the IMF was a closed organization that operated without effective oversight (Weaver 2010). It conducts examinations of the IMF and its work and reports directly to the Executive Board. The IEO generally completes two reports a year, which are posted on its Web site.[3]

The IMF's governance procedures were also the subject of discussions among the members. The Interim Committee, established in 1974 (Chapter 3), had continued to serve in an advisory capacity to the IMF's Board of Governors, with membership that reflected the distribution of seats on the Executive Board. Managing Director Camdessus had proposed transforming it into a body with decision making authority (Shakow 2008). However, his proposal never gained sufficient support among the member governments, although the committee was turned into a permanent institution in 1999 with a new name, the International Monetary and Financial Committee (IMFC).[4] The reform of quotas to allocate larger shares to the rapidly growing emerging markets was another topic of discussion, but progress was glacial.

In addition, the IMF sought to deal with sovereign debt crises on a systemic basis. In 1999 the G7 leaders at their summit in Cologne endorsed a

---

[3]   The Web site's URL is www.ieo-imf.org. The IEO is administered by a director with an initial term of four years renewable for another three years, and the staff is composed of economists on temporary assignment from the IMF and others recruited from outside the Fund on fixed-term contracts.

[4]   The inclusion of "Financial" in the committee's title reflected Cadmessus's belief that the IMF's responsibilities should encompass that area.

report of their finance ministers that set out a broad framework for private sector involvement in crisis resolutions and called upon the IMF to develop specific processes to implement the framework (Kenen 2001). First Deputy Managing Director Anne Krueger responded in 2001 with a proposal for a new procedure, called the Sovereign Debt Resolution Mechanism (SDRM), to resolve cases of potential default on sovereign bonds. Under the original version of the SDRM, the IMF could issue a standstill on creditor actions and would also have the power of approval of a debt restructuring agreement between the debtor government and a majority of its creditors. The proposal was subsequently revised in response to initial criticisms that the Fund would not be viewed as an impartial adjudicator. A later version of the proposal (Krueger 2002) shifted the decisions for the activation of a legal stay and a restructuring agreement to a majority of the creditors.

The United States had indicated an interest in statutory solutions to the issue of restructuring sovereign debt. But after Krueger made her initial proposal, U.S. Treasury Undersecretary John Taylor (2002) endorsed the use of collective action clauses in bond contracts to allow a restructuring of the debt by a majority of the bondholders (Eichengreen 2002, Eichengreen and Rühl 2001). Once the United States expressed its interest in an alternative mechanism, the prospects of an IMF-based SDRM dwindled. The SDRM was sent off for further study, and the need for revisions in the IMF's duties and capabilities in dealing with a sovereign debtor's inability (or unwillingness) to pay its obligations was not addressed.[5]

9.2 International Lender of Last Resort

Another aspect of the IMF's activities that became a topic of discussion and debate was its ability to function as an international lender of last resort (ILOLR). The classic role of a domestic lender of last resort, based on Bagehot's (1873) characterization, is to lend freely to temporarily illiquid but nonetheless solvent banks at a penalty rate with good collateral. Central banks serve this role within national borders to prevent disruption of financial flows due to the collapse of a bank.

There are several justifications for the IMF to act as an ILOLR, lending foreign exchange to governments with external sector crises (Jeanne, Ostry, and Zettelmeyer 2008). First, there are externalities resulting from the occurrence of crises that are not incorporated in domestic decisions

---

[5] The IMF played no role in Argentina's negotiations with its bondholders to restructure its debt (Chapter 8).

on crisis prevention (Weithöner 2006). The IMF can provide a safety net for those countries affected by spillovers. Second, multilateral lenders such as the IMF may be able to stop speculative runs due to coordination failures by supplying adequate liquidity (Chang and Velasco 2000, Corsetti, Guimarães, and Roubini 2006, Morris and Shin 2006). Third, the IMF can deal with informational problems in private financial markets (Marchesi and Thomas 1999). Finally, the IMF can strengthen the position of domestic reformers through its lending programs (Mayer and Mourmouras 2004, 2005, 2008).

However, there are important differences between the capabilities of a domestic central bank and what an IGO can do in the face of an international crisis (De Bonis, Giustiniani, and Gomel 1999, Giannini 1999). First, an IGO such as the IMF cannot draw upon unlimited financial resources as can a central bank, which creates money (or bank reserves). Concerns arose during the late 1990s regarding the size of the IMF's financial resources after the Fund committed large amounts of credit to the countries with capital crises.

Second, the IMF has traditionally been reluctant to charge a penalty rate, since an excessively high rate would deter countries from approaching the IMF at a time when its advice and financial resources may be most needed. On the other hand, the Fund has sought to avoid charging a rate so low that it encouraged members to borrow frequently and in large amounts, thereby creating a situation of moral hazard.[6] It would also be politically difficult for a sovereign government to offer the Fund ownership of a country's natural resources or other assets as collateral.

Third, the concepts of liquidity and solvency are ambiguous in the case of countries where the public sector has issued international debt. A sovereign borrower has the ability to make debt payments by raising taxes. If the debt is denominated in a foreign currency, the government must acquire foreign exchange. Therefore, continued solvency depends on a government's ability and willingness to engage in the policy adjustments needed to satisfy its debt obligations. The case for debt relief arises when the costs of those adjustments are politically unacceptable to the country's citizens.

Fischer (1999), who claimed that the IMF served many of the functions of an ILOLR, responded to the alleged constraints on its actions. First, he pointed out that the IMF could borrow additional financial resources from

---

[6]   The interest charge on credit obtained through the IMF's SBA is linked to an SDR interest rate, which is based on short-term interest rates for the *euro*, the Japanese yen, the British pound, and the U.S. dollar.

its members. Moreover, in its role as a crisis manager the Fund had assembled financial rescue packages that included credit from other multilateral institutions and national governments. There was also the possibility of using SDRs to augment the pool of available credit.

Second, Fischer (1999) asserted that a program's conditions take the place of a penalty rate, as governments must implement the conditions to receive the credit. Moreover, the IMF was willing to charge higher interest rates and had done so with the SRF. Conditionality also takes the place of the collateral a private lender or domestic central bank might demand (Khan and Sharma 2003). In addition, the IMF has senior status in its claims on a country and could effectively deny access to the global financial markets to any governments that did not repay their loans.

Fischer conceded that it is difficult to differentiate between illiquid and insolvent sovereign borrowers. There is no legal bankruptcy status for a sovereign borrower, thus leaving an institutional vacuum for the resolution of debtors' claims. National attempts to restore solvency could result in the "measures destructive of national or international prosperity" that the IMF's Articles of Agreement sought to avoid. The IMF sought to fill the institutional gap through the proposed SDRM but was rebuffed (Chapter 9.1). In addition, unlike a domestic central bank that can deter risky borrowing through its regulatory oversight of the private institutions under its purview, the IMF has no such preemptive authority over its principals.

Another version of how an ILOLR should function was advocated by the International Financial Institution Advisory Commission (IFIAC), also named the "Meltzer Commission" after its chair, Allen H. Meltzer of Carnegie-Mellon University. The U.S. Congress had established the committee in 1998 as part of its legislation to authorize an increase in the IMF's quota and gave the committee the charge of reviewing the work of the IMF, the World Bank, and other intergovernmental organizations. The *Report of the International Financial Institution Advisory Commission (IFIAC)* (2000) recommended that the IMF be restructured as a smaller institution with three responsibilities: to act as a quasi-lender of last resort, to collect and publish data from its members, and to provide policy advice to members during Article IV consultations.[7]

Under the IFIAC's proposal, eligible emerging market countries would receive loans during a liquidity crisis for 120 days with only one allowable rollover at a penalty rate. Eligibility was based on meeting standards, which

---

[7] The IFIAC *Report* (2000) also recommended that the IMF's concessionary program, the Poverty and Growth Facility, be closed and long-term loans be eliminated.

included freedom of entry for foreign banks, adequate capitalization of domestic banks, publication of the maturity structure of sovereign debt, and an unspecified fiscal requirement. The recommendation of the majority of the IFIAC to limit lending was based on their concern that the IMF itself had indirectly contributed to the crises through moral hazard.[8]

The two views of how ILOLR lending should be conducted – the IMF's traditional approach with *ex post* conditionality and the IFIAC's guidelines for *ex ante* conditions – reflected different conceptions of the sources of international financial instability. After the East Asian crisis, the IMF accepted that crises could be transmitted across national boundaries via contagion and required a response managed by the IMF with the contributions of other IFIs and national governments. Meltzer and others believed that crises were the result of imprudent domestic policies, and the burden of proof was on a government that sought to borrow from the IMF to prove otherwise (Schwartz 1998). To "reward" governments that had implemented irresponsible policies with financial assistance, they believed, only promoted similar behavior. The IMF agreed that some crises were the result of rash actions, but in these cases the extensive conditions attached to the IMF's programs were needed to reform the domestic governmental structure.

The IMF took action to solidify its role as a lender of last resort by instituting new lending facilities. The SRF had been created in 1998 to provide large amounts of credit to countries facing capital account outflows (Chapter 7). The 1997 arrangement with Korea, which began before the establishment of the SRF, was converted to one, and the SRF was subsequently used with Russia (1997), Brazil (1998), and Turkey (2000).[9]

The IMF also established a means to provide rapid financing in the case of a sudden stop of capital flows. Precautionary arrangements, which allowed members to apply for an arrangement without intending to draw down on them, already existed. A new facility, the Contingent Credit Line (CCL), was introduced in 1999 with several unique features. In the case of a capital market shock, a member with a CCL would ask for an "activation review." Upon approval of its request, the country could borrow up to 500 percent of its quota. Applicants needed to satisfy eligibility criteria, which included no current need for Fund resources, a positive assessment of the country's policies at the last Article IV consultation, no disputes with private

---

[8]   The IFIAC *Report* (2000: 122), however, also contained a dissenting minority report, which claimed that that there was a "dearth of empirical evidence" that moral hazard was a factor in the crises of the 1990s, with the exception of that in Russia.

[9]   The SRF was abolished in 2009 when the IMF reorganized its lending facilities, including an expansion of the access limits (Chapter 9).

creditors, and a satisfactory economic and financial program ready to be implemented if needed.

However, no member ever applied for a CCL, and the facility expired in 2003. Potential borrowers were concerned that a request for a CCL would be interpreted as an indication of financial weakness. Moreover, the termination of a CCL by the IMF could be seen as an indication of a deterioration in a country's economic status. Finally, many countries adopted other means to ensure adequate financing in the event of a sudden reversal of capital flows or speculative currency attack (Chapter 9.4).

The establishment of the CCL, however, revealed a shift in the IMF's perception of its responsibilities in the event of a financial crisis. The Fund was willing to explore new ways of providing credit with much less conditionality. While the experience with the CCL demonstrated that devising the appropriate mechanism would be a complicated task, the IMF's evolving position would give it more flexibility at the time of the next crisis (Chapter 10).

9.3 FSF and Basel II

The G7 leaders responded to the financial crises with yet another call for upgrading financial standards and the establishment of another agency in Basel, the Financial Stability Forum (FSF).[10] The goal in this case was the prevention of further crises through more transparency and adherence to financial codes. The advanced economies used their two-tier approach to financial regulation, with the Basel-based agencies formulating new guidelines and the IMF and World Bank overseeing their implementation in the emerging market economies.

The membership of the forum included national authorities from the advanced economies and representatives of IFIs and other IGOs, international associations of financial regulators, and committees of central bankers.[11] The forum provided an opportunity for its members to assess

---

[10] The G20 was also founded in the wake of the Asian crisis to discuss responses to international financial crises. However, until 2008 it only met at the ministerial level on an annual basis and undertook no policy initiatives.

[11] The national members at the time of the inception of the FSF were the G7 nations and Australia, Hong Kong, the Netherlands, and Singapore. The international organizations were the BIS, which provided administrative support, and the European Community Bank, the IMF, the OECD, and the World Bank. The regulatory associations were the BCBS, the International Association of Securities Commissions (IOSCO), and the International Association of Insurance Supervisors (IAIS). The committees of central bankers were two other Basel Hub agencies, the Committee on the Global Financial System and the Committee on Payments and Settlement Systems (CPSS).

vulnerabilities in the international financial system, identify actions to address these vulnerabilities, and improve the coordination and exchange of information (Davies and Green 2008). The FSF identified twelve key areas of standards, grouped into three main categories: macropolicy and data transparency, institutional and market infrastructure, and financial regulation and supervision (Table 9.1). The standards represent intermediate public goods, and the FSF delegated their establishment to the institutions seen as best qualified to do so, an example of the "best-shot" public goods technology (Chapter 1).

The IMF was assigned the task of devising appropriate standards for the first category. The IMF had created the *Special Data Dissemination Standard* and the *General Data Dissemination Standard* to encourage data transparency after the Mexican crisis (Chapter 6). In response to the FSF's call for policy standards the Fund published its *Code on Good Practices in Monetary and Financial Policies* and *Code on Good Practices on Fiscal Transparency*. These dealt with the process of devising policy goals and the appropriate strategies for achieving them, as well as providing information on their status.

The standards developed under the direction of the FSF marked an expansion of "international soft law," that is, norms and principles that are recognized and accepted by a group of nations (Abbott and Snidal 2000, Alexander, Dhumale, and Eatwell 2006). Since these rules do not have the legal status of binding treaties, they allow nations flexibility in their application. However, governments in emerging markets may feel obliged to comply with international standards because of pressure from private markets or IGOs.

The exclusion of emerging markets from the FSF raised concerns regarding the use of its standards in those nations. Effective application of the standards on a national basis depends on country "ownership" of the policies (Schneider 2008). But ownership depends on participation in the determination of the guidelines, and the contribution of the emerging markets to this process was (at most) limited. There were also questions regarding the suitability of standards largely based on the experience of upper-income countries in nations with very different institutional frameworks.

The FSF assigned the task of reviewing the enactment of the standards to the IMF and the World Bank. The two IGOs jointly established the Financial Sector Assessment Program (FSAP) in 1999. FSAP teams from the two organizations visit nations that request an assessment and examine a country's financial standards and codes and its ability to withstand financial stress. They provide their respective organizations with reports

Table 9.1. *Standards for Sound Financial Systems*

Area	Standard	Issuing Body
I. Macroeconomic Policy and Data Transparency		
Monetary and Fiscal Policy Transparency	*Code of Good Practices on Transparency in Monetary and Financial Policies*	IMF
Fiscal Policy Transparency	*Code of Good Practices on Fiscal Transparency*	IMF
Data Dissemination	*Special Data Dissemination Standard* *General Data Dissemination System*	IMF
II. Financial Regulation and Supervision		
Banking Supervision	*Core Principles for Effective Banking Supervision*	BCBS
Securities Regulation	*Objectives and Principles of Securities Regulation*	IOSCO
Insurance Regulation	*Insurance Core Principles*	IAIS
III. Institutional and Market Infrastructure		
Crisis Resolution and Deposit Insurance	*Core Principles of Effective Deposit Insurance Systems*	BCBS/International Association of Deposit Insurers
Insolvency	*Insolvency and Creditor Rights*	World Bank
Corporate Governance	*Principles of Corporate Governance*	OECD
Accounting and Auditing	*International Financial Reporting Standards* *International Standards on Auditing*	International Accounting Standards Board International Auditing and Assurance Standards Board
Payment, Clearing, and Settlement	*Core Principles for Systematically Important Payment Systems* *Recommendations of Securities Settlement Systems* *Recommendation for Central Counterparties*	CPSS CPSS/IOSCO CPSS/IOSCO
Market Integrity	*FATF Recommendations on Combatting Money Laundering and the Financing of Terrorism & Proliferation*	Financial Action Task Force

Source: BIS.

summarizing their findings and recommendations to improve the resiliency of the financial system: a Financial System Stability Assessment (FSSA) for the IMF and a Financial Sector Assessment for the World Bank. In addition, the Fund and the bank collaborate on the *Reports on the Observance of Standards and Codes,* which evaluate a country's observance of the key areas identified by the FSF.[12]

By April 2008, three-quarters of the membership of the Fund had participated in a FSAP, and about two-thirds of these countries had posted their FSSAs on the IMF's Web site. But several countries of systemic importance to the global financial markets had not yet taken part, most prominently China and the United States (IMF IEO 2006b). The nonparticipation of these two large countries stemmed in part from a reluctance to allow outside observers to form judgments on their national policies.[13]

The establishment of codes for the dissemination of data can decrease uncertainty and contribute to lower volatility in the financial markets.[14] But the delegation by the FSF to the IMF and the World Bank of the tasks of devising such codes and monitoring their implementation rested on the assumption that these institutions should ascertain whether satisfactory procedures for promoting private financial flows had been established. U.S. Treasury Secretary Lawrence Summers (1999b) called for such an expansion in the focus of IMF surveillance from sharing information among governments to "promoting the collection and dissemination of information for investors and markets." But China and Indonesia's avoidance of the FSAP demonstrated that some emerging markets did not agree that it was necessary to conform to the practices of the global financial markets.

The expansion and revision of capital standards for banks represented another area of increased financial regulation. The BCBS spent much of the 1990s updating the Basel I guidelines. The simplicity of the first standard, which dealt only with credit risk, had made it straightforward to apply. However, financial innovation had led to the creation of new types of assets and their riskiness was uncertain. Awareness of other types of risk, such as market risk due to fluctuations in asset prices, had increased as well. Private

---

[12] The IMF also assesses compliance with the measures developed by the Financial Action Task Force on Money Laundering, an IGO established in 1989 to combat money laundering and the financing of terrorism.

[13] The G20 national leaders announced in November 2008 that all its members would undertake an FSAP (Chapter 10).

[14] Eichengreen (2009a) summarizes the evidence on the effectiveness of standards and codes. The IMF and the World Bank (IMF and World Bank 2011) provide a post–global crisis review.

banks claimed that they could assess the amount of capital they would need to hold against the various forms of risk through their own statistical models, such as the Value at Risk (VaR). But these tools had been tested only for short periods and their properties in the event of excessive volatility were unknown.

A new capital accord, known as Basel II, was released in 2004 after a long period of negotiations among national authorities and banks (Tarullo 2008). The complexity of its requirements reflected the great diversity among the banks that would be subject to its provisions. Basel II has three components: Pillar I dealt with capital requirements and retained the minimum capital adequacy ratio of 8 percent and the definition of regulatory capital that satisfied the requirement. The changes included new capital requirements for market and operational risk, and the assessment of credit risk. Banks could choose to perform the latter by utilizing a standardized approach with risk weights determined by credit rating agencies, or by using one of two approaches, both based on the banks' own internal ratings. Pillar II addressed the issue of supervisory review by national regulators of their banks' capital adequacy, including the requirements of Pillar I. Pillar III established guidelines for the public disclosure of information on the banks' financial conditions.

The implementation date for Basel II was set for December 2006, but its realization was slowed in part by uncertainties about its provisions.[15] Many of the reporting options available under Basel II would only be appropriate for large banks, and concerns about the suitability of the Basel II framework for emerging markets and developing countries were raised (Powell 2004). The volatile economic and financial environments of many of these countries made risk assessment difficult to measure (Rojas-Suarez 2008). In addition, a lack of adequately trained personnel would slow enforcement of the new regulations. The IMF (2005b) foresaw an increase in the need for its technical assistance to members if they sought to adopt the advanced provisions of Basel II.

In retrospect, the Basel II guidelines allowed banks too much latitude in assessing their exposure to risk and need for capital. Problems with the evaluation of risk due to asymmetric information and a lack of transparency proved to be endemic in the financial markets of the upper-income countries as well as the emerging markets, and the credit rating agencies

---

[15] In the United States, for example, there were numerous discussions among the government agencies responsible for regulatory oversight of whether all the banks would be required to adopt the standards.

made serious errors of judgment. In addition, there was little attention paid to the risk of the overall financial system, that is, "macroprudential" risk. The global financial crisis of 2008–9 would result in plans for yet another set of revised guidelines, Basel III (Chapter 11).

9.4 Reserves and Regional Arrangements

While the IMF engaged in self-study and reform and the G7 governments established new regulatory bodies and standards, the emerging market nations drew their own conclusions from the international financial crises. They sought to escape their "weaker link" status and avoid the need for IMF programs through the accumulation of foreign reserves as well as the development of alternative sources of liquidity. These actions represented a turning away from the IMF and its resources, which had far-reaching implications for the global economy.

During the period after the Argentine crisis, the emerging markets and developing countries recorded increases in real growth rates and declines in inflation (Chapter 10) Private capital flows to these countries tripled between 2002 and 2003 and rose again in 2004 and 2005. The World Bank (2007) attributed the surge of private flows to a combination of global factors, including low interest rates and increased liquidity, as well as robust growth in the recipient countries. The absence of crises resulted in a decline in the number of IMF programs (Figure A.2), and former IMF borrowers took advantage of their prosperity to pay off their loans.

The rise in capital inflows and changes from current account deficits to surpluses allowed emerging market countries to build up their holdings of foreign reserves. The most notable increases occurred in the case of China, where the foreign exchange reserves of the People's Bank of China surpassed $1 trillion in 2006 and approached $2 trillion by 2008. The foreign exchange reserves of the middle-income economies exceeded $4 trillion by 2008 (Figure 9.1), while Japan held an additional $1 trillion. Some of the countries also used their foreign exchange to establish sovereign wealth funds, portfolios of assets to be used for future generations or to fund projects of national interest.

The increase in reserve holdings was interpreted as a form of "self-insurance" by the central banks of those countries concerned about the occurrence of currency crises (Aizenman and Lee 2007, De Beaufort Wijnholds and Kapteyn 2001, Durdu, Mendoza, and Terrones 2009, Feldstein 1999). A central bank with sufficient reserves can defend its

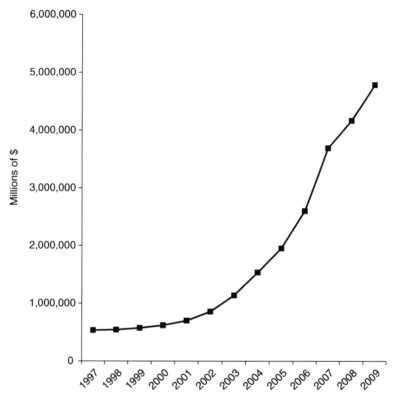

Figure 9.1. Foreign Reserves of Emerging Markets: 1997–2009.
Note: Gold excluded.
Source: World Bank, *World Development Indicators*, March 2012.

exchange rate from speculative selling. Moreover, the possession of the reserves serves as an indicator that a bank has good "fundamentals," which in the second-generation currency crisis model would deter speculators (Chapter 6) and insulate a country from contagion. Reserves also allow the monetary authorities to assist domestic banks with liabilities denominated in foreign currencies if they face large withdrawals.

Reserves, however, also carry costs for the country holding them. A country must sacrifice current spending in order to run a balance of payments surplus to acquire the reserves. Maintaining the reserve holdings imposes a further opportunity cost in the form of forgone spending. If a central bank sterilizes the monetary impact of the inflows by issuing domestic bonds, it generally pays a higher interest rate than it receives on its own holdings of foreign bonds, usually U.S. Treasury securities.

Avoiding such costs was one of the reasons for establishing the IMF (Chapter 2). The IMF could pool the foreign exchange of its members, lending them out as needed. But the emerging market governments effectively decided that the costs of acquiring and holding reserves were less than those of entering an IMF program. The accumulation of reserves for the purpose of self-insurance, therefore, represented a sign of "no confidence" by the emerging markets in the IMF in the wake of the financial crises of the 1990s.

The buildup of foreign exchange in the emerging markets may also have been a response to the lack of change in their quotas (Joyce and Razo-Garcia 2011). Quotas determine access limits to Fund resources, and while the IMF had been willing to bypass these in past crises, there was no assurance that they would do so again. Moreover, larger drawings could involve stricter conditionality as well as explicit surcharges.

There is an intermediary stage between the national accumulation of foreign reserves and using the facilities of the IMF: a regional monetary fund. The proposal of the Japanese government to establish an Asian Monetary Fund had failed in 1998 because of opposition from the United States (Chapter 7). However, in the aftermath of the East Asian crisis the countries in that region continued discussions of establishing an alternative to the IMF. In 2000 the members of the Association of Southeast Asian Nations (ASEAN)[16] joined China, Korea, and South Korea to form a network of bilateral swap arrangements, known collectively as the Chiang Mai Initiative (CMI) after the town in Thailand where the finance ministers of the countries met to finalize the agreement. The swap arrangements allowed the participants to draw upon the foreign currency reserves of their partners in the arrangements for up to six months in the event of a currency crisis.

The number of arrangements eventually grew to sixteen, and the total amount that could be borrowed totaled $50 billion–$60 billion (Henning 2009). The CMI, however, was not divorced from the IMF. The participating countries agreed that after the first 10 percent of a swap (later raised to 20 percent) was disbursed, the country drawing funds was required to participate in an IMF program. Activation of the agreement was also dependent on the creditor country's approval.

---

[16] The ASEAN current members are Brunei, Cambodia, Indonesia, Laos, Malaysia, Myanmar, the Philippines, Singapore, Thailand, and Vietnam.

In 2009 the CMI was expanded through the Chiang Mai Initiative Multilateralization (CMIM) Agreement (Henning 2009, Sussangkam 2010). The CMIM represents a multilateral financial commitment by its members of a total of $120 billion. China and Japan each provide 32 percent of the funds, South Korea 16 percent, and the other governments contribute smaller shares. Each participant is entitled to swap its own currency for U.S. dollars for an amount that equals its contribution times a purchasing multiplier, which ranges up to 5. However, the funds are still held at each participant's central bank.

Other regional arrangements exist, such as the Latin American Reserve Fund with seven members and the Arab Monetary Fund with twenty-two member countries. However, these have not been drawn upon; nor was the CMI active during the recent global crisis. Instead, South Korea and Singapore drew upon swap lines established by the U.S. Federal Reserve (Chapter 10). The total size of the amount of funds committed to the CMIM may be too small to be effective in the face of large capital outflows.

These regional arrangements raise the issue of "subsidiarity," that is, the appropriate range of policy jurisdiction for IGOs that transcend national boundaries. In general, coordination should be done over the same geographic range where the spillover of the public good takes place in order to ensure the proper allocation of benefits and costs and to deal with information problems (Sandler 2004). The regional provision of a public good may also resolve some of the multistage agency issues that arise with IGOs (Chapter 1). On the other hand, economies of scale or scope may justify the provision of a public good on a global basis. In the case of the former, for example, unit costs may fall as a result of providing the IPG in different regions. An IGO may experience economies of scope as a result of supplying more than one public good. Moreover, a global financial crisis could overwhelm the resources of a regional arrangement and require an international response (Joyce and Sandler 2008).

There is no inherent reason why regional organizations and IGOs need act independently (Desai and Vreeland 2011, Henning 2006). The IMF, for example, has increased its regional surveillance activities and could work with the CMIM as well as the other organizations in addressing regional issues. Moreover, there have been proposals for reorganizing the Fund's Executive Board on a regional as well as national basis.

But during the 2000s, the IMF's members diverged in a number of ways. The upper-income nations deepened their financial ties after further domestic deregulation, particularly in the United States and several European nations, while using international agencies to coordinate their actions. The emerging market countries, on the other hand, increased their holdings of foreign exchange to strengthen their ability to deter currency and financial crises and avoid dependence on the IMF. The next chapter examines the IMF's concerns over the emergence of "global imbalances" and the Fund's response to the global financial crisis that ultimately erupted.

10

The Great Recession

The era of economic stability that prevailed during the middle 2000s came to an end with the Great Recession of 2008–9. The shock emanating from the United States and other advanced economies swept through the global economy, contracting trade and financial flows and depressing economic activity. This chapter describes the IMF's attempts to avert a crisis and its response when the collapse occurred.

The "Great Moderation," described in the first section, was characterized by declines in inflation and output volatility in most nations. Moreover, growth rates accelerated in the emerging market economies. The one discordant note was the increase in current account deficits in several advanced economies, most notably the United States. These were matched by surpluses in many emerging market economies as well as the oil exporters, which were accompanied by increased foreign exchange reserves. The reasons for and implications of these "global imbalances" have been widely debated. Some viewed them as the result of the transfer of funds from emerging nations with high savings rates to advanced economies with liquid financial markets and did not believe that they posed a threat to international financial stability. Others emphasized the role of diminished private and public savings in the advanced economies that left those nations vulnerable to capital outflows.

The IMF's forecasting record in the period leading up to the Great Recession is reviewed in the second section. The IMF warned of economic repercussions of the buildup of global imbalances. The IMF was also aware that housing prices in many advanced economies had reached levels that did not reflect economic fundamentals. But it did not recognize the buildup of financial fragility as banks and other institutions developed new instruments that were vulnerable to the collapse of housing values. The IMF forecast continuing economic growth and stable conditions in financial markets up until the outbreak of the global crisis.

The IMF sought to address the global imbalances through consultations with its principal members, and these discussions are summarized in the third section. The Fund organized a meeting of China, Japan, and the oil exporters with the Eurozone membership and the United States, but it proved impossible to persuade these countries to change their policies. The distrust among them spilled over to the discussions of the IMF's surveillance of currency values, with China castigating the IMF for its focus on the role of exchange rates in addressing external imbalances. These events demonstrated once again the limitations of agency over sovereign principals with divergent policies.

The crisis that swept through the global economy is described in the third section. Declining housing prices led to a collapse in liquidity in the financial markets of the advanced economies. Central bankers and financial policy makers responded with lower interest rates and the provision of liquidity, but financial institutions in the United States and Western Europe were unable to finance their exposed balance sheets. After the failure of Lehman Brothers in September 2008, the financial collapse became a global economic crisis. The IMF responded by supplying substantial amounts of credit to distressed members. The conditionality attached to these loans was based on the circumstances of the borrowing countries, and in many cases the IMF allowed members to use macroeconomic policies to offset declines in private expenditures. The IMF was supported by the G20 leaders, who increased the IMF's financial resources and assigned it new duties in the postcrisis global economy.

The IMF's performance in the precrisis period and its subsequent activities once the crisis broke out are analyzed in the last section. The IMF's failure to foresee the fragility of the financial sectors of the advanced economies reflected its focus on the emerging markets, as well as an unwillingness to criticize the policies of its most important members. But the IMF responded rapidly to the weakening in global economic activity and furnished ample credit on a wide basis with limited conditionality. It also accepted the effectiveness of capital controls to deal with financial turbulence. Its activities in these areas reflected the preoccupation of the upper-income nations with their own economic situations and the ascendance of those emerging market economies that recovered quickly from the crisis.

10.1 Global Imbalances

The period following the financial crises in the emerging markets was one of decreased economic volatility in these nations. This stability was part

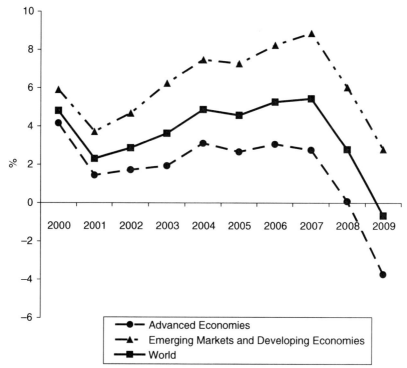

Figure 10.1. Real GDP Growth: 2000s.
Source: IMF, *World Economic Outlook* Database, September 2011.

of a broader phenomenon known as the "Great Moderation," which was marked by steady real growth and moderate inflation during the early and mid-2000s (Figures 10.1, 10.2). The possible causes advanced to explain this phenomenon included an absence of negative international shocks and better macroeconomic policies (Summer 2005). The then–Federal Reserve Board governor (and later chair) Ben S. Bernanke (2004) attributed the reduction in macroeconomic volatility to improved monetary control procedures. Many central banks in advanced economies adopted the practice of inflation targeting by setting explicit limits on price rises and were rewarded with lower inflation rates and a decline in the public's expectations of future price changes.

Moreover, the emerging markets and developing economies recorded increases in real growth during the decade of the 2000s that exceeded those of the advanced economies (Figure 10.1). Part of their growth was due to increased commodity prices and export-oriented policies, but it

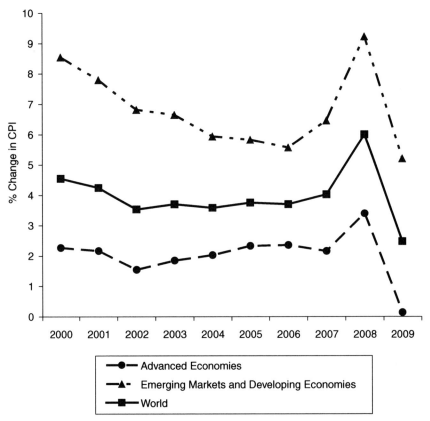

Figure 10.2. Inflation: 2000s.
Source: IMF, *World Economic Outlook* Database, September 2011.

also resulted from more stable macropolicies. Central bankers in some of these countries also switched to inflation targeting, while others sought to control price rises by a commitment to a fixed exchange rate. Foreign direct investment to these countries rose steadily, while portfolio and other forms of capital flows were more volatile (Figure 10.3). As a result of the improvements in economic conditions, the demand for IMF credit fell and the number of arrangements for new programs declined to the lowest level since 1973 (Figure A.2).

There were concerns regarding long-run stability, however, due to the emergence of what were called "global imbalances." The United States and several other upper-income economies such as the United Kingdom registered current account deficits that were matched by surpluses in emerging

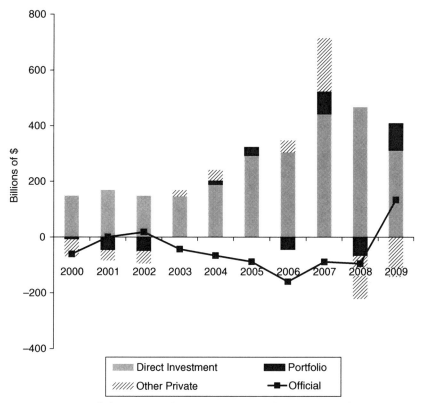

Figure 10.3. Capital Flows to Developing Economies and Emerging Markets: 2000s.
Source: IMF, *World Economic Outlook* Database, September 2011.

markets as well as oil exporters (Figures 10.4, 10.5), and capital flows from
the latter to the upper-income countries. This phenomenon challenged
expectations, as the neoclassical model predicted that capital would flow
from advanced economies to lower- and middle-income countries, where
it would earn higher returns. A vigorous debate ensued over the causes of
the divergent balance of payment positions and the need (if any) for cor-
rective policies.[1]

On the one hand, some analysts pointed to increases in savings that took
place after the financial crises of the 1990s, particularly in Asia (Bernanke
2005). The higher savings surpassed private investment expenditures

---

[1] There is a large literature devoted to this subject. Wolf (2008) provides one of the best
overviews.

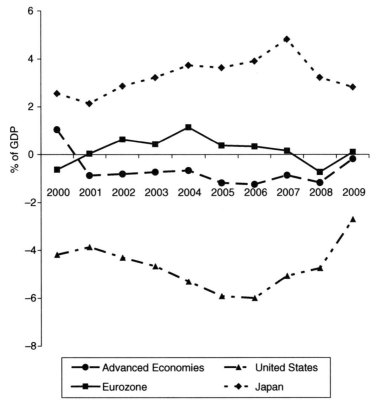

Figure 10.4. Current Accounts of Advanced Economies: 2000–2009.
Source: IMF, *World Economic Outlook* Database, September 2011.

in these countries, and as a consequence there was a swing to surpluses in their current accounts.[2] Savings also grew in several advanced economies with aging populations, such as Germany and Japan. These trends were reinforced by rising oil prices, which contributed to surpluses in the oil-exporting countries. The "global glut" of savings flowed to the United States because that country possessed the largest and most liquid financial markets in the world, and there was a dearth of alternatives (Caballero, Farhi, and Gourinchas 2008a, 2008b, Cooper 2008). According to this line of analysis, the resulting increases in the external liabilities of the United

---

[2]   The exception to this phenomenon occurred in China, where investment expenditures increased during this period. However, its current account also recorded surpluses due to very high rates of household and business savings.

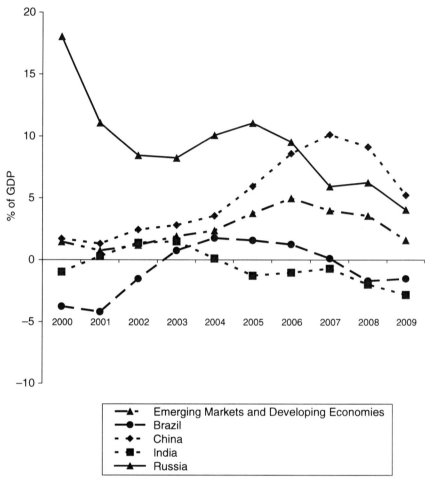

Figure 10.5. Current Accounts of Developing Economies and Emeging Markets: 2000–2009.
Source: IMF, World Economic Outlook, September 2011.

States did not pose a cause for concern, as the capital inflows would eventually reverse themselves as savers drew upon their assets.

Another interpretation of the global imbalances stressed the decline in savings in the United States as the primary determinant of that country's current account deficit (Feldstein 2008). Part of the fall reflected the change in the federal government's budget position from a surplus to a deficit after 2001. This shift was accompanied by a decrease in the household savings rate, due in part to the upsurge in the real estate prices. Households used the increased value of their homeownership as collateral for loans to finance consumption expenditures. Consequently, there were increases in the debt of both the government and households.

Much of the debt was held by private and official purchasers outside the United States (Chapter 9). This debt represented a vulnerability in the eyes of those who emphasized the contribution of the United States to generating the global imbalances, since foreign debt holders could decide at any time to diversify their portfolios with assets in other currencies. This would result in a currency depreciation with deleterious consequences for the global economy if the fall were precipitous. Higher interest rates in the United States might preserve the value of the dollar, but borrowers in that country would pay the cost. Those who identified the decline in U.S. savings as the cause of the imbalances sought to raise government and household savings to reduce the current account deficit. On the other hand, there was less concern about the current account deficit of the United States among those who held the global savings glut responsible, although Bernanke (2005) favored a reduction in the budget deficit for other reasons.

Other analysts, however, focused on the role of China and its exchange rate policy (Goldstein and Lardy 2008, 2009). The Chinese central bank had fixed the value of its currency, the *yuan*, against the U.S. dollar until 2005, when a crawling peg was instituted. The Chinese currency subsequently appreciated against the dollar, but that country's current account surpluses and foreign exchange reserves continued to grow.

Another perspective was that of those who viewed the accumulation of foreign reserves as evidence of the emergence of a new fixed exchange rate regime, which they named "Bretton Woods II" (Dooley, Folkerts-Landau, and Garber 2004, Dooley and Garber 2005). They pointed out that after World War II, the United States served as the financial center surrounded by a periphery of European countries and Japan. These countries adopted a growth strategy based on undervalued currencies, controls on trade and capital flows, and FDI flows from the United States. Once their economies had grown, they became part of the global economy's center, and the Bretton Woods system ended when they were no longer willing to finance further U.S. deficits. Proponents of this view claimed that the Asian countries were following a similar strategy, using their exports to boost growth rates while financing the U.S. deficits.

Empirical analyses of the global imbalances, such as those of Chinn and Ito (2007, 2008) and Gruber and Kamin (2007), found government budget balances to be highly significant determinants of current accounts. But the scale of the U.S. deficits recorded in the period of 2001–4 was greater than the imbalances predicted by their models. These results suggest that factors not included in conventional macroeconomic analyses may have contributed to the deficits during this period.

The unexplained surge in the current account deficits may have reflected the expansions in credit that occurred in many of the deficit countries. While previous lending booms had been concentrated in the emerging markets, these increases mainly occurred in advanced economies such as Greece, Ireland, Spain, the United Kingdom, and the United States (Hume and Sentence 2009). An increase in household credit was a distinguishing feature of this expansion in lending.[3] The concerns that were raised about the sovereign debt of the United States had usually overlooked the mounting debt of the household sector. Within the United States, the increase in mortgage-related lending was seen as a beneficial development that boosted homeownership. The development of new financial instruments linked to these mortgages and the holdings of these securities by foreign institutions were generally overlooked but would prove to be a source of financial instability (see later discussion).

10.2 Premonitions

The IMF's crisis prevention responsibilities include issuing warnings of growing financial or economic instability. The IMF uses its traditional tools of multilateral surveillance, the *WEO* and the *GFSR*,[4] as well as its bilateral surveillance to draw its members' attention to incipient sources of vulnerability. But the IMF's record in forecasting the 2008–9 global crisis is, at best, mixed. The IMF's economists were concerned about the impact of the global imbalances and were aware of the potential for collapses in housing prices. However, they did not link the capital flows to the advanced economies and their expanding housing sectors to the growth in financial instruments that heightened the fragility of the balance sheets of their financial institutions. The IMF's forecasts on the eve of the Global Recession were overly optimistic and only began to incorporate the impact of the weakening in mortgage values in the United States in their projections in the fall of 2007 after the crisis was under way.

---

[3] See Reinhart and Rogoff (2009) on the historical role of housing prices in asset bubbles.
[4] See IMF (1999a) and IMF IEO (2006a) for reviews of the IMF's multilateral surveillance.

While the IMF's economists welcomed the broad-based growth observed during the 2000s, they emphasized the need for changes in national policies to correct the imbalances. They specifically called for fiscal consolidation in the United States, structural reforms in European countries, and exchange rate flexibility in Asian countries. The *WEO* published several analyses of the risks posed by the continuation of the global imbalances (IMF 2002b, 2005f, 2005g, 2006f, 2007e).

The IMF also took note of the pattern of booms and busts in the prices of financial assets and housing. In 2003, for example, the *WEO* (IMF 2003) presented an analysis of the impact of downturns in equity and housing prices. The authors reported that housing price busts were associated with steeper economic downturns than stock market declines, and that bank-based financial systems suffered more than market-based systems during collapses in housing prices. In the following year, the *WEO* (IMF 2004c) included an examination of the global real estate boom, which found that housing prices had become synchronized across countries in response to common global factors, particularly low interest rates and sustained growth, and were vulnerable to a correction.

But the IMF's analyses of financial stability in the *GFSR* were generally optimistic about the stability of financial markets and institutions. The authors of the 2005 *GFSR* (IMF 2005a: 1), for example, found that the resilience of the global financial system had improved in response to "solid global economic growth, buoyant financial markets, and continued improvements in the balance sheets of the corporate, financial, and household sectors." The following year, the *GFSR* (IMF 2006b) reported that the dispersion of credit risk by banks had left the financial system more resilient and better able to absorb shocks. The authors of the report made this claim even though, as they admitted, the identities of those who held the risk were not transparent. The IMF subsequently admitted that it had underrated the combined risk of financial complexity and increased leverage (IMF 2009d).

The *WEO*s offered positive economic forecasts in the period leading up to the global crisis. In April 2007, for example, the IMF forecast global economic growth in 2008 of 4.9 percent (IMF 2007e), and in July this projection was raised to 5.2 percent (IMF 2007f). The IMF responded to the volatility in the mortgage markets in the United States that fall by revising their 2008 global growth forecast downward to 4.8 percent (IMF 2007g) but claimed that "sound fundamentals would continue to support solid global growth" (IMF 2007g: 6). The Fund's forecasters hedged their projections by cautioning that continued financial turbulence could "generate a deeper 'credit crunch' than envisaged in the baseline scenario, with considerably greater macroeconomic impact" (IMF 2007g: 7).

The IMF's record on bilateral surveillance, as expressed in the *Staff Reports* of the Article IV consultations with the United States, is not more prescient.[5] The *Staff Reports* for the 2004 (IMF 2004b), 2005 (IMF 2005e), and 2006 (IMF 2006e) consultations offered positive assessments of the resiliency of the financial sector in the United States and saw little risk resulting from household borrowing. In the summer of 2007 the IMF's team of economists expressed concerns about systemic risks from tail events, the management of counterparty risks, and the use of credit agency ratings (IMF 2007d). But they also reported that "*core commercial and investment banks are in a sound financial position, and systemic risks appear low*" (IMF 2007d: 14).[6]

It is legitimate to ask whether the IMF's record in this area is any worse than those of other IFIs. The IMF's analysis can be contrasted with that of the BIS, which had consistently raised concerns regarding booms in private credit and their impact on asset prices and balance sheets (Borio, Furfine, and Lowe 2001, Borio and Lowe 2003). The BIS recognized that banks in some advanced economies had distributed risk through securitization but was more apprehensive than the IMF about the ramifications of this practice. The BIS (BIS 2007: 145) pointed out that much of the risk was embodied in "securities of growing complexity and opacity" and that the high credit ratings assigned to these securities did not reflect the probability of tail events.

Like the IMF, the BIS was uneasy about vulnerable sectors of the global economy, including real estate in the United States. It also took a cautious view of the potential risks posed by the boom in real estate prices in the United States and the relatively untested financial derivatives linked to them. The BIS realized that the outcome of a simultaneous occurrence of adverse economic and financial developments would be quite perilous and concluded that "tail events affecting the global economy might at some point have much higher costs than is commonly supposed" (BIS 2007: 145).

The IMF's lack of foresight of the coming collapse is even more startling in view of the fact that one of the most perceptive critics of financial innovation was Raghuram G. Rajan, economic counselor and director of research at the IMF during the years 2003 through early 2007. In 2005, Rajan delivered a speech (Rajan 2005) at a conference honoring the retiring Federal

---

[5] The IMF's IEO (2011) found similar assessments in the bilateral surveillance of other advanced economies with large financial sectors.

[6] Italics in original.

Reserve Board chair Alan Greenspan. He addressed the issue of financial development and warned that changes in financial technology, regulations, and institutions had combined to bring about an increase in the amount of risk borne by the financial system. As a result, the system was exposed to large systemic shocks, and Rajan warned of the possibility of a "low probability but highly costly downturn" (Rajan 2005: 360). Rajan's views were vigorously contested at the conference by the former U.S. Treasury Secretary Summers and others (*Wall Street Journal* 2009), and his prescience appears to have had no impact on his colleagues at the Fund.

Why did the IMF not anticipate the financial crisis? A full appraisal of the IMF's precrisis activities is provided later, but several reasons can be cited here. First, the IMF continued to believe that financial development played an important role in economic growth, and offering a more measured view of its benefits and costs could be seen as obfuscating that message. Second, the IMF's largest members were not interested in warnings of the risks of asset bubbles and credit booms, as Summers's reaction to Rajan's warnings demonstrates. Even if the IMF believed that there had been an increase in the probability of a manifestation of financial instability, the IMF was reluctant to engender a confrontation with its major principals. Third, the IMF's focus was on dealing with global imbalances and exchange rates, not the development of new financial instruments.

10.3 Impasse

In addition to its traditional tools of surveillance, the IMF sought to use other methods to draw attention to the phenomenon of global imbalances and coordinate a response by its members. The IMF's Medium-Term Strategy (Chapter 9) had included "new directions in surveillance" as a priority (IMF 2006c: 1) and proposed a multilateral procedure to supplement the bilateral Article IV consultations with member governments. The new forum, called a "multilateral consultation," allowed the IMF to address global issues with several countries or a regional association.

In 2006 the IMF sought to use its new consultation process to address the issue of global imbalances (Bird and Willett 2007). The invited participants were China, representatives of the Eurozone, Japan, Saudi Arabia, and the United States. There were bilateral meetings of the IMF and each country (or area) and multilateral meetings that culminated in a joint public statement in April 2007. The respective national and regional authorities publicly agreed that the reduction of the imbalances required new policy measures, but none altered their existing policies in response to the calls for coordinated action. Their unwillingness to undertake joint action reflected deep disagreements over the root causes of the imbalances. The United States, for example, pointed to Chinese exchange rate practices as the primary reason for the continued pattern of Chinese current account surpluses and U.S. deficits, while the Chinese held fiscal policy in the United States responsible for the imbalances (Giles 2007).

The IMF staff report (IMF 2007c) on these consultations sought to present them as successful. It reported that the format of the multilateral consultations had worked well and resulted in a better understanding by the participants of the others' positions. However, the report also candidly admitted that "participants emphasized that national policies were driven primarily by domestic requirements, although a positive impact on global imbalances was a welcome additional benefit" (IMF 2007c: 9). There was nothing the IMF could do to change policies that were based on the perceived national interests of its members. The multilateral consultations were dropped and their place in the IMF's work agenda reduced.

But the dispute between China and the United States had not been resolved, and it carried over into the deliberations over another aspect of IMF surveillance: its review of exchange rate policies. The Fund's 1977 *Decision on Surveillance over Exchange Rate Policies* had survived virtually intact over thirty years despite many reviews (IMF 2006d).[7] Over time the IMF's surveillance of exchange rate practices had come to be widely seen as inadequate. A report from the IEO of the IMF's activities in this area, for example, had concluded, "*In the period reviewed (1999–2005), the IMF was simply not as effective as it needs to be to fulfill its responsibilities for exchange rate surveillance*" (IMF IEO 2007a: 35).[8] The authors of the report recommended that the "rules of the game" with respect to exchange rate practices be clarified, and that practical policy guidance be given to members regarding the stability of exchange rate arrangements and the proper use of exchange market intervention.

Members of the U.S. Congress had threatened to impose trade restrictions as that country's trade deficit with China widened, and its government sought to use the IMF to rectify the imbalance through changes in Chinese exchange rates. Timothy Adams, the undersecretary for international affairs at the U.S. Department of the Treasury, had bluntly warned

---

[7] One potentially substantive change had been made in 1995 after the Mexican crisis when the list of indicators that were monitored was expanded to include "unsustainable flows of private capital," but the term was not defined.

[8] Italics in original.

that "the perception that the IMF is asleep at the wheel on its most fundamental responsibility – exchange rate surveillance – is very unhealthy for
the institution and the international monetary system" (Adams 2006: 135).[9]
The IMF was caught in a dispute between its largest principal and one of the
fastest-growing members.

The Medium-Term Strategy (Chapter 9) called for an updating of the
1977 *Decision*, and in June 2007 the Executive Board issued a new *Decision
on Bilateral Surveillance over Members' Policies* (IMF 2007a). The first part
of the new *Decision* established "external stability" as an obligation of the
members under Article IV, and the accompanying Companion Paper (IMF
2007b) elaborated on the concept of external stability. A balance of payment position was judged to be consistent with external stability when
the underlying current account was "broadly in line with its equilibrium"
and when the capital account was not vulnerable to "abrupt shifts in capital flows"(IMF 2007b: 2). The second part of the new *Decision* carried
over from the 1977 *Decision* several principles to provide guidance for the
members in their exchange rate policies. Part II added a new guideline,
Principle D, which recommended (but did not oblige) members to "avoid
exchange rate policies that result in external instability." This section also
spelled out circumstances that might require a review by the IMF of a country's practices. These included protracted exchange market intervention, a
"fundamental exchange rate misalignment,"[10] or prolonged current account
surpluses or deficits.

Many of the conditions that could justify a Fund review could be interpreted as relevant to China's situation, and the *Decision* was widely seen as
the product of pressure from the United States on the IMF to target China
for its exchange rate policies. The People's Bank of China responded to the
new decision with a sharp statement that declared its opposition to the
Decision, "as it does not fully reflect the developing countries' opinions."[11]
The Chinese central bank's statement noted that exchange rate adjustment
has a "role to play in resolving external imbalances, but it is not the ultimate
and only policy instrument." It urged the IMF to undertake its surveillance
function "by strengthening communications and dialogue with members

[9] Mussa (2007), a former director of the IMF's Research Department, offers a critique of the
     IMF's surveillance of China's exchange rate policies.
[10] The IMF established a Consultative Group on Exchange Rate Issues to provide exchange
     rate assessments in its surveillance activities. Three different methodologies are utilized in
     the analysis (Lee *et al.* 2008).
[11] The announcement was posted at www.pbc.gov.cn/english/renhangjianjie/.

on the basis of mutual understanding and respect." The government of China subsequently refused to allow publication of its Article IV consultations with the Fund because of its opposition to the IMF's position that the Chinese currency was undervalued.

Fischer (2008) noted that the *Decision* focused on exchange rate policies rather than a country's overall policy stance and pointed out that there can be other sources of exchange rate instability besides overt exchange rate manipulation.[12] He claimed that a government's failure to use fiscal policy to correct an unsustainable balance of payments position should be as worthy of Fund censure as the manipulation of an exchange rate. By this criterion, U.S. policies were as problematic as Chinese exchange rate practices.

The result of this controversy was gridlock in the surveillance of exchange rates. The IMF's ability to identify national policies that were inconsistent with members' obligations publicly was constrained by the ability of governments to withhold their permission to publish the results of Article IV consultations. Truman (2008) claimed that the IMF's staff had identified several cases of exchange rate policies that deserved further investigation, but no action was taken by the IMF's Executive Board.

In 2009, the IMF backtracked on its earlier position on exchange rates. The Fund announced that the term "fundamental misalignment" would no longer be utilized in its surveillance of exchange rates and that uncertainty in interpreting the causes of exchange rate movements would be acknowledged. The changes were attributed to a desire to avoid the use of "labels" that distracted attention from policy discussions. But the IMF's retreat from its earlier positions also showed the impact of the Great Recession on the relative positions of the IMF's members. China's economy had recovered from the initial shocks to its exports, and its resurgence contributed to growth in other Asian countries. There was little to be gained from criticism of its exchange rate practices, although that issue had not been settled to the satisfaction of the United States.

10.4 Implosion

The global financial crisis that erupted in 2008 shared some similarities with the East Asian crisis of 1997–8 (Chapter 7). In both cases, capital inflows and lax monetary policies had resulted in private credit booms. These led to

---

[12] Fischer had left the IMF in 2001. In 2005 he became governor of the Bank of Israel.

increases in asset prices and distortions in investment expenditures. Once these bubbles burst, the balance sheets of domestic banks and other financial institutions deteriorated as loans and other assets were marked down or written off. The IMF's response in the case of the global collapse, however, was larger in magnitude, was more rapid, and carried fewer conditions than it had during the previous emergency.

Housing prices peaked in the United States in 2006 and then began to fall.[13] The write-downs of mortgages and their derivative securities forced financial institutions that were widely leveraged to sell assets. The sell-offs extended outside the United States to institutions in Europe that also held these securities, and the spreads on credit default swaps rose in response to growing volatility. Central bankers in the upper-income countries responded by lowering interest rates and providing credit. The Federal Reserve established swap facilities with the ECB and the central bank of Switzerland so that those institutions could supply dollars to their banks that needed to finance dollar-denominated holdings. The emerging market nations and developing economies, however, were generally seen as insulated from the financial turbulence because of their strong growth and their ability to "decouple" from advanced economies. In addition, their own banks were generally more regulated and less likely to hold exotic financial instruments.

The government-assisted purchase of the investment bank Bear Stearns by JPMorgan Chase in March 2008 revealed the precarious positions of financial institutions in the upper-income countries. Central banks continued to cut policy rates but also intervened directly in the financial markets as asset prices fell and credit spreads for private borrowers widened. The continuing weakening of the real estate market in the United States contributed to fears about the viability of the government-sponsored mortgage agencies "Fannie Mae" (Federal National Mortgage Association) and "Freddie Mac" (Federal Home Loan Mortgage Association). Concerns about a synchronized disruption of national economies also increased, although the emerging markets continued to be seen as insulated from the financial crisis.

However, the takeover by the U.S. government of Fannie Mae and Freddie Mac in September, followed by the bankruptcy of Lehman Brothers, the sale of Merrill Lynch to the Bank of America, and the bailout

---

[13] There are many excellent accounts of the causes and events of the Great Recession. The chronology presented here is based on the work of Bean (2010), the BIS (2009), and Mishkin (2011).

of American Insurance General, resulted in a global loss of confidence in the financial markets. In response, governments undertook massive intervention schemes to shore up their financial institutions. The U.S. Treasury Department initially announced that it would purchase distressed assets from domestic banks. However, the regulators eventually followed the example of European authorities by injecting capital onto the banks' balance sheets. In addition, the Federal Reserve instituted new programs to provide liquidity to domestic institutions while increasing the size of its existing swap lines and inaugurating similar arrangements with the central banks of other upper-income countries.

In October, the ECB, the Federal Reserve, and several other central banks announced a coordinated reduction in their policy interest rates. The G7 finance ministers met in Washington, D.C., and announced their determination to cooperate to "stabilize financial markets and restore the flow of credit." They also supported the IMF's role in assisting the countries most affected by the financial collapse. However, the lame duck status of the U.S. president, George W. Bush, limited their ability to coordinate their national plans for economic recovery.

While the national authorities moved to halt the shutdown of their financial systems, the ensuing economic collapse quickly spread outside the G7 area. World trade fell in the latter part of the year, and economic growth in the emerging markets slowed as their exports collapsed. In September the IMF issued a forecast for world GDP growth of 3.9 percent in 2008 and 3.0 percent in 2009. One month later it revised those figures to 3.7 percent and 2.2 percent, respectively. By January 2009, the world economic growth rate for the year that had ended was revised downward again to 3.4 percent, and growth for the new year fell to 0.5 percent. The actual 2008 growth rate was later reported to be 2.9 percent.

The IMF and its managing director, Dominique Strauss-Kahn, who had taken office in November 2007, had watched the intensification of the crisis with mounting concern over possible spillover effects. During the early stages, the IMF's role was confined to issuing calls for a coordinated response in national financial policies and a broad-based fiscal stimulus. Once the global economy began to contract, however, governments turned to the IMF for assistance.[14] The Fund responded rapidly with large amounts of credit in front-loaded disbursements. The IMF instituted seventeen

---

[14] In several cases governments approached the IMF only after being refused elsewhere. Pakistan, for example, had been rebuffed by China (*New York Times* 2008).

Table 10.1. *IMF Stand-By Arrangements Post–September 2008*

Date of Program Agreement	Country	Amount (Millions of U.S. dollars)	% of Quota	Total Financing (Millions of U.S. dollars)
September 15, 2008	Georgia	1,172	497	2,290
November 5, 2008	Ukraine	17,253	802	21,253
November 6, 2008	Hungary	16,529	1,015	26,229
November 14, 2008	Seychelles	28	200	28
November 19, 2008	Iceland	2,196	1,190	11,296
November 24, 2008	Pakistan	11,349	700	21,549
December 23, 2008	Latvia	2,387	1,200	10,584
January 12, 2009	Belarus	3,560	587	4,760
January 16, 2009	El Salvador*	806	300	2,156
January 16, 2009	Serbia	4,108	560	4,869
March 6, 2009	Armenia	838	580	2,000
April 1, 2009	Mongolia	240	300	425
April 11, 2009	Costa Rica*	772	300	1,772
April 22, 2009	Guatemala*	989	300	1,743
May 4, 2009	Romania	17,948	1,111	27,118
July 8, 2009	Bosnia and Herzegovina	1,592	600	2,062
July 24, 2009	Sri Lanka	2,594	400	2,594

Sources: IMF 2009a, 2009e.
Note: * denotes a precautionary agreement

SBAs, almost all with exceptional access, during the period of September 2008 and through the following summer (Table 10.1).[15]

The Ukraine, for example, which faced falling export prices and a cutoff of foreign credit, received an SBA of $17.3 billion, which represented 802 percent of its quota. Hungary's SBA included a $16.5 billion loan, 1,015 percent of its quota. Iceland, the first upper-income country to enter a Fund program since the 1970s, suffered a spectacular collapse of its banking system and received $2.2 billion, 1,190 percent of its quota. Pakistan received $11.3 billion, 700 percent of its quota. In many cases the IMF credit was augmented by funds from the World Bank and other multilateral agencies; several European governments supplied additional financing to those European nations that borrowed from the Fund.

---

[15] In several cases the amounts available to the countries were augmented after the initial agreements.

The policy conditions that were part of these programs reflected an awareness of the origin and severity of the global downturn. The crisis was a true sudden stop that originated in the upper-income countries, although a few emerging markets had experienced unsustainable domestic booms (Ghosh *et al.* 2009, Ghosh *et al.* 2011).[16] The contraction in economic activity due to falling international trade required an easing of macroeconomic policies, including lower interest rates and some fiscal stimulus, in countries with records of stable policies. Exchange rate devaluations could be useful, but their size depended on a country's conditions, and the IMF warned of possible contractionary effects. Moreover, the IMF agreed that capital account controls could be utilized as a last resort if negotiations with creditors for rescheduling were unsuccessful (Ghosh *et al.* 2009).

The crisis hit East European countries particularly hard. Capital inflows in the form of bank loans had fueled credit booms there, including surges in real estate investment, similar to the conditions in East Asia before its crisis (Chapter 7). The collapse in Western Europe disrupted the financial sectors in the Eastern countries that had relied on short-term capital flows to finance current account deficits. The IMF's programs for these countries focused on the need for fiscal consolidation and monetary restraint (Ghosh *et. al* 2011). The three Baltic countries (Estonia, Latvia, and Lithuania) were particularly hard hit, suffering declines in output of 14–18 percent in 2009 (Åslund 2010). The IMF provided assistance to Hungary, Latvia, and Romania, partnering with the EU. The one area of contention occurred over Latvia, where the IMF initially sought a currency devaluation. But its government wanted to preserve its currency board to stay on track to adopt the *euro* and was supported in its position by the EU. The IMF withdrew its opposition, and the country adjusted to the external shock through fiscal tightening and wage cuts.

Subsequent reviews of the nonconcessionary programs undertaken during this period found that credit was disbursed more quickly and in larger amounts than had occurred in past crises (IMF 2009e, 2010c). There were fewer structural conditions attached to the programs than in previous arrangements, and these were often in the form of structural benchmarks rather than performance criteria. Fiscal policy in the program countries was utilized to respond to falling private demand when appropriate and feasible, although their governments avoided the large increases in budget

---

[16] The countries most affected by the spread of the crisis had larger current account deficits and faster private sector credit growth before the crisis occurred (Lane and Milesi-Ferretti 2010).

deficits that occurred in the advanced economies.[17] Countries in Asia and Latin America with credible records of macroeconomic policies were able to boost domestic spending to offset the decline in exports while drawing upon their reserve holdings to stabilize their exchange rates. Interest rate increases designed to prevent a run on exchange rates were limited when compared to past crises, and exchange rates stabilized after initial periods of volatility.[18] Even longtime critics of the IMF admitted that the Fund had allowed countries to run countercyclical policies and retain capital controls (Stiglitz *et al.* 2010).

In addition, the IMF created a new lending facility, the Short-Term Liquidity Facility (SLF). The program allowed the IMF to lend to countries with strong macroeconomic policies that faced liquidity constraints because of strains in the global financial markets. Eligibility was based on a positive assessment of a country's macropolicies, its access to the capital markets, and the sustainability of its debt burden. Eligible countries could draw up to 500 percent of their quotas, and there would be no conditions attached to the loans. The maturity of an SLF was only three months, although a country could draw up to three times in one year.

The IMF also disbursed funds to developing economies particularly affected by the crisis (IMF 2009b, 2010a). In 2006 the IMF had established a new facility, the Exogenous Shocks Facility (ESF), to provide credit to low-income members facing exogenous shocks to their balance of payments. The Fund subsequently refined the new facility by creating a rapid-access component that allowed countries to receive quickly up to 25 percent of their quota for each shock. After September 2008, the IMF disbursed funds to Cameroon, Comoros, the Republic of the Congo, Ethiopia, and Kenya under the new arrangement and agreed to make credit available for the Kyrgyz Republic, Malawi, Mozambique, Senegal, and Tanzania through the ESF. Another group of developing economies borrowed funds through the PRGF. In January 2010, the IMF revamped its facilities for low-income members, replacing the PRGF and ESF with the Extended Credit Facility for medium-term needs, the StandBy Credit Facility for short-term financing support, and the Rapid Credit Facility for urgent financing.[19]

---

[17] However, there were exceptions. Iceland and Latvia suffered, for example, record large deficits because of revenue declines.

[18] Again, exceptions occurred, in this case in Hungary, Iceland, and the Ukraine.

[19] The World Bank also provided substantial assistance to the low-income nations. The World Bank's Independent Evaluation Group (2010) provided a review of the World Bank's response to the crisis.

While the IMF was providing financial assistance and overhauling its facilities, the leaders of the G20 nations met in Washington, D.C., in November 2009. The meeting itself was historic since it marked the end of the era when the G7 leaders would convene to arrange the response to a financial crisis. The summit allowed the leaders of China, Brazil, India, and other emerging markets to ensure that their countries' interests were taken into account when measures to address the global downturn were formulated.

The national leaders announced their determination to work together to restore growth and reform the world's financial systems (G20 2008). The G20 communiqué acknowledged the importance of the IMF's role in the response to the crisis and instructed the Fund to review the adequacy of its instruments and facilities. The leaders pledged that the IFIs would have sufficient financial resources to meet the demands for their assistance. The G20 governments also made a commitment to reform the governance of the IMF and announced that all of its members would undergo an FSAP.[20]

Over the winter of 2008–9, the IMF continued to modify the terms of its lending. It sought to "modernize" its conditionality by cutting back on the number of conditions and discontinuing structural performance criteria. It doubled the limits on access to IMF credit to 200 percent over a year and 600 percent cumulatively. The Fund eliminated facilities that were not often used, including the new SLF, which had not been well received by members because of its limits on access.

To replace the SLF, the IMF established the Flexible Credit Line (FCL). This new facility allows countries with strong fundamentals to draw funds without conditions that can be repaid over a period of up to five years. There is no access limitation and the arrangement can be renewed after six months. The FCL was more acceptable than its predecessor, and Mexico, Poland, and Colombia signed up for one-year precautionary arrangements. The IMF also created High Access Precautionary Access (HAPA) SBAs for countries that did not qualify for the FCL, and HAPA arrangements were approved during the crisis with Costa Rica, El Salvador, and Guatemala.[21]

---

[20] In April 2010, the IMF's Executive Board announced that FSAP assessments would be mandatory for all members with "systemically important financial sectors."

[21] The IMF subsequently established a Precautionary Credit Line for countries with good policy records but that did not qualify for the FCL. The new facility included pre-qualification with conditionality if the arrangement was activiated. This facility was replaced by the Precautionary and Liquidity Line in 2012.

One unusual aspect of the response to the crisis was the extension by the Federal Reserve of a total of fourteen swap lines to central banks in other countries (IMF 2010d). The swap lines served as an alternative source of dollars for the few emerging markets (Brazil, South Korea, Mexico, and Singapore) that were able to make such arrangements with the Federal Reserve.[22] In addition, news stories after the crisis (*Financial Times* 2010) revealed that foreign banks with branches in the United States had drawn upon the Federal Reserve's emergency credit facilities. Foreign borrowers included Barclays and the Bank of Scotland of the United Kingdom, Société Générale of France, and UBS of Switzerland. The extensive borrowing demonstrated how interconnected large financial institutions are, and how easily financial distress can spread across borders. It also revealed the existence of a two-tier response to financial crises, with the Federal Reserve lending to those nations and private institutions that it viewed as systematically important to the functioning of private capital markets, while the IMF provided credit to others.

By the spring of 2009, the crisis had moderated. There were signs of financial stabilization as the volatility of asset prices fell, although the indicators of economic recovery were mixed. The world economic growth rate of 5.0 percent masked differences among the IMF's members. The contractions in the advanced economies had been more severe than those recorded in the emerging market countries, with the exception of the downturns in the East European countries (Figures 10.6, 10.7). In a study of the performance of emerging market economies, the IMF (2010f) claimed that the middle-income economies with lower precrisis vulnerabilities were further ahead in their recoveries than the upper-income nations. Similarly, low-income countries were in much better shape than they had been in previous crisis periods. The IMF (2010a) attributed their relatively stronger performance to better macroeconomic conditions going into the crisis and the use of countercyclical policy responses assisted by substantial IMF support.

The G20 national leaders met again in April in London with the newly elected U.S. president, Barack Obama, in attendance. The summit's communiqué (Group of Twenty 2009) contained a broad policy agenda to address the crisis, including a number of measures designed to reinforce the IMF's lending capabilities. First, the G20 leaders approved an increase in the IMF's financial resources of $500 billion. Immediate financing of $250

---

[22] Aizenman and Pasricha (2010) show that exposure to U.S. banks was the key distinguishing features of these four countries.

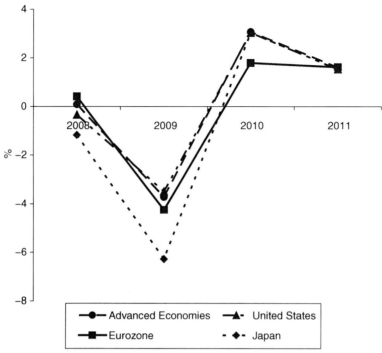

Figure 10.6. Real GDP Growth Rates of Advanced Economies: 2008–2011.
Source: IMF, World Economic Outlook Database, September 2011.

billion would be made available by Japan and the EU, and these amounts would be the basis of an expanded NAB. Second, a general SDR allocation of $250 billion would be made to the IMF's membership to increase global liquidity, and the IMF's Fourth Amendment ratified.[23] Third, IMF gold would be sold to raise another $6 billion for concessional finance for the poorest countries.

The IMF was also assigned new duties. The national leaders called on the IMF to monitor their own progress in their recovery measures. They supported "candid, even-handed, and independent IMF surveillance of our economies and financial sectors" (G20 2009). However, the IMF would be working with a new partner, as the G20 converted the FSF to the Financial Stability Board (FSB). The revitalized organization includes the FSF members, all the G20 countries not currently members of the FSF, and Spain and

---

[23] The Fourth Amendment, which became effective in August 2009, allocated SDRs to countries that became members of the IMF after the initial allocation in 1981.

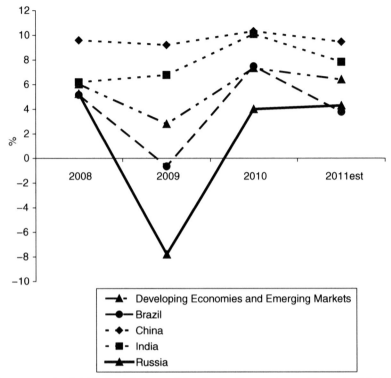

Figure 10.7. Real GDP Growth Rates of Developing Economies and Emerging Markets: 2008–2011.
Source: IMF, *World Economic Outlook* Database, September 2011.

the European Commission.[24] The FSB was given a wide range of responsibilities, including monitoring progress in strengthening national financial systems and collaborating with the IMF to provide early warning of macroeconomic and financial risks (Chapter 11).

The G20 leaders also dealt with the governance of the IMF. They agreed on the implementation of a package of IMF quota reforms and called on the Fund to move up the next review of quotas by two years (Table A.2). They also agreed that the heads of the IFIs should be appointed in an open and merit-based selection process. If such a process were followed, the managing director of the IMF need not be a European (Table A.1), while the World Bank would not necessarily be headed by a citizen of the United States.

---

[24] The broadening of the membership of the revamped organization was matched by similar expansions at other agencies of the Basel Hub, such as the BCBS.

When the G20 leaders met again in Pittsburgh in September 2009, they announced that their joint efforts to ensure economic recovery had been successful and designated the G20 as the "premier forum" for future international economic governance. The heads of government called for international financial regulatory reform, including changes in the Basel capital standards. They also confirmed many of the changes at the IMF that were endorsed at the previous summit. The national leaders supported the establishment of a process for the mutual assessment by the G20 governments of their economic policies, assisted by the IMF. They approved a shift in the quota positions of the IMF of at least 5 percent to the underrepresented countries, and an increase in the NAB of more than $500 billion. The G20 repeated the call for the selection of the next managing director through a merit-based process and agreed that other governance-related issues, including the size and composition of the Executive Board, needed to be addressed.

10.5 IMF and the Great Recession: Appraisal

A review of the IMF's activities before and during the Great Recession of 2008–9 reveals the weaknesses and strengths of the IMF's capabilities. On the one hand, the IMF underestimated the fragility of the financial systems in the advanced economies and the potential for their disruption. The IMF was unable to move its members toward policies, such as a consensus on exchange rate practices or the accumulation of reserves, that may have lessened the crisis. On the other hand, once the crisis erupted, the IMF moved rapidly to provide assistance on liberal terms and contributed to the subsequent recovery.

The IMF's failure to foresee the collapse in the advanced economies reflected its views of the stability of its members' financial sectors. The IMF believed that financial development furthered economic growth and that the new derivatives and other instruments fostered the stability of financial markets.[25] The IMF shared the confidence of regulators in many upper-income nations that their financial sectors were robust and resilient. The IMF focused its surveillance on possible vulnerabilities in the emerging market countries, the "weaker links" in international finance. In 2001,

---

[25] The long-awaited FSAP report for the United States, which appeared in 2010 (IMF 2010h), concluded that the financial crisis revealed important weaknesses in that country's financial sector, including the existence of a shadow banking system, a decline in underwriting standards, failures in risk management, and the use of complex derivatives whose properties were poorly understood. European banks had engaged in many of the same practices.

for example, the IMF conducted vulnerability exercises in these countries to assess weaknesses in economic fundamentals and financial stability. But the advanced economies were not included in these exercises until after the global crisis.

The IMF's multilateral consultations on global imbalances faltered as a result of the inherent difficulty that an agent faces in convincing its principals to undertake joint actions. Some analysts have argued that the IMF should have done more to encourage the formulation of joint policies. Subramanian (2009), for example, awarded the IMF a grade of C in crisis prevention due in part to its ineffectiveness in resolving the global imbalances. But the IMF could only propose policy initiatives to its members and therefore devised bureaucratic procedures for consultations on the bilateral and multilateral levels that had little consequence. However, these forums did have the side benefit of justifying the Fund's existence at a time when the demand for the IMF's financial assistance had declined.

The IMF was much more successful in dealing with the fallout of the global crisis, effectively serving as an ILOLR (Chapter 9). The IMF's crisis management in the Great Recession of 2008–9 clearly differed from its responses to previous crises (Chapters 6, 7, 8). This time the IMF had the opportunity to prepare before the crisis expanded outside the financial centers of the United States and Europe, and it was ready to take quick action on a large scale. It lent to the countries most deeply affected, providing large amounts of credit at the beginning of the programs. The Fund reformulated its lending facilities to make them more effective, avoided unnecessary program conditions, and supported policies to restore growth in countries that were caught in the economic and financial maelstrom. Consequently, the IMF's reputation soared, and talk of a "comeback" and a phoenixlike rise became widespread (Chapter 1).

Subramanian (2009) awarded the IMF a grade of A minus for its response to the crisis, noting that it mobilized the resources to make much-needed loans and advocated a strong fiscal stimulus to counteract the global recession. He withheld a straight A only because the IMF allowed Latvia to avoid a currency devaluation despite a massive current account deficit, raising the question of whether its treatment of European and other borrowers was evenhanded. Some observers also questioned the partiality of the IMF in providing large amounts of credit to the European nations. The scale of the lending can be justified by the magnitudes of the capital flow reversals. On the other hand, the IMF had not adequately warned these nations of the potential risks of the precrisis borrowing that occurred in countries such as Hungary and Romania.

The IMF's own review (2009e) of its nonconcessionary programs during the crisis reported signs of stabilization in the program countries and claimed that the IMF's policies were "broadly right in most cases" (IMF 2009e: 43).[26] The authors of the report advanced two explanations for the relative success of the IMF's programs: first, the crisis emanated from outside the countries that needed to borrow from the IMF, which meant that there were not as many domestic weaknesses to address as in past crises. Consequently, the IMF did not need to require significant changes in domestic policies. In addition, the report admitted, the IMF's design of its own programs had embodied the lessons of the past. The IMF may also have had more latitude because of the preoccupation of its advanced members with their own economic situations, which allowed the IMF to operate more freely.

Another factor that may have accounted for the IMF's rapid and effective response was the leadership of Managing Director Strauss-Kahn. Strauss-Kahn was a prominent member of the French Socialist Party and had served as the French minister of the economy, finance, and industry in the 1990s. He sought but did not receive the nomination of his party for the presidential election of 2007. Although his appointment to the IMF's top position was initially viewed by some as a setback to any further advancement in France, Strauss-Kahn's record of management during the crisis established a global profile for him and boosted his reputation in France.

The IMF subsequently used the crisis as an opportunity to reformulate its own policy positions. In a remarkable turnaround, Ostry *et al.* (2010) admitted that capital controls could be useful as a tool to manage capital inflows. The Fund's economists presented evidence that countries with larger stocks of debt liabilities or nonfinancial FDI saw smaller declines in GDP in 2008–9, which buttressed the claim that capital controls could help prevent financial fragility.[27] The alteration of its position on capital controls marked a break with the previous stance that posited unregulated capital accounts as the optimal long-run regime. The change reflected both an intellectual evolution within the IMF as well as the influence of those members such as China and India that had never accepted the old orthodoxy.

Moreover, the G20 had pledged substantial changes in the governance of the IMF that would make it more equitable and presumably more credible

---

[26] The U.S. General Accountability Office (2009) also gave the IMF's program a positive assessment.

[27] Financial FDI, on the other hand, was associated with steeper declines in growth, possibly due to capital outflows to parent banks.

with its middle- and lower-income members. The leaders of these nations also promised to engage in a process of mutual surveillance in which the IMF would have a prominent role. Whether or not the IMF would be able to play that role, however, depended on whether the promises of the G20 governments made during the crisis were fulfilled. As we will see in the next chapter, the assurances that are given in the midst of a crisis often lose urgency once the crisis passes. In addition, the IMF soon faced a new onset of financial instability in Europe that split the IMF's members.

11

The World Turned Upside Down

While the IMF was successful in assisting nations to deal with the crisis of 2008–9, it could not (even if it had wanted to) stem the systemic changes that marked a turning point in the global economy. The post–Bretton Woods configuration of economic power has been turned upside down.[1] The advanced economies are burdened with the cost of repairing the damage done by their financial institutions while their recoveries have stalled. The emerging market and developing countries emerged from the crisis relatively unscathed but can no longer count on exports to the United States to fuel their economic growth. This chapter reviews the challenges the IMF will face as its members deal with changes in their economic and political positions.

A tepid economic recovery left fiscal burdens in many advanced economies, and the effects of this legacy are explored in the first section. Ireland, Greece, and Portugal are saddled with large sovereign debt liabilities and have required assistance from the IMF and other European governments. The IMF faces the danger of being caught in a crossfire among the debtor governments, those that contributed to their relief, and its other members concerned about the Fund's exposure to the European borrowers.

Further fiscal challenges will arise in future decades in those upper-income countries with aging populations. If government expenditures on health and income support programs continue at current rates, their debt burdens will also become unsustainable. The IMF in its crisis prevention role must continue to urge these countries to keep their fiscal situations manageable without inducing another downturn. Delays in facing this issue will raise its future cost and at some point engender a negative market reaction.

[1] The chapter title comes from an English ballad supposedly played at the surrender of Lord Charles Cornwallis and British troops to Americans under General George Washington at the Battle of Yorktown in 1781.

The emerging markets must deal with developments in their financial sectors, which are examined in the second section. Capital flows have been a source of volatility, and many of these countries have imposed controls on capital account transactions. The IMF now recognizes such measures as one of the macroprudential tools available to policy makers. More generally, these countries are considering whether they should seek to integrate their financial sectors with global markets or retain some degree of autonomy over their activities. The IMF's guidance in this area would be useful both for the middle-income countries as well as for its low-income members that seek to become the next generation of emerging markets.

The IMF itself requires reform of its governance procedures, and some advances in this area are reviewed in the third section. But a more fundamental overhaul of the IMF's perspective on global financial issues is needed if it is to be a credible agent for advancing the public goods of financial and economic stability. The IMF's membership must also show a willingness to engage in collective decision making that continues after crises have passed if they seek to forestall another global calamity.

11.1 Debt Again

The advanced economies' slow recovery from the global crisis had troublesome consequences for their fiscal positions. Increased government expenditures and declining tax revenues resulted in budget deficits that were financed through the issuance of debt. Rising sovereign debt levels also reflected the absorption by governments of distressed assets on their banks' balance sheets. The bond markets responded to the increases in debt levels by demanding higher returns from sovereign borrowers.

Their initial target was Greece, which had taken advantage of the relatively low borrowing rates that members of the Eurozone paid to finance their government deficits. The Greek deficits averaged 5 percent of GDP per year between 2001 and 2008, exceeding the 3 percent ceiling established by the EU's Stability and Growth Pact and the Eurozone average of 2 percent (Nelson, Belkin, and Mix 2010). Borrowing to cover these deficits drove the country's debt levels past the pact's limit of 60 percent of GDP, and current account deficits climbed to more than 14 percent by 2008.

Greece initially fared relatively well during the global crisis. However, in October 2009, its government announced that the fiscal year's budget deficit would be 12.7 percent of GDP, twice as large as had been previously estimated; this figure was later further revised upward to 15.4 percent. The ratings on Greek sovereign bonds were downgraded and their spreads over

German bonds escalated, leading to concerns about a spiral of rising interest rates and expanded financing needs.

European officials met over the winter of 2009–10 to consider the extension of financial assistance to Greece. The EU did not possess an institutional mechanism for a bailout of a sovereign borrower, but its political leaders felt the need to deal with Greece's situation, as a default by its government would have severe ramifications for European financial institutions. Their banks had not fully recovered from the global crisis, and another round of write-downs would strain their weakened positions. The European governments also addressed the issue of whether the IMF should be included in any financial rescue arrangement. The argument in favor of the IMF's involvement was that a global agency would have more credibility and acceptance as an external monitor than a European entity. Moreover, the IMF was experienced in dealing with sovereign debt crises, and the IMF's financial contribution would lower the costs paid by the European governments. By March 2010, the European leaders made the decision that they would extend credit if asked and that the IMF would join them.

The following month the Greek government requested support from the other European governments and the IMF. This was the first request from a West European country to the IMF since those of the United Kingdom and Spain in the late 1970s and Portugal in 1984. The IMF joined the European Commission and the ECB in providing $145 billion in financing, with $40 billion from the IMF in the form of a three-year SBA. The IMF's commitment was equal to about 3,200 percent of Greece's IMF quota at that time, a record amount.[2]

The IMF's program with Greece included conditions that were similar to those the Fund had sought in the 1980s and 1990s (Chapters 4, 6, 7, 8). For example, the program stipulated a reduction in the general government deficit from 13.6 percent in 2009 to below 3 percent of GDP by 2014. The decrease in the deficit would be accomplished through spending reductions, increases in the collection of taxes, and the curtailment of entitlement programs (IMF 2010e). Greece's situation was mainly the result of its own fiscal policies rather than an external shock and therefore needed to be addressed through comprehensive domestic adjustments. But there was also the possibility that the cutbacks in spending would lead to an economic contraction that actually worsened the country's debt/GDP

---

[2] Greece will receive an increase in its quota as part of the reassessment of quotas (Chapter 11.2). The credit to Greece through the EFF represented 2,400 percent of its new quota.

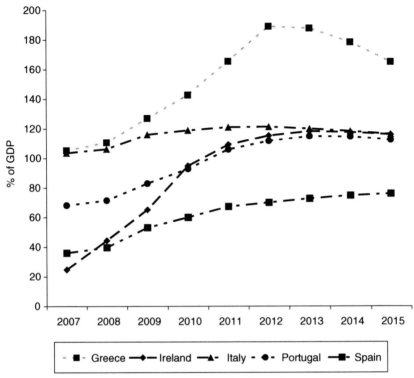

Figure 11.1. Government Gross Debt of Selected Advanced Economies: 2007–2015.
Note: Data include future projections.
Source: IMF *Fiscal Monitor*, September 2011.

position. Greece's membership in the Eurozone ruled out the use of currency devaluation or monetary stimulus to offset the impact of the contractionary fiscal policies.

Other European sovereign borrowers came under scrutiny by bondholders. Portugal, Ireland, Italy, and Spain in particular all had escalating debt, and with Greece formed the group dubbed "PIIGS" (Figure 11.1). Ireland and Spain had experienced tremendous housing bubbles before the global crisis that left them with the fiscal bills for failed banks. Italy and Portugal suffered from low growth and mounting public borrowing. The interest rates on their debt rose to levels that would make refinancing difficult, and their governments announced policies of fiscal austerity. The European governments established a new entity, the European Financial Stability Facility (EFSF), to raise funds for further bailouts of indebted countries.

Ireland became the next country to require a financial rescue by other European governments and the IMF in December 2010. The amount committed under the agreement totaled about $113 billion, which included a three-year EFF from the IMF to provide $30 billion, worth about 2,322 percent of Ireland's IMF quota.[3] Since the source of Ireland's debt problems was very different from the fiscal deficits in Greece, the program had a different focus. It required a restructuring and downsizing of the banking sector, although fiscal consolidation was also a component.

Portugal followed in May 2011. The IMF and the EU approved a financing package of $116 billion, including a three-year EFF for $39 billion, worth 2,306 percent of its quota. The policy conditions include a reduction in the government's deficit from 9.1 percent in 2010 to 3 percent by 2013. The fiscal curtailments included cuts in public sector wages and staff positions.

These arrangements with the European governments placed the IMF in a sensitive position. On the one hand, the Fund needed to ensure that the policies of the governments borrowing from it were realistic, in terms of both achieving the programs' goals and gaining political acceptance. But to lower debt/GDP ratios in the absence of rapid growth requires large swings from deficits to surpluses in the primary budgets of the governments most affected. The domestic distress caused by enacting such policies is heightened when a country is already recovering from a substantial economic shock. A lack of confidence by investors in governments with austerity programs to make the necessary adjustments results in higher interest rates, which make the task more difficult.

If a government backtracked from its commitments, the IMF would be under enormous pressure not to terminate its assistance. Continuing to lend, however, would endanger the newly won credibility the IMF earned during the global crisis (Rogoff 2010). Moreover, receipt of IMF credit does not ensure the avoidance of default, as the case of Argentina demonstrates. Qian, Reinhart, and Rogoff (2010), in a study of default episodes over the period of 1952–2008, reported that almost half (42%) of the countries in default had IMF programs one to two years before the default.

The Fund's traditional "crisis manager" role in previous crises had given it control over the recovery programs and subsequent disbursements of credit. But in Europe it worked in partnership with governments that also gave assistance, particularly Germany and France, two of the IMF's largest principals. Their national leaders faced domestic pressures from indignant

---

[3]   The subsequent increase in Ireland's quota lowered the relative size of its EFF credit to 1,548 percent of its quota.

taxpayers who did not want to pay the bills of profligate governments and differed with each other over the degree of involvement of the private sector in any debt restructurings. The ECB was also a major player in these negotiations and sometimes took an independent position. Consequently, the IMF was forced to reconcile the efforts of governments and organizations with different interests and goals.

Following the initial arrangements with the European debtor governments, there were periodic waves of speculation about debt defaults or restructuring, accompanied by denials by government officials that such moves were being contemplated. The IMF issued a paper in September 2010 (Cottarelli *et al.* 2010) claiming that sovereign defaults were "unnecessary, undesirable, and unlikely." Its position aligned it with those who believed that a combination of external financing coupled with sufficient domestic austerity measures would allow the debtor countries to make full payment on their obligations. This belief was similar to the view in the early 1980s that the debt crisis of that era was due to insufficient liquidity, which could be resolved through concerted lending arranged by the Fund (Chapter 4).

But the measures designed for Greece proved to be inadequate. In 2012, a new financing package, which was linked to a substantial restructuring of Greece's sovereign debt, was arranged. Bondholders agreed to a write-down of about 75 percent of the present value of their bonds. The government of Greece received a commitment for $170 billion in new financing from the official sector. The IMF's share took the form of a four-year EFF of $36.7 billion, which replaced the cancelled SBA of 2010. The program established a new fiscal target of a primary budget deficit of 1 percent of GDP in 2012, and a primary surplus in the following years. These would be achieved through spending cuts and increased tax collection and sought to reduce the debt/GDP level to 120 percent by 2020. But a youth unemployment rate of 50 percent raised doubts about the viability of these measures, and a similar situation in Spain showed that Greece was not alone. Several European countries faced the prospect of a new "lost decade."

The PIIGS are not the only advanced economies with debt problems. The combination of slow growth and recurring deficits occurred in virtually all the upper-income economies. Reinhart and Rogoff (2009) in their analysis of financial crises demonstrated that a worsening of fiscal balances, driven largely by a falloff in tax collections, is a legacy of such crises, and this leads to steep increases in sovereign debt. The IMF (IMF 2010c) projected that the general government debt/GDP ratio for the advanced economies would reach about 110 percent in 2015, an increase from a precrisis level of 37

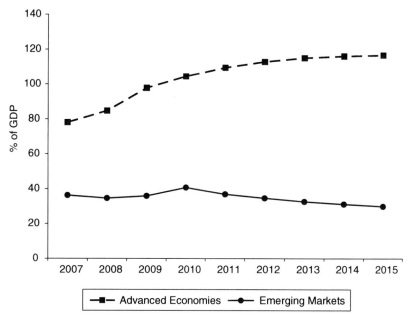

Figure 11.2. Government Gross Debt of Advanced Economies and Emerging Markets: 2007–2015.
Note: Data include future projections.
Source: IMF *Fiscal Monitor*, September 2011.

percentage points.[4] The debt/GDP ratios for the emerging markets, on the other hand, were projected to decline in response to a resumption in growth and relatively low interest rates (Figure 11.2).

Even more challenging prospects for the advanced economies are embedded in the future course of their public finances. The substantial cyclical deficits will diminish as economic growth resumes and revenues rise. But these countries have aging populations, and demographic trends will increase government expenditures on income support and medical programs. The IMF, for example, projects expansions in health care spending by 4.5 percent as a percentage of GDP for the United States over the next twenty years, and by about 3 percent for Canada, the EU, and Japan (Cottarelli and Schaechter 2010). If the governments of these countries allow public expenditures to evolve as projected, their debt levels will escalate to unsustainable levels.

---

[4] General debt includes all governmental obligations, while net debt includes only those held by the public. Projections of net debt moved in line with those for general debt.

While calling for short-run fiscal measures to hasten recovery from the global crisis, the IMF has also drawn attention to the need for longer-term fiscal reform and consolidation. The IMF has urged its upper-income members to address the costs of supporting their aging populations and introduced a new publication, the *Fiscal Monitor* (IMF 2010c), to provide analyses of members' fiscal policies. The *Fiscal Monitor* has dealt with the use of specific measures to deal with age-related spending, such as increasing retirement ages, introducing broad-based taxes, and improving tax compliance.

The advent of an era of increasing expenditures on pensions and health care in the advanced economies when their debt has already risen to historically high levels and growth has stalled is producing a transition in the global economy. These nations are becoming the new "weaker links" of international economic and financial stability, as the events in Europe have demonstrated. The IMF's advice may be better heeded now that these governments are current or potential borrowers.

Further sovereign debt crises will occur, however, and the IMF will be called upon to provide assistance. The Fund must be cautious with the economic and political viability of any rescue plans it joins. The governments of advanced economies that urged strict conditionality when they were not borrowing from the IMF may adopt a different position when they need credit. But the leaders of the emerging market nations will be highly sensitive to any signs that the Europeans receive better terms than those imposed during previous crises. The IMF is also concerned about its financial ability to meet further calls for assistance, as the amount of credit committed by the IMF to the new arrangements already far exceeds the commitments made during previous crises (Figure A.3).

11.2 Integration or Autonomy?

The IMF's dealings with the emerging markets in the postcrisis era reflect their continuing growth and integration into the global economy, particularly in the financial sphere. Many of their governments feel vindicated by the depth of the downturn in those countries that had substantially deregulated their financial markets before the crisis. The shocks that originated in the United States and other advanced economies were transmitted to the middle- and low-income countries in part through financial links, and the extent of the pass-through depended on the depth of these linkages (Balakrishnan *et al.* 2009, Claessens *et al.* 2010a). The emerging markets accept the need to develop their financial sectors but expect the IMF to advise them how to do so without exposing their economies to excessive volatility.

These concerns correspond with a new emphasis in financial regulation. Domestic regulation of financial sectors had traditionally focused on microprudential risk, that is, threats to the solvency of individual financial institutions. But the turbulence that swept through the financial markets in 2008 demonstrated that there may also be systemic risk. The attempts by banks and other financial institutions to rebalance their balance sheets and raise capital led to falling asset prices and diminished market liquidity. Consequently, there is a need for macroprudential policies to reduce aggregate risk in the financial sector (Borio 2005, 2006, Borio and Lowe 2003, White 2006). The G20 called upon the BIS, the FSB, and the IMF to develop a macroprudential policy framework (IMF 2011c).

Capital flows raise the prospects of macroprudential risk, as they can lead to credit booms and asset bubbles. Higher interest rates, a central bank's traditional response to rising demand, only induce further flows. As interest rates in the United States remained at extraordinarily low levels in the wake of the global crisis, capital flowed to those emerging markets that had resumed their vigorous growth. Under these circumstances, capital controls may be a useful tool of policy (Moreno 2011), and many of the recipients of inflows experimented with different types of controls.

The IMF now recognizes the possible efficacy of such measures. The policy note written by Ostry *et al.* (2010) represented a new stage in the IMF's stance on the use of capital controls (Chapter 10). Rodrik (2010a) characterized it as "a stunning reversal," paralleling a shift in economic analysis in this area (Jeanne and Korinek 2010, Korinek 2011, Stiglitz 2010). Subsequent studies from the IMF (Habermeier, Kokenyne, and Baba 2011, IMF 2011a, Ostry *et. al* 2011, Pradhan *et al.* 2011) have explored the circumstances that would justify the use of capital controls. Ostry *et al.* (2011), for example, examined the policy options available to a country facing capital inflows. They claimed that capital controls would be appropriate if other actions, including exchange rate appreciation, exchange market intervention, and tighter fiscal policy, were ineffective in mitigating the risks associated with capital inflows. Habermeier, Kokenyne, and Baba (2011), however, caution that the impact of such policies varies across countries and the effects may be short-lived.

The Fund's acceptance of the use of controls was reinforced by the growth in influence of the emerging market members that take a different position in this area from the advanced economies. Duvvuri Subbarao (Subbarao 2010), head of the Reserve Bank of India, noted the correlation between the extent of capital account openness in emerging markets and the adverse impact of the global crisis in these countries. He praised the IMF for its flexibility in allowing members to use capital controls and urged the Fund to undertake research on the negative externalities of large and volatile capital flows and the use of regulations to address these externalities. Subbarao's statement demonstrates how far the positions of the emerging markets differ from those taken in the past by the advanced economies (Chapter 8).

The changes in the assessment of capital controls can be seen as part of an overall reconsideration of the appropriate degree of integration with global financial markets. Since the onset of the debt crisis of the 1980s, the advanced economies have responded with calls for international standards and regulatory cooperation (Chapter 9). These have been justified on the grounds that the status of financial stability as an IPG requires a harmonization of policies and responses (Summers 1999a). The most recent initiative was the establishment of the FSB by the G20 leaders (Chapter 10). Its specific duties include promoting coordination among national financial authorities, advising national authorities on best practices to meet regulatory standards, and undertaking reviews of the work of international standard-setting bodies (FSB 2009). The IMF has also supported the creation and implementation of common standards and codes of conduct, which the Fund would monitor as part of its surveillance of its members' financial sectors (Claessens *et al.* 2010b, IMF 2009d, IMF 2010b, Kodres and Narain 2010).[5]

However, the development of international standards historically has been undertaken by the policy makers of those economies with broad financial markets, using the Basel-based agencies to organize their efforts. The regulations appropriate for these economies may not be suitable for countries with different financial structures and policies. The recent increase in the membership of the FSB to include all the G20 nations increases the representation of the emerging markets but contributes to a divergence in the interests of the members and multiplies the opportunities for disagreements that slow down the process of coordination (Masson and Pattison 2009, Rottier and Véron 2010).

The case for retaining some national autonomy in designing regulatory frameworks has been made by Rodrik (2009, 2010b), who argues that

---

[5]   The FSB and the IMF were also assigned the task of jointly developing early warning exercises to identify vulnerabilities in financial systems and work with governments to forestall a crisis.

financial regulations should depend on national preferences. He also points out that the record of regulation demonstrates that the most appropriate set of standards are not always chosen. Rodrik (2009, 2010b) suggests that countries should agree on a minimal set of guidelines, and those countries that want to engage in deeper financial integration retain the option of doing so. Similarly, Stiglitz *et al.* (2010) would also allow some degree of national autonomy for national regulatory structures.

The issue of the optimal degree of financial and regulatory integration is not confined to the middle-income nations. Many developing nations seek to emulate their example in developing domestic financial markets and attracting FDI. Countries such as Kenya and Vietnam, which have moved in this direction, are known as "frontier markets." These countries look to the IMF for guidance on how to attract foreign capital and whether to align their institutions with their foreign counterparts. The IMF must develop a position on these issues that respects the different policy aspirations of its members and allows them to establish the boundaries of their integration with the global financial markets.

Despite the efforts of the IMF, there will be new crises in the emerging markets. These are more likely to resemble the East Asian crisis in 1997–8 and the recent financial crisis rather than sovereign debt crises. These countries will continue to attract foreign capital, which contributes to the expansion of private credit and asset booms that are followed by collapses in values and threats to the solvency of private financial institutions. In such circumstances the IMF should play the role of an ILOLR as it did in 2008–9 to minimize contagion across frontiers, while working with governments to salvage their financial sectors without incurring massive increases in their own debt liabilities.

11.3 What Is to Be Done?

The IMF's efforts during the global crisis of 2008–9 contributed to the restoration of its reputation from the criticisms it had received in the 1990s. During the crisis the IMF served as an effective ILOLR, providing large amounts of credit rapidly with restrained and targeted conditionality. Its officials were sensitive to domestic conditions, and the IMF urged its member governments to enact stimulative policies to counteract the global contraction that followed the financial collapse. The IMF adjusted its position on capital controls, showing an intellectual and ideological flexibility that few thought the institution possessed.

However, the IMF does not consider itself only – or even primarily – as a lender of funds to countries during a crisis. The first purpose set out in its Articles of Agreement reads, "Promote international monetary cooperation through a permanent institution which provides the machinery for consultation and collaboration on international monetary problems." The attenuation of the IMF during the Great Moderation of the 2000s demonstrated that its members thought that they could maintain stability without the explicit coordination of the IMF, despite major differences over global imbalances. The events of the Great Recession proved otherwise, and the chastened members of the G20 promised to incorporate the IMF in their plans for the postcrisis global economy.

To be effective at crisis prevention as well as crisis lending and management, however, requires major reforms at the IMF. There are a number of basic governance issues that must be addressed if the Fund is no longer to be seen as the agent of the G7 countries rather than the entire membership. These aspects of the IMF's organizational arrangements are widely recognized, and specific measures have been proposed in studies and reports on the IMF's governance (Truman 2006), including one commissioned by the IMF itself (Committee on IMF Governance Reform 2009) as well as an evaluation report by the IMF's IEO (2009).[6]

Among the proposals are plans for recalculating the members' quotas, and the IMF has made changes in this area. The IMF's Board of Governors approved a series of quota measures in 2011 that will transform the IMF's governance, although not as far as some have suggested. A doubling of quotas under the Fourteenth General Review of Quotas to about $767 billion is being accompanied by an increase in the relative quotas of fifty-four emerging market and developing countries.[7] The ten largest quotas will be held by the United States (17.41%), Japan (6.46%), China (6.39%), Germany (5.59%), France (4.23%), the United Kingdom (4.23%), Italy (3.16%), India (2.75%), Russia (2.71%), and Brazil (2.32%). A new quota review formula will be decided by January 2013, to be followed by another quota review in January 2014. The basic votes held by each member to compensate partially for the inequality of the quotas in determining voting shares will be increased. In addition, Europeans will hold two fewer seats on the Executive Board, and all directors must be elected. The composition of the board will be reviewed every eight years.

---

[6]   Many of the reports have been summarized in IMF (2009c).

[7]   The enlargement of the total quotas will be accompanied by a reduction in the size of the NAB, which was enlarged in March 2011 to accommodate the increased demand for IMF credit.

No progress has been made, however, on the issue of the selection of a non-European managing director. The abrupt resignation of Strauss-Kahn in May 2011 left the position vacant, and the G20 had promised an open and transparent selection process. But the European members quickly coalesced around a single candidate, Christine Lagarde of France, while the other members failed to agree on an alternative choice. Lagarde became the IMF's eleventh managing director in July 2011, the first woman in that position. Her appointment marked an advance for the professional recognition of women, but a major opportunity to establish the geographic impartiality of the Fund was missed.

Other governance issues remain unresolved. The role of the Executive Board, for example, has been widely criticized. The board's current structure and procedures make it ineffective in exercising oversight while participating in the conduct of the IMF's activities with the staff. The directors are usually midlevel representatives of their governments, who serve a median term in office of about two years (IMF IEO 2008). Their relatively short tenure gives them little time to master the organizational intricacies of the IMF and increases their dependence on the IMF's staff to obtain information. Moreover, the size of the twenty-four-member board, double the IMF's original Executive Board, is too large for effective group decision making.

The IMFC, which has the same organization as the Executive Board, draws its membership from the Board of Governors and therefore has more status. But the IMFC meets only twice a year, during the IMF and World Bank's fall and spring meetings, and has no administrative powers. The Second Amendment to the IMF's Articles of Agreement, however, allows the member governments to appoint a ministerial-level council to "supervise the management and adaptation of the international monetary system, including the continuing operation of the adjustment process and developments in global liquidity."[8] A council would allow the member governments to provide more oversight and strategic direction than the IMFC or Executive Board has. The lack of progress in actually establishing such a council may reflect the G7's antipathy to the existence of a rival forum to provide leadership.

Serious reform must extend beyond rearranging the constituencies of the executive directors or relative quotas. The financial architecture that separates the IMF and other Washington-based agencies with a comparative advantage in economic issues from the Basel-based agencies with an expertise in financial issues should be reconsidered. Before the crisis the

---

[8] This provision appears in Schedule D of the Articles of Agreement.

BIS showed a greater appreciation of financial risks than the IMF did, and this perspective needs to be integrated into the IMF's analyses.

The IMF must continue to assess the benefits and risks associated with the globalization of financial markets and prove that it possesses relevant expertise that it can use to assist its members. The IMF should address vulnerabilities in the global economy in its surveillance activities, and the Fund has promised to broaden the scope of these activities (IMF 2010g). The IMF has also expanded its surveillance of regional economic trends and will issue analyses of spillover effects from major economies. The Fund has promised (again) to strengthen its surveillance of financial activities and will publish more studies related to capital flows (IMF 2010b). It also intends to do more multilateral consultations, as well as continue its work with the G20's mutual assessment process (IMF 2011b).

These changes in the Fund's governance and outlook are necessary but not sufficient if the IMF is to serve as an effective agent in promoting financial and economic stability. While the global economy has grown in recent decades, financial deregulation has contributed to an increase in all forms of crises in the post–Bretton Woods era. A recent database compiled by Fund economists (Laeven and Valencia 2012) reveals that there were 147 systemic banking crises over the period of 1970 to 2011, 218 currency crises, and 28 instances of twin crises that combined the two. There were also 66 episodes of sovereign debt default.[9]

A systemic response to the increase in financial instability requires major renovations in international monetary arrangements, which necessitate a willingness of the IMF's members to respond to and engage with the Fund and each other. The evidence to date of progress in this area is, at best, mixed. The G20 governments expressed their readiness at the height of the crisis to undertake joint policies, and much work has been done on such issues as international financial regulations and macroprudential policies. But in subsequent meetings the G20 leaders have not shown a willingness to promote the rebalancing of their economies to prevent a repetition of global imbalances. The European debt crises threaten to add volatility to financial markets and threaten the integrity of the *euro*.

Other initiatives by the IMF could enhance the stability of the international monetary system but require the active involvement of the IMF's members. The experience of the emerging markets during the crisis appeared to vindicate their belief that foreign reserves buffer a country from global shocks. The IMF has not convinced these governments that it could

---

[9]   See Chapter 2 for the comparable Bretton Woods figures.

provide an adequate safety net in the event of another crisis.[10] The Fund has proposed further enhancements to its lending facilities, such as a regional financing arrangement, in order to make them more attractive and reduce the need for reserves (IMF 2010d, Jeanne 2010, Mateos y Lago, Duttagupta, and Goyal 2009). Another option would be greater use of central bank swap agreements, with the IMF serving in a coordination role (Obstfeld 2009b).

The use of the SDR as an alternative reserve asset to the dollar had been raised before the crisis, and Chinese officials have expressed an interest in giving the SDR a greater role (Zhou 2009). However, there are (at least) two impediments to the wider use of the SDR. First, there are no private markets in SDR-denominated assets that would enhance their liquidity, and central banks are unlikely to hold assets that are not easily sold. The currency composition of international reserves, with approximately 64 percent denominated in dollars and 27 percent in euros, reflects the continuing widespread use of those currencies in international transactions. Second, the IMF would need the authority to issue SDRs when needed, thus acting more as a global central bank (Eichengreen 2009b, 2010). It is highly doubtful that the IMF's principals would be willing to grant such autonomy to an agent.

These changes, particularly those related to the activities of the IMF, can only be undertaken with the assent of its principals, the 188 member governments. The IMF has the potential to monitor and coordinate its members' policies, but it cannot achieve these goals on its own. The "phoenix" can only continue to rise if it is supported by the membership. The member governments will determine whether the IMF will serve as an effective agent for achieving the public good of international financial stability.

The case for collective decision making to provide the IPGs of financial and economic stability is as strong today as it was at Bretton Woods in 1944. The discussions among the G7 governments that took place in the 1970s and resulted in the revision of Article IV of the IMF's Articles of Agreement should be revived with a broader range of participants. The obligations of the IMF's members to develop "the orderly underlying conditions that are necessary for financial and economic stability" (IMF Article of Agreement IV) must be clarified, a process that in turn requires a better understanding of those conditions. The recent global crisis shows the need to address the volatility of the financial linkages of the global economy and demonstrates that an empowered IMF can provide valuable services to its members.

---

[10] A recent study of the IMF's interactions with its members (IMF IEO 2009) found that IMF interactions have been least effective with advanced economies and the large emerging market countries.

Appendix: IMF Data

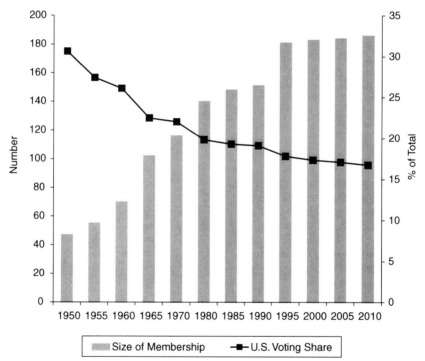

Figure A.1. Size of IMF Membership and U.S. Voting Share: 1950–2010.
Source: IMF *Annual Report*, various issues.

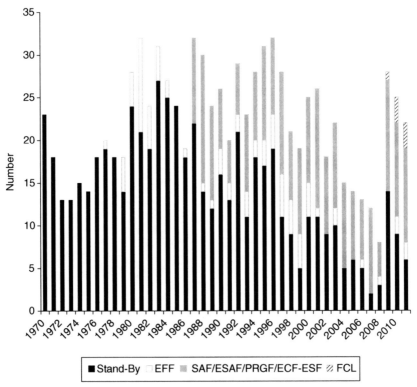

Figure A.2. Arrangements Approved: 1970–2011.

Source: IMF *Annual Report*, various issues.

Note: EFF = Extended Credit Facility; SAF = Structural Adjustment Facility; ESAF = Enhanced Structural Adjustment Facility; PRGF = Poverty Reduction and Growth Facility; ECF = Extended Credit Facility; ESF = Exogenous Shocks Facility; FCL = Flexible Credit Line.

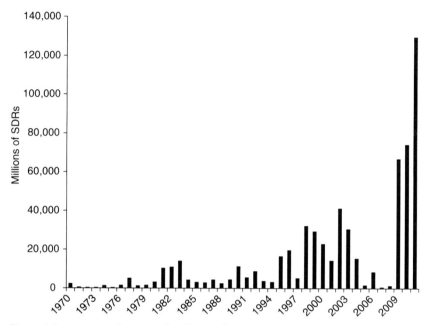

Figure A.3. Amounts Committed under Lending Arrangements: 1970–2011.
Source: IMF *Annual Report,* various issues.

Table A.1. *Managing Directors.*

Name	Country of Origin	Years of Service
Camille Gutt	Belgium	1946–1951
Ivar Rooth	Sweden	1951–1956
Per Jacobsson	Sweden	1956–1963
Pierre-Paul Schweitzer	France	1963–1973
H. Johannes Witteveen	Netherlands	1973–1978
Jacques de Larosière	France	1978–1987
Michel Camdessus	France	1987–2000
Horst Köhler	Germany	2000–2004
Rodrigo de Rato	Spain	2004–2007
Dominique Strauss-Kahn	France	2007–2011
Christine Lagarde	France	2011–

Source: IMF.

Appendix

Table A.2. *Quota Reviews.*

Review of Quotas	Date Resolution Adopted	Overall Increase in Quotas
First Quinquennial	No increase proposed	–
Second Quinquennial	No increase proposed	–
1958/59	February and April 1959	60.7
Third Quinquennial	No increase proposed	–
Fourth Quinquennial	March 1965	30.7
Fifth General	February 1970	35.4
Sixth General	March 1976	33.6
Seventh General	December 1978	50.9
Eighth General	March 1983	47.5
Ninth General	June 1990	50.0
Tenth General	No increase proposed	–
Eleventh General	January 1998	45.0
Twelfth General	No increase proposed	–
Thirteenth General	No increase proposed	–
Fourteenth General	December 2010	100.0

Note: Quota reviews are conducted every five years. The 1958/59 review was conducted outside the five-year cycle.
Source: IMF.

References

Abbott, Kenneth W., and Duncan Snidal. 1998. "Why States Act through Formal International Organizations." *Journal of Conflict Resolution* 42 (1): 3–32.

2000. "Hard and Soft Law in International Governance." *International Organization* 54 (3): 421–56.

Abdelal, Rawi. 2007. *Capital Rules: The Construction of Global Finance.* Cambridge, MA, and London: Harvard University Press.

Abiad, Abdul, and Ashoka Mody. 2005. "Financial Reform: What Shakes It? What Shapes It?" *American Economic Review* 95 (1): 66–88.

Adams, Timothy. 2006. "The IMF: Back to Basics." In Edwin M. Truman (ed.), *Reforming the IMF for the 21st Century.* Washington, DC: Peterson Institute for International Economics, pp. 133–8.

Agénor, Pierre-Richard. 2004. *The Economics of Adjustment and Growth.* 2nd ed. Cambridge, MA, and London: Harvard University Press.

Agénor, Pierre-Richard, Jagdeep S. Bhandari, and Robert P. Flood. 1992. "Speculative Attacks and Models of Balance of Payments Crises." *IMF Staff Papers* 39 (2): 357–94.

Aggarwal, Vinod K. 1987. "International Debt Threat: Bargaining among Creditors and Debtors in the 1980s." Institute of International Studies Policy Paper in International Affairs No. 29. Berkeley: University of California Press.

Aggarwal, Vinod. 1996. *Debt Games: Strategic Interactions in International Debt Rescheduling.* Cambridge and New York: Cambridge University Press.

Aizenman, Joshua, and Gurnain Kaur Pasricha. 2010. "Selective Swap Arrangements and the Global Financial Crisis: Analysis and Interpretation." *International Review of Economics and Finance* 19 (3): 353–65.

Aizenman, Joshua, and Jaewoo Lee. 2007. "International Reserves: Precautionary versus Mercantilist Views, Theory and Evidence." *Open Economies Review* 18 (2): 191–214.

Akyüz, Yilmaz, and Korkut Boratav. 2003. "The Making of the Turkish Financial Crisis." *World Development* 31 (9): 1549–66.

Alexander, Kern, Rahul Dhumale, and John Eatwell. 2006. *Global Governance of Financial Systems: The International Regulation of Systemic Risk.* Oxford and New York: Oxford University Press.

Alexander, Sidney. 1952. "The Effects of Devaluation on a Trade Balance." *IMF Staff Papers* 2 (2): 359–73.

Allen, William A., and Geoffrey Wood. 2006. "Defining and Achieving Financial Stability." *Journal of Financial Stability* 2 (2): 152–72.

Archer, Clive. 2001. *International Organizations*. 3rd ed. London and New York: Routledge.

Arpac, Ozlem, and Graham Bird. 2009. "Turkey and the IMF: A Case Study in the Political Economy of Policy Implementation." *Review of International Organizations* 4 (2): 135–57.

Åslund, Anders. 2000. "Russia and the International Financial Institutions." Paper Presented to the International Financial Institution Advisory Committee. Available at www.carnegieendowment.org/publications.

2010. *The Last Shall Be the First: The East European Financial Crisis, 2008–10.* Washington, DC: Peterson Institute for International Economics.

Axelrod, Robert, and Robert O. Keohane. 1986. "Achieving Cooperation under Anarchy: Strategies and Institutions." In Kenneth A. Oye (ed.), *Cooperation under Anarchy*. Princeton, NJ: Princeton University Press, pp. 226–54.

Bagehot, Walter. 1873. *Lombard Street*. London: Henry S. King.

Bakker, Age F. P. 1996. *International Financial Institutions*. London and New York: Longman.

Balakrishnan, Ravi, Stephen Danniger, Selim Elekdag, and Irina Tytell. 2009. "The Transmission of Financial Stress from Advanced to Emerging Economies." IMF Working Paper No. 09/133. Washington, DC: International Monetary Fund.

Baldacci, Emanuele, Luiz de Mello, and Gabriela Inchauste. 2002. "Financial Crises, Poverty, and Income Distribution." IMF Working Paper No. 02/4. Washington, DC: International Monetary Fund.

Bank for International Settlements. 1998. *68th Annual Report*. Basel: Bank for International Settlements.

1999. *69th Annual Report*. Basel: Bank for International Settlements.

2002. *72nd Annual Report*. Basel: Bank for International Settlements.

2007. *Bank for International Settlements 77th Annual Report*. Basel: Bank for International Settlements.

2009. *Bank for International Settlements 79th Annual Report*. Basel: Bank for International Settlements.

Barnett, Michael, and Martha Finnemore. 2004. *Rules for the World: International Organizations in Global Politics*. Ithaca, NY, and London: Cornell University Press.

Bartolini, Leonardo, and Allan Drazen. 1997. "Capital-Account Liberalization as a Signal." *American Economic Review* 87 (1): 138–54.

Bayne, Nicholas. 2005. *Staying Together: The G8 Summit Confronts the 21st Century*. Aldershot, UK, and Burlington, VT: Ashgate.

Bean, Charles. 2010. "The Great Moderation, the Great Panic, and the Great Contraction." *Journal of the European Economic Association* 8 (2–3): 289–325.

Beattie, Alan. 2010. "A Reach Regained." *Financial Times*, April 22.

Berg, Andrew. 1999. "The Asia Crisis: Causes, Policy Responses, and Outcomes." IMF Working Paper No. 99/138. Washington, DC: International Monetary Fund.

Bernanke, Ben S. 2004. "The Great Moderation." Remarks at meetings of the Eastern Economic Association. Available at www.federalreserve.gov.

2005. "The Global Savings Glut and the U.S. Current Account Deficit." Sandridge Lecture to Virginia Association of Economics. Available at www.federalreserve.gov.

Bhagwati, Jagdish. 1988. *Protectionism*. Cambridge, MA: MIT Press.

1998. "The Capital Myth: The Difference between Trade in Widgets and Dollars." *Foreign Affairs* 77 (3): 7–12.

Bird, Graham. 1980. "The Mix between Adjustment and Financing: Geometrical Presentations of the Factors Accounting for Different Choices Made by Developing and Developed Countries." *Indian Economic Review* 15 (2): 155–64.

2007. "The IMF: A Bird's Eye View of Its Role and Operations." *Journal of Economic Surveys* 21 (4): 683–745.

Bird, Graham, and Dane Rowlands. 1997. "The Catalytic Effect of Lending by the International Financial Institutions." *World Economy* 20 (7): 967–91.

2000. "The Catalyzing Role of Policy-Based Lending by the IMF and the World Bank: Fact or Fiction?" *Journal of International Development* 12 (7): 951–73.

Bird, Graham, and Thomas D. Willett. 2007. "Multilateral Surveillance: Is the IMF Shooting for the Stars?" *World Economics* 8 (4): 1–23.

Blustein, Paul. 2001. *The Chastening: Inside the Crisis That Rocked the Global Financial System and Humbled the IMF*. New York: Public Affairs.

2005. *And the Money Kept Rolling In (and Out): Wall Street, the IMF, and the Bankrupting of Argentina*. 2005. New York: Public Affairs.

Blyth, Mark. 2002. *Great Transformations: Economic Ideas and Institutional Change in the Twentieth Century*. Cambridge and New York: Cambridge University Press.

Boorman, Jack, Timothy Lane, Marianne Schulze-Ghattas, Aleš Bulíř, Atish R. Ghosh, Javier Hamann, Alex Mourmouras, and Steven Phillips. 2000. "Managing Financial Crises: The Experience in East Asia." *Carnegie-Rochester Conference Series on Public Policy* 53 (1): 1–67.

Bordo, Michael D. 1993. "The Bretton Woods International Monetary System: A Historical Overview." In Michael D. Bordo and Barry Eichengreen (eds.), *A Retrospective on the Bretton Woods System: Lessons for International Monetary Reform*. Chicago: University of Chicago Press, pp. 3–98.

Bordo, Michael D., and Barry Eichengreen. 2003. "Crises Now and Then: What Lessons from the Last Era of Financial Globalization?" In Paul Mizen (ed.), *Monetary History, Exchange Rates and Financial Markets: Essays in Honor of Charles Goodhart*. Vol. 2. Cheltenham, UK, and Northampton, MA: Edward Elgar, pp. 52–91.

Bordo, Michael D., Ashoka Mody, and Nienke Oomes. 2004. "Keeping Capital Flowing: The Role of the IMF." *International Finance* 7 (3): 421–50.

Bordo, Michael D., Barry Eichengreen, and Jongwoo Kim. 1998. "Was There Really an Earlier Period of International Financial Integration Comparable to Today?" In Seongtae Lee (ed.), *The Implications of Globalization of World Financial Markets*. Seoul: Bank of Korea, pp. 27–75.

Bordo, Michael, Barry Eichengreen, Daniela Klingebiel, and Maria Soledad Martinez-Peria. 2001. "Is the Crisis Problem Growing More Severe?" *Economic Policy* 16 (32): 53–82.

Borio, Claudio. 2005. "Monetary and Financial Stability: So Close and Yet So Far?" *National Institute Economic Review* No. 192, pp. 84–101.

2006. "Monetary and Prudential Policies at a Crossroads? New Challenges in the New Century." BIS Working Paper No. 216. Basel: Bank for International Settlements.

Borio, Claudio, Craig Furfine, and Philip Lowe. 2001. "Procyclicality of the Financial System and Financial Stability: Issues and Policy Options." In *Marrying the Macro- and Micro-Prudential Dimensions of Financial Stability*. BIS Paper No. 1. Basel: Bank for International Settlements.

Borio, Claudio, and Philip Lowe. 2003. "Imbalances or 'Bubbles'? Implications for Monetary and Financial Stability." In William C. Hunter, George G. Kaufman, and Michael Pomerleano (eds.), *Asset Price Bubbles: The Implications for Monetary, Regulatory and International Policies*. Cambridge, MA, and London: MIT Press, pp. 247–70.

Boughton, James M. 1998. "Harry Dexter White and the International Monetary Fund." *Finance and Development* 35 (3): 39–41.

2000. "From Suez to Tequila: The IMF as Crisis Manager." *Economic Journal* 110 (460): 273–91.

2001a. "Northwest of Suez: The 1956 Crisis and the IMF." *IMF Staff Papers* 48 (3): 425–46.

2001b. *Silent Revolution: The International Monetary Fund, 1979–1989*. Washington, DC: International Monetary Fund.

2003. "On the Origins of the Fleming-Mundell Model." *IMF Staff Papers* 50 (1): 1–9.

Boughton, James M., and Domenico Lombardi (eds.). 2009. *Finance, Development, and the IMF*. Oxford and New York: Oxford University Press.

Boughton, James M., and Suchitra Kumarapathy. April 2006. "Recycling Petrodollars in the 1970s." In IMF, *World Economic Outlook: Oil Prices and Global Imbalances*. Washington, DC: International Monetary Fund.

Bowe, Michael, and James W. Dean. 1997. *Has the Market Solved the Sovereign-Debt Crisis?* Princeton Study in International Finance No. 83. Princeton, NJ: Princeton University Press.

Boyd, John H., Sungkyu Kwak, and Bruce Smith. 2005. "The Real Output Losses Associated with Modern Banking Crises." *Journal of Money, Credit and Banking* 37 (6): 977–99.

Browne, Lynn Elaine, Rebecca Hellerstein, and Jane Sneddon Little. 1998. "Inflation, Asset Markets, and Economic Stabilization: Lessons from Asia." *New England Economic Review*, September/October, pp. 3–32.

Bryant, Ralph. 2003. *Turbulent Waters: Cross-Border Finance and International Governance*. Washington, DC: Brookings Institution Press.

Caballero, Ricardo J., Emmanuel Farhi, and Pierre-Olivier Gourinchas. 2008a. "An Equilibrium Model of 'Global Imbalances' and Low Interest Rates." *American Economic Review* 98 (1): 358–93.

2008b. "Financial Crash, Commodity Prices, and Global Imbalances." *Brookings Papers on Economic Activity*, Fall, pp. 1–55.

Calomiris, Charles. 1998. "The IMF's Imprudent Role as Lender of Last Resort." *Cato Journal* 17 (3): 275–94.

Calvo, Guillermo A. 2002. "Globalization Hazard and Delayed Reform in Emerging Markets." *Economía* 2 (2): 1–29.

Calvo, Guillermo A., and Enrique G. Mendoza. 1996. "Mexico's Balance-of-Payments Crisis: A Chronicle of a Death Foretold." *Journal of International Economics* 41 (3–4): 235–64.

Camdessus, Michel. 1995. "Drawing Lessons from the Mexican Crisis – the Role of the IMF." Speech to 25th Washington Conference of the Council of the Americas. Available at www.imf.org.

Cerra, Valerie, and Sweta C. Saxena. 2005. "Did Output Recover from the Asian Crisis?" *IMF Staff Papers* 52 (1): 1–23.

2008. "Growth Dynamics: The Myth of Economic Recovery." *American Economic Review* 98 (1): 439–57.

Chang, Roberto, and Andrés Velasco. 2000. "Liquidity Crises in Emerging Markets: Theory and Policy." In Ben S. Bernanke and Julio J. Rotemberg (eds.), *NBER Macroeconomics Annual 1999*. Cambridge, MA, and London: MIT Press, pp. 11–58.

Chinn, Menzie D., and Hiro Ito. 2007. "Current Account Balances, Financial Development and Institutions: Assaying the World 'Saving Glut.'" *Journal of International Money and Finance* 26 (4): 546–69.

2008. "Global Current Account Imbalances: American Fiscal Policy versus East Asian Savings." *Review of International Economics* 16 (3): 479–98.

Chwieroth, Jeffrey M. 2010. *Capital Ideas: The IMF and the Rise of Financial Liberalization.* Princeton, NJ, and Oxford: Princeton University Press.

Claessens, Stijn, and Kristin J. Forbes (eds.). 2001. *International Financial Contagion.* Boston, Dordrecht, and London: Kluwer Academic.

Claessens, Stijn, Giovanni Dell'Ariccia, Deniz Igan, and Luc Laeven. 2010a. "Cross-Country Experiences and Policy Implications from the Global Financial Crisis." *Economic Policy* No. 62, pp. 269–93.

2010b. *"Lessons and Policy Implications from the Global Financial Crisis."* IMF Working Paper No. 10/44. Washington, DC: International Monetary Fund

Cline, William R. 1981. "Economic Stabilization in Peru, 1975–78." In William R. Cline and Sidney Weintraub (eds.), *Economic Stabilization in Developing Countries.* Washington, DC: Brookings Institution, pp. 297–326.

1995. *International Debt Reexamined.* Washington, DC: Institute for International Economics.

2010. *Financial Globalization, Economic Growth, and the Crisis of 2007–09.* Washington, DC: Peterson Institute for International Economics

Committee on IMF Governance Reform. 2009. *Final Report.* Washington, DC: International Monetary Fund

Cooper, Richard N. 1983. "Panel Discussion." In John Williamson (ed.), *IMF Conditionality.* Washington, DC: Institute for International Economics, p. 571.

2008. "Global Imbalances: Globalization, Demography, and Sustainability." *Journal of Economic Perspectives* 22 (3): 93–112.

Copelovitch, Mark S. 2010. *The International Monetary Fund in the Global Economy: Banks, Bonds, and Bailouts.* Cambridge and New York: Cambridge University Press.

Corden, W. Max. 1994. *Economic Policy, Exchange Rates, and the International System.* Chicago and London: University of Chicago Press.

2001. "The World Financial Crisis: Are the IMF Prescriptions Right?" In Shale Horowitz and Uk Heo (eds.), *The Political Economy of International Financial Crisis.* Lanham, MD: Rowman & Littlefield, pp. 41–61.

Cornes, Richard, and Todd Sandler. 1984. "Easy Riders, Joint Production, and Public Goods." *Economic Journal* 94 (3): 580–98.

1996. *The Theory of Externalities, Public Goods, and Club Goods*. 2nd ed. Cambridge and New York: Cambridge University Press.

Corsetti, Giancarlo, Bernardo Guimarães, and Nouriel Roubini. 2006. "International Lending of Last Resort and Moral Hazard: A Model of IMF's Catalytic Finance." *Journal of Monetary Economics* 53 (3): 441–471.

Corsetti, Giancarlo, Paolo Pesenti, and Nouriel Roubini. 1999a. "Paper Tigers? A Model of the Asian Crisis." *European Economic Review* 43 (7): 1211–36.

1999b. "What Caused the Asian Currency and Financial Crisis?" *Japan and the World Economy* 11 (3): 305–73.

Cottarelli, Carlo, and Curzio Giannini. 2003. "Bedfellows, Hostages, or Perfect Strangers? Global Capital Markets and the Catalytic Effect of IMF Crisis Lending." *Cahiers d'Economie Politique* No. 45, pp. 211–50.

Cottarelli, Carlo, and Andrea Schaechter. 2010. *Long-Term Trends in Public Finances in the G-7 Economies*. IMF Staff Position Note No. 10/13. Washington, DC: International Monetary Fund.

Cottarelli, Carlo, Lorenzo Forni, Jan Gottschalk, and Paolo Mauro. 2010. *Default in Today's Advanced Economies: Unnecessary, Undesirable, and Unlikely*. Washington, DC: International Monetary Fund

Crockett, Andrew. 1997. "Why Is Financial Stability a Goal of Public Policy?" In Federal Reserve Bank of Kansas City (ed.), *Managing Financial Stability in a Global Economy*. Kansas City, MO: Federal Reserve Bank of Kansas City, pp. 7–36.

Cuddington, John T. 1989. "The Extent and Causes of the Debt Crisis of the 1980s." In Ishrat Husain and Ishac Diwan (eds.), *Dealing with the Debt Crisis*. Washington, DC: World Bank, pp. 15–44.

Daseking, Christina, and Robert Powell. 1999. "From Toronto Terms to the HIPC Initiative: A Brief History of Debt Relief for Low-Income Countries." IMF Working Paper No. 99/142. Washington, DC: International Monetary Fund.

Daseking, Christina, Atish Ghosh, Timothy Lane, and Alun Thomas. 2004. *Lessons from the Crisis in Argentina*. Occasional Paper No. 236. Washington, DC: International Monetary Fund.

Davies, Howard, and David Green. 2008. *Global Financial Regulation: The Essential Guide*. Cambridge, UK, and Malden, MA: Polity.

De Beaufort Wijnholds, Onno. 2011. *Fighting Financial Fires: An IMF Insider Account*. Houndmills, Basingstoke, Hampshire, UK, and New York: Palgrave Macmillan.

De Beaufort Wijnholds, Onno, and Arend Kapteyn. 2001. "Reserve Adequacy in Emerging Market Economies." IMF Working Paper no. 01/143. Washington, DC: International Monetary Fund.

De Bonis, Riccardo, Alessandro Giustiniani, and Giorgio Gomel. 1999. "Crises and Bail-Outs of Banks and Countries: Linkages, Analogies, and Differences." *World Economy* 22 (1): 55–86.

De Cervantes, Miguel Saavedra. 1966. *Don Quixote*. Translated by Peter Anthony Motteux. London: Dent and New York: Dutton.

Dell, Sidney. 1981. *On Being Grandmotherly: The Evolution of IMF Conditionality*. Essay in International Finance No. 144. Princeton, NJ: Princeton University Press.

DeLong, J. Bradford, Christopher L. DeLong, and Sherman Robinson. 1996. "The Case for Mexico's Rescue." *Foreign Affairs* 75 (3): 8–14.

De Menil, George, and Anthony Solomon. 1983. *Economic Summitry.* New York: Council on Foreign Relations.

Demirgüç-Kunt, Asli, and Enrica Detragiache. 2010. "Basel Core Principles and Bank Risk: Does Compliance Matter?" IMF Working Paper No. 10/81. Washington, DC: International Monetary Fund.

Desai, Padma. 2003. *Financial Crisis, Contagion, and Containment.* Princeton, NJ: Princeton University Press.

Desai, Raj M., and James Raymond Vreeland. 2011. "Global Governance in a Multipolar World: The Case for Regional Monetary Funds." *International Studies Review* 13 (1): 109–21.

De Vries, Margaret Garritsen. 1976. *The International Monetary Fund, 1966–1971: The System under Stress.* Washington, DC: International Monetary Fund.

1985. *The International Monetary Fund, 1972–1978: Cooperation on Trial.* Vol. I. Washington, DC: International Monetary Fund.

1987. *Balance of Payments Adjustment, 1945 to 1986: The IMF Experience.* Washington, DC: International Monetary Fund.

Diaz-Alejandro, Carlos. 1985. "Good-bye Financial Repression, Hello Financial Crash." *Journal of Development Economics* 19 (1/2): 1–24.

Diwan, Ishac, and Dani Rodrik. 1992. *External Debt, Adjustment, and Burden Sharing: A Unified Framework.* Princeton Study in International Finance No. 73. Princeton, NJ: Princeton University Press.

Dominguez, Kathryn M. 1993. "The Role of International Organizations in the Bretton Woods System." In Michael D. Bordo and Barry Eichengreen (eds.), *A Retrospective on the Bretton Woods System: Lessons for International Monetary Reform.* Chicago: University of Chicago Press, pp. 357–404.

Dooley, Michael P. 1995. "A Retrospective on the Debt Crisis." In Peter B. Kenen (ed.), *Understanding Interdependence: The Macroeconomics of the Open Economy.* Princeton, NJ: Princeton University Press, pp. 262–87.

1996. "A Survey of Literature on Controls over International Capital Transactions." *IMF Staff Papers* 43 (4): 639–87.

Dooley, Michael, and Peter Garber. 2005. "Is It 1958 or 1968? Three Notes on the Longevity of the Revised Bretton Woods System." *Brookings Papers on Economic Activity* No. 1, pp. 147–87.

Dooley, Michael P., David Folkerts-Landau, and Peter Garber. 2004. "The Revised Bretton Woods System." *International Journal of Finance and Economics* 9 (4): 307–13.

Dornbusch, Rudiger. 1986. *Dollars, Debts, and Deficits.* Leuven, Belgium: Leuven University Press and Cambridge, MA, and London: MIT Press.

1993. "Comment on Bordo." In Michael D. Bordo and Barry Eichengreen (eds.), *A Retrospective on the Bretton Woods System: Lessons for International Monetary Reform.* Chicago: University of Chicago Press, pp. 99–104.

2001. "A Primer on Emerging Market Crises." NBER Working Paper No. 8326. Cambridge, MA: National Bureau of Economic Research.

Dornbusch, Rudiger, and Alejandro Werner. 1994. "Mexico: Stabilization, Reform and No Growth." *Brookings Papers on Economic Activity* No. 1, pp. 253–97.

Drazen, Allen. 2000. *Political Economy in Macroeconomics*. Princeton, NJ: Princeton University Press.

Dreher, Axel. 2003. "The Influence of Elections on IMF Programme Interruptions." *Journal of Development Studies* 39 (6): 101–20.

Durdu, Ceyhun Bora, Enrique G. Mendoza, and Marco E. Terrones. 2009. "Precautionary Demand for Foreign Assets in Sudden Stop Economies: An Assessment of the New Mercantilism." *Journal of Development Economics* 89 (2): 194–209.

Easterly, William. 2006. "An Identity Crisis? Examining IMF Financial Programming." *World Development* 34 (6): 964–80.

Easterly, William, Roumeen Islam, and Joseph E. Stiglitz. 2001. "Shaken and Stirred: Explaining Growth Volatility." In Boris Pleskovic and Nicholas Stern (eds.), *Annual World Bank Conference on Development Economics 2000*. Washington, DC: World Bank, pp. 191–211.

Eckes, Alfred E., Jr. 1975. *A Search for Solvency*. Austin and London: University of Texas Press.

Edison, Hali J., Michael W. Klein, Luca Antonio Ricci, and Torsten Sløk. 2004. "Capital Account Liberalization and Economic Performance: Survey and Synthesis." *IMF Staff Papers* 51 (2): 220–56.

Edwards, Martin S. 2005. "Investor Responses to IMF Program Suspensions: Is Noncompliance Costly?" *Social Science Quarterly* 86 (4): 857–73.

Edwards, Sebastian. 1998. "The Mexican Peso Crisis: How Much Did We Know? When Did We Know It?" *World Economy* 21 (1): 1–30.

      2003. "Review of Joseph E. Stiglitz's *Globalization and Its Discontents*." *Journal of Development Economics* 70 (1): 252–7.

Edwards, Sebastian, and Moisés Naím. 1998. *Mexico 1994: Anatomy of an Emerging Market Crash*. Washington, DC: Carnegie Endowment for International Peace.

Eichengreen, Barry. 1989. "Hegemonic Stability Theories of the International Monetary System." In Richard Cooper (ed.), *Can Nations Agree? Issues in International Economic Cooperation*. Washington, DC: Brookings Institution, pp. 255–98.

      1991. "Historical Research on International Lending and Debt." *Journal of Economic Perspectives* 5 (2): 149–69.

      1993. "Epilogue: Three Perspectives on the Bretton Woods System." In Michael D. Bordo and Barry Eichengreen (eds.), *A Retrospective on the Bretton Woods System: Lessons for International Monetary Reform*. Chicago: University of Chicago Press, pp. 621–57.

      2001. "Capital Account Liberalization: What Do Cross-Country Studies Tell Us?" *World Bank Economic Review* 15 (3): 341–65.

      2002. *Financial Crises and What to Do about Them*. Oxford and New York: Oxford University Press.

      2008. *Globalizing Capital: A History of the International Monetary System*. 2nd ed. Princeton, NJ: Princeton University Press.

      2009a. "From the Asian Crisis to the Global Credit Crisis: Reforming the International Financial Architecture Redux." *International Economics and Economic Policy* 6 (1): 1–22.

      2009b. "*Out of the Box Thoughts about the International Financial Architecture*." IMF Working Paper No. 09/116. Washington, DC: International Monetary Fund.

2010. "The Financial Crisis and Global Policy Reforms." In Reuven Glick and Mark Spiegel (eds.), *Asia and the Global Financial Crisis*. San Francisco: Federal Reserve Bank of San Francisco, pp. 299–334.

Eichengreen, Barry, and Albert Fishlow. 1998. "Contending with Capital Flows: What Is Different about the 1990s?" In Miles Kahler (ed.), *Capital Flows and Financial Crises*. Ithaca, NY: Cornell University Press, pp. 23–68.

Eichengreen, Barry, and Christof Rühl. 2001. "The Bail-In Problem: Systematic Goals, Ad Hoc Means." *Economic Systems* 25 (1): 3–32.

Eichengreen, Barry, Andrew K. Rose, and Charles Wyplosz. 1995. "Exchange Market Mayhem: The Antecedents and Aftermath of Speculative Attacks." *Economic Policy* 10 (21): 249–96.

Eichengreen, Barry, Kenneth Kletzer, and Ashoka Mody. 2006. "The IMF in a World of Private Capital Markets." *Journal of Banking & Finance* 30 (5): 1335–57.

Feldstein, Martin. 1999. "A Self-Help Guide for Emerging Markets." *Foreign Affairs* 78 (2): 93–109.

2002. "Argentina's Fall." *Foreign Affairs* 81 (2): 8–14.

2008. "Resolving the Global Imbalance: The Dollar and the U.S. Saving Rate." *Journal of Economic Perspectives* 22 (3): 113–25.

Financial Stability Board. 2009. "Financial Stability Board Holds Inaugural Meeting in Basel." Press Release No. 28/2009. Basel: Financial Stability Board.

Financial Times. 2010. "European Banks Took Big Slice of Fed Aid." December 2.

Finch, C. David. 1989. *The IMF: The Record and the Prospect*. Essay in International Finance No. 175. Princeton, NJ: Princeton University Press.

Fischer, Stanley. 1987. "Sharing the Burden of the International Debt Crisis." *American Economic Review* 77 (2): 165–70.

1997. *Capital Account Liberalization and the Role of the IMF*. Washington, DC: International Monetary Fund.

1998. "In Defense of the IMF: Specialized Tools for a Specialized Task." *Foreign Affairs* 77 (4): 103–6.

1999. "On the Need for an International Lender of Last Resort." *Journal of Economic Perspectives* 13 (4): 85–104.

2000. "Remarks Given at the Bretton Woods Committee Meeting." Available at www.imf.org/external/np/speeches/2000.

2001. "The Russian Economy: Prospects and Retrospect." Speech at Higher School of Economics, Moscow. June 19, 2001. Available at www.imf.org/external/np/speeches/2001/061901.htm.

2003. "Globalization and Its Challenges." *American Economic Review* 93 (2): 1–30.

2004. *IMF Essays from a Time of Crisis: The International Financial System, Stabilization, and Development*. Cambridge, MA, and London: MIT Press.

2008. "Mundell-Fleming Lecture: Exchange Rate Systems, Surveillance, and Advice." *IMF Staff Papers* 55 (3): 367–83.

Fishlow, Albert. 1986. "Lessons from the Past: Capital Markets during the 19th Century and the Interwar Period." In Miles Kahler (ed.), *The Politics of International Debt*. Ithaca, NY, and London: Cornell University Press, pp. 37–93.

Fleming, Marcus. 1962. "Domestic Financial Policies under Fixed and under Floating Exchange Rates." *IMF Staff Papers* 9 (3): 369–79.

Flood, Robert P., and Peter M. Garber. 1984. "Collapsing Exchange-Rate Regimes: Some Linear Examples." *Journal of International Economics* 17 (1–2): 1–13.

Flood, Robert P., and Nancy Marion. 1999. "Perspectives on the Recent Currency Crisis Literature." *International Journal of Finance and Economics* 4 (1): 1–26.

——— 2000. "Self-Fulfilling Risk Predictions: An Application to Speculative Attacks." *Journal of International Economics* 50 (1): 245–68.

Folkerts-Landau, David. 1985. "The Changing Role of International Bank Lending in Development Finance." *IMF Staff Papers* 32 (2): 317–63.

Fratianni, Michele, and John Pattison. 1982. "The Economics of International Organizations." *Kyklos* 35 (2): 244–62.

——— 2001. "The Bank for International Settlements: An Assessment of Its Role in International Monetary and Financial Policy Coordination." *Open Economies Review* 12 (2): 197–222.

Frenkel, Roberto. 2003. "Globalization and Financial Crises in Latin America." *CEPAL Review* No. 80, pp. 31–51.

Frey, Bruno S. 1997. "The Public Choice of International Organizations." In Dennis C. Mueller (ed.), *Perspectives on Public Choice: A Handbook*. Cambridge and New York: Cambridge University Press, pp. 106–23.

Frieden, Jeffry A. 1991. "Invested Interests: The Politics of National Economic Policies in a World of Global Finance." *International Organization* 45 (4): 425–51.

——— 2006. *Global Capitalism: Its Fall and Rise in the Twentieth Century*. New York and London: W. W. Norton.

Fritz-Krockow, Bernhard, and Ramlogan Parmeshwar (eds.). 2007. *International Monetary Fund Handbook: Its Functions and Operations*. Washington, DC: International Monetary Fund.

Furman, Jason, and Joseph E. Stiglitz. 1998. "Economic Crises: Evidence and Insights from East Asia." *Brookings Papers on Economic Activity* No. 2: 1–114.

Gandolfo, Giancarlo. 2002. *International Finance and Open-Economy Macro-economics*. Berlin: Springer.

Ghosh, Atish R., Marcos Chamon, Christopher Crowe, Jun I. Kim, and Jonathan D. Ostry. 2009. *Coping with the Crisis: Policy Options for Emerging Market Countries*. IMF Staff Position Note No. 09/08. Washington, DC: International Monetary Fund.

Ghosh, Atish R., Christopher Crowe, Jun Il Kim, Jonathan D. Ostry, and Marcos Chamon. 2011. "IMF Policy Advice to Emerging Market Economies During the 2008–09 Crisis: New Fund or New Fundamentals?" *Journal of International Commerce, Economics and Policy* 2 (1): 1–17.

Ghosh, Atish, Timothy Lane, Marianne Schulze-Ghattas, Aleš Bulíř, Javier Hamann, and Alex Mourmouras. 2002. *IMF-Supported Programs in Capital Account Crises*. Occasional Paper No. 210. Washington, DC: International Monetary Fund.

Giannini, Curzio. 1999. *"Enemy of None but a Common Friend of All"? An International Perspective on the Lender-of-Last-Resort Function*. Essay in International Finance No. 214. Princeton, NJ: Princeton University Press.

Giles, Chris. 2007. "IMF Yet to Risk Talking Tough." *Financial Times,* January 23.

Glick, Reuven, and Michael M. Hutchison. 2001. "Banking and Currency Crises: How Common Are Twins?" In Reuven Glick, Ramon Moreno, and Mark M. Spiegel (eds.), *Financial Crises in Emerging Markets*. Cambridge and New York: Cambridge University Press, pp. 35–69.

Goldfajn, Ilan. 2003. "The Swings in Capital Flows and the Brazilian Crisis." In Stephany Griffith-Jones, Ricardo Gottschalk, and Jacques Cailloux. *International Capital Flows in Calm and Turbulent Times: The Need for International Architecture*. Ann Arbor: University of Michigan Press, pp. 267–90.

Goldfajn, Ilan, and André Minella. 2007. "Capital Flows and Controls in Brazil: What Have We Learned?" In Sebastian Edwards (ed.), *Capital Controls and Capital Flows in Emerging Economies: Policies, Practices and Consequences*. Chicago and London: University of Chicago Press, pp. 349–420.

Goldstein, Morris. 1998. *The Asian Financial Crisis: Causes, Cures, and Systemic Implication*. Washington, DC: Institute for International Economics.

2003. "IMF Structural Programs." In Martin Feldstein (ed.), *Economic and Financial Crises in Emerging Market Economies*. Chicago and London: University of Chicago Press, pp. 363–437.

Goldstein, Morris, and Nicholas R. Lardy (eds.). 2008. *Debating China's Exchange Rate Policy*. Washington, DC: Peterson Institute for International Economics.

Goldstein, Morris, and Nicholas R. Lardy. 2009. *The Future of China's Exchange Rate Policy*. Washington, DC: Peterson Institute for International Economics.

Goodman, John B., and Louis W. Pauly. 1993. "The Obsolescence of Capital Controls? Economic Management in an Age of Global Markets." *World Politics* 46 (1): 50–82.

Gould, Erica R. 2003. "Money Talks: Supplementary Financiers and International Monetary Fund Conditionality." *International Organization* 57 (3): 551–86.

Grenville, Stephen. 2004. "The IMF and the Indonesian Crisis." *Independent Evaluation Office Background Paper*. Washington, DC: International Monetary Fund.

Griffith-Jones, Stephany. 2003. "International Financial Stability and Market Efficiency as a Global Public Good." In Inge Kaul, Pedro Conceição, Katell Le Goulven, and Ronald U. Mendoza (eds.), *Providing Global Public Goods: Managing Globalization*. New York and Oxford: Oxford University Press, pp. 435–54.

Group of Twenty. 2008. *Summit Declaration on Financial Markets and the World Economy*. Available at www.g20.org.

2009. *The Global Plan for Recovery and Reform*. Available at www.g20.org.

Gruber, Joseph W., and Steven B. Kamin. 2007. "Explaining the Global Pattern of Current Account Imbalances." *Journal of International Money and Finance* 26 (4): 500–522.

Guitián, Manuel. 1982. "Economic Management and International Monetary Fund Conditionality." In Tony Killick (ed.), *Adjustment and Financing in the Developing World: The Role of the International Monetary Fund*. Washington, DC: International Monetary Fund, pp. 73–104.

1992. *The Unique Nature of the Responsibilities of the International Monetary Fund*. Pamphlet Series No. 46. Washington, DC: International Monetary Fund.

1995. "Capital Account Liberalization: Bringing Policy in Line with Reality." In Sebastian Edwards (ed.), *Capital Controls, Exchange Rates, and Monetary Policy in the World Economy*. Cambridge and New York: Cambridge University Press, pp. 71–90.

Guttentag, Jack M., and Richard Herring. 1985. "Commercial Bank Lending to Developing Countries: From Overlending to Underlending to Structural Reform." In Gordon W. Smith and John T. Cuddington (eds.), *International Debt and the Developing Countries*. Washington, DC: World Bank, pp. 129–50.

Habermeier, Karl, Annamaria Kokenyne, and Chikako Baba. 2011. *The Effectiveness of Capital Controls and Prudential Policies in Managing Large Inflows*. Washington, DC: International Monetary Fund.

Haggard, Stephan. 2000. *The Political Economy of the Asian Financial Crisis*. Washington, DC: Institute for International Economics.

Haggard, Stephan, and Sylvia Maxfield. 1993. "The Political Economy of Capital Account Liberalisation." In Helmut Reisen and Bernhard Fischer (eds.), *Financial Opening: Policy Issues and Experiences in Developing Countries*. Paris: OECD, pp. 65–83.

1996. "The Political Economy of Financial Internationalization in the Developing World." *International Organization* 50 (1): 35–68.

Hahm, Joon-Ho, and Frederic S. Mishkin. 2000. "The Korean Financial Crisis: An Asymmetric Information Perspective." *Emerging Markets Review* 1 (1): 21–52.

Hajnal, Peter I. 1999. *The G7/G8 System: Evolution, Role and Documentation*. Aldershot, UK, and Burlington, VT: Ashgate.

Hallwood, C. Paul and Ronald MacDonald. 2000. *International Money and Finance*. 3rd ed. Malden, MA and Oxford, UK: Blackwell Publishers.

Hausman, Ricardo, and Andés Velasco. 2002. "Hard Money's Soft Underbelly: Understanding the Argentine Crisis." *Brookings Trade Forum*, pp. 59–104.

Hawkins, Darren G., David A. Lake, Daniel L. Nielson, and Michael J. Tierney (eds.). 2006. *Delegation and Agency in International Organizations*. Cambridge and New York: Cambridge University Press.

Helleiner, Eric. 1994. *States and the Reemergence of Global Finance: From Bretton Woods to the 1990s*. Ithaca, NY, and London: Cornell University Press.

2005. "The Strange Story of Bush and the Argentine Debt Crisis." *Third World Quarterly* 26 (6): 951–69.

Henning, C. Randall. 2006. "Regional Arrangements and the International Monetary Fund." In Edwin M. Truman (ed.), *Reforming the IMF for the 21st Century*. Washington, DC: Peterson Institute for International Economics, pp. 171–84.

2009. *The Future of the Chiang Mai Initiative: An Asian Monetary Fund?* Policy Brief No. 09-5. Washington, DC: Peterson Institute for International Economics.

Hnatkovska, Viktoria, and Norman Loayza. 2005. "Volatility and Growth." In Joshua Aizenman and Brian Pinto (eds.), *Managing Economic Volatility and Crises: A Practitioner's Guide*. Cambridge and New York: Cambridge University Press, pp. 65–100.

Hoggarth, Glenn, Ricardo Reis, and Victoria Saporta. 2002. "Costs of Banking System Instability: Some Empirical Evidence." *Journal of Banking & Finance* 26 (5): 825–55.

Honohan, Patrick, and Luc Laeven. 2005. "Introduction and Overview." In Patrick Honohan and Luc Laeven (eds.), *Systemic Financial Crises: Containment and Resolution*. Cambridge and New York: Cambridge University Press, pp. 3–22.

Horsefield, J. Keith, Margaret Garritsen de Vries, Joseph Gold, Mary H. Gumbart, Gertrud Iovasy, and Emil G. Spitzer. 1969. *The International Monetary Fund,*

1945–1965: Twenty Years of International Monetary Cooperation. Washington, DC: International Monetary Fund.

Houben, Aerdt, Jan Kakes, and Garry Schinasi. 2004. *Toward a Framework for Safeguarding Financial Stability*. IMF Working Paper No. 04/101. Washington, DC: International Monetary Fund.

Hovaguimian, Catherine. 2003. "The Catalytic Effect of IMF Lending: A Critical Review." *Financial Stability Review* No. 15, pp. 160–9.

Hume, Michael, and Andrew Sentence. 2009. "The Global Credit Boom: Challenges for Macroeconomics and Policy." *Journal of International Money and Finance* 28 (8): 1426–61.

Hutchison, Michael M., and Ilan Noy. 2005. "How Bad Are Twins? Output Costs of Currency and Banking Crises." *Journal of Money, Credit and Banking* 37 (4): 725–52.

International Financial Institution Advisory Commission. 2000. *Report of the International Financial Institution Advisory Commission*. Washington, DC: United States Congress.

International Monetary Fund. 1977. *Decision on Surveillance over Exchange Rate Policies*. Washington, DC: International Monetary Fund.

1987. *Theoretical Aspects of the Design of Fund-Supported Adjustment Programs*. IMF Occasional Paper No. 55. Washington, DC: International Monetary Fund.

1993. *Articles of Agreement*. Washington, DC: International Monetary Fund.

December, 1998. *World Economic Outlook and International Capital Markets: Interim Assessment*. Washington, DC: International Monetary Fund.

1999a. *External Evaluation of IMF Surveillance: Report by a Group of Independent Experts*. Washington, DC: International Monetary Fund.

May, 1999b. *World Economic Outlook*. Washington, DC: International Monetary Fund.

2001. *Structural Conditionality in Fund-Supported Programs*. Washington, DC: International Monetary Fund.

2002a. *Guidelines on Conditionality*. Washington, DC: International Monetary Fund.

September, 2002b. *World Economic Outlook*. Washington, DC: International Monetary Fund.

April, 2003. *World Economic Outlook*. Washington, DC: International Monetary Fund.

2004a. *Signaling by the Fund – a Historical Review*. Washington, DC: International Monetary Fund.

2004b. *United States of America: Staff Report for the 2004 Article IV Consultation*. Washington, DC: International Monetary Fund.

September, 2004c. *World Economic Outlook*. Washington, DC: International Monetary Fund.

April, 2005a. *Global Finance Stability Report*. Washington, DC: International Monetary Fund.

2005b. *Implementation of Basel II – Implications for the World Bank and IMF*. Public Information Notice No. 05/154. Washington, DC: International Monetary Fund.

2005c. *The Managing Director's Report on the Fund's Medium-Term Strategy*. Washington, DC: International Monetary Fund.

2005d. *Review of the 2002 Conditionality Guidelines*. Washington, DC: International Monetary Fund.

2005e. *United States of America: 2005 Staff Report for the Article IV Consultation.* Washington, DC: International Monetary Fund.

April, 2005f. *World Economic Outlook.* Washington, DC: International Monetary Fund.

September, 2005g. *World Economic Outlook.* Washington, DC: International Monetary Fund.

2006a. *Article IV of the Fund's Articles of Agreement: An Overview of the Legal Framework.* Washington, DC: International Monetary Fund.

April, 2006b. *Global Finance Stability Report.* Washington, DC: International Monetary Fund.

2006c. *The Managing Director's Report on Implementing the Fund's Medium-Term Strategy.* Washington, DC: International Monetary Fund.

2006d. *Review of the 1977 Decision over Exchange Rate Policies Background Information.* Washington, DC: International Monetary Fund.

2006e. *United States: Staff Report for the 2006 Article IV Consultation.* Washington, DC: International Monetary Fund.

April, 2006f. *World Economic Outlook.* Washington, DC: International Monetary Fund.

2007a. *Decision on Bilateral Surveillance over Members' Policies.* Washington, DC: International Monetary Fund.

2007b. *Review of the 1977 Decision – Proposal for a New Decision Companion Paper.* Washington, DC: International Monetary Fund.

2007c. *Staff Report on the Multilateral Consultation on Global Imbalances with China, the Euro Area, Japan, Saudi Arabia, and the United States.* Washington, DC: International Monetary Fund.

2007d. *United States: Staff Report for the 2007 Article IV Consultation.* Washington, DC: International Monetary Fund.

April, 2007e. *World Economic Outlook.* Washington, DC: International Monetary Fund.

July, 2007f. *World Economic Outlook Update.* Washington, DC: International Monetary Fund.

September, 2007g. *World Economic Outlook.* Washington, DC: International Monetary Fund.

2009a. *Annual Report 2009.* Washington, DC: International Monetary Fund.

2009b. *Creating Policy Space – Responsive Design and Streamlined Conditionality in Recent Low-Income Country Programs.* Washington, DC: International Monetary Fund.

2009c. *IMF Governance – Summary of Issues and Reform Options.* Washington, DC: International Monetary Fund.

2009d. *Initial Lessons of the Crisis for the Global Architecture and the IMF.* Washington, DC: International Monetary Fund.

2009e. *Review of Recent Crisis Programs.* Washington, DC: International Monetary Fund.

2010a. *Emerging from the Global Crisis: Macroeconomic Challenges Facing Low-Income Countries.* Washington, DC: International Monetary Fund.

2010b. *Financial Sector Surveillance and the Mandate of the Fund.* Washington, DC: International Monetary Fund.

2010c. *Fiscal Monitor: Navigating the Fiscal Challenges Ahead.* Washington, DC: International Monetary Fund.

2010d. *The Fund's Mandate – Future Financing Role.* Washington, DC: International Monetary Fund.

2010e. *Greece: Staff Report on Request for Stand-By Arrangement.* Washington, DC: International Monetary Fund.

2010f. *How Did Emerging Markets Cope in the Crisis?* Washington, DC: International Monetary Fund.

2010g. *Modernizing the Surveillance Mandate and Modalities.* Washington, DC: International Monetary Fund.

2010h. *United States: Publication of Financial Sector Assessment Program Documentation – Financial Stability Assessment.* Country Report No. 10/247.

2011a. *Recent Experiences in Managing Capital Inflows – Cross-Cutting Themes and Possible Policy Framework.* Washington, DC: International Monetary Fund.

2011b. *Review of the Fund's Involvement in the G-20 Mutual Assessment Process.* Washington, DC: International Monetary Fund.

2011c. *Macroprudential Policy: An Organizing Framework.* Washington, DC: International Monetary Fund.

International Monetary Fund. Independent Evaluation Office. 2003. *The IMF and Recent Capital Account Crises: Indonesia, Korea, Brazil.* Washington, DC: International Monetary Fund.

2004. *The IMF and Argentina, 1991–2001.* Washington, DC: International Monetary Fund.

2005. *Report on the Evaluation of the IMF's Approach to Capital Account Liberalization.* Washington, DC: International Monetary Fund.

2006a. *An Evaluation of the IMF's Multilateral Surveillance.* Washington, DC: International Monetary Fund.

2006b. *Report on the Evaluation of the Financial Sector Assessment Program.* Washington, DC: International Monetary Fund.

2007b. *Structural Conditionality in IMF-Supported Programs.* Washington, DC: International Monetary Fund.

2009. *IMF Interactions with Member Countries.* Washington, DC: International Monetary Fund.

2011. *IMF Performance in the Run-Up to the Financial and Economic Crisis: IMF Surveillance in 2004–07.* Washington, DC: International Monetary Fund.

International Monetary Fund and the World Bank. 2011. *2011 Review of the Standards and Codes Initiative.* Washington, DC: International Monetary Fund and World Bank.

Isard, Peter. 2005. *Globalization and the International Financial System: What's Wrong and What Can Be Done.* Cambridge and New York: Cambridge University Press.

Ishii, Shogo, Karl Habermeier, and Staff Team. 2002. *Capital Account Liberalization and Financial Sector Stability.* IMF Occasional Paper No. 211. Washington, DC: International Monetary Fund.

Ivanova, Anna, Wolfgang Mayer, Alex Mourmouras, and George Anayiotos. 2006. "What Determines the Implementation of IMF-Supported Programs?" In Ashoka Mody and Alessandro Rebucci (eds.), *IMF-Supported Programs: Recent Staff Research.* Washington, DC: International Monetary Fund, pp. 160–86.

James, Harold. 1996. *International Monetary Cooperation since Bretton Woods*. New York and Oxford: Oxford University Press.

Jeanne, Olivier. 2000. *Currency Crises: A Perspective on Recent Theoretical Developments*. Special Paper in International Macroeconomics No. 20. Princeton, NJ: Princeton University Press.

2010. *Dealing with Volatile Capital Flows*. Peterson Institute for International Economics No. PB10–18. Washington, DC: Peterson Institute for International Economics.

Jeanne, Olivier, and Anton Korinek. 2010. "Excessive Volatility in Capital Flows: A Pigouvian Taxation Approach." *American Economic Review* 100 (2): 403–7.

Jeanne, Olivier, Jonathan D. Ostry, and Jerome Zettelmeyer. 2008. "A Theory of International Crisis Lending and IMF Conditionality." IMF Working Paper No. 08.236. Washington, DC: International Monetary Fund.

Johnson, G. G., and Richard K. Abrams. 1983. *Aspects of the International Banking Safety Net*. Washington, DC: International Monetary Fund.

Johnson, Simon, and James Kwak. 2010. *13 Bankers: The Wall Street Takeover and the Next Financial Meltdown*. New York: Pantheon Books.

Joyce, Joseph P. 2006. "Promises Made, Promises Broken: A Model of IMF Program Implementation." *Economics & Politics* 18 (3): 339–65.

Joyce, Joseph P., and Ilan Noy. 2008. "The IMF and the Liberalization of Capital Flows." *Review of International Economics* 16 (3): 413–30.

Joyce, Joseph P., and Malhar Nabar. 2009. "Sudden Stops, Banking Crises and Investment Collapses." *Journal of Development Economics* 90 (2): 314–22.

Joyce, Joseph P., and Raul Razo-Garcia. 2011. "Reserves, Quotas and the Demand for International Liquidity." *Review of International Organizations* 6 (3–4): 393–413.

Joyce, Joseph P., and Todd Sandler. 2008. "IMF Retrospective and Prospective: A Public Goods Viewpoint." *Review of International Organizations* 3 (3): 221–38.

Kahler, Miles. 1995. *International Institutions and the Political Economy of Integration*. Washington, DC: Brookings Institution Press.

Kamin, Steven B. 2004. "Identifying the Role of Moral Hazard in International Financial Markets." *International Finance* 7 (1): 25–59.

Kaminsky, Graciela L., and Carmen M. Reinhart. 1999. "The Twin Crises: The Causes of Banking and Balance-of-Payments Problems." *American Economic Review* 89 (3): 473–500.

Kaminsky, Graciela L., Carmen M. Reinhart, and Carlos A. Végh. 2005. "When It Rains, It Pours; Procyclical Capital Flows and Macroeconomic Policies." In Mark Gertler and Kenneth Rogoff (eds.), *NBER Macroeconomic Annual* 2004. Cambridge, MA, and London: MIT Press, pp. 11–52.

Kapstein, Ethan B. 1994. *Governing the Global Economy: International Finance and the State*. Cambridge, MA, and London: Harvard University Press.

Kaul, Inge, Isabelle Grunberg, and Marc A. Stern. 1999a. "Defining Global Public Goods." In Inge Kaul, Isabelle Grunberg, and Marc A. Stern (eds.), *Global Public Goods: International Cooperation in the 21st Century*. New York and Oxford: Oxford University Press, pp. 2–19.

1999b. *Global Public Goods: International Cooperation in the 21st Century*. New York and Oxford: Oxford University Press.

Kaul, Inge, Pedro Conceição, Katell Le Goulven, and Ronald U. Mendoza. 2003. *Providing Global Public Goods: Managing Globalization*. New York and Oxford: Oxford University Press.

Kenen, Peter B. 1986. *Financing, Adjustment and the International Monetary Fund*. Washington DC: Brookings Institution Press.

2001. *The International Financial Architecture: What's New? What's Missing?* Washington, DC: Peterson Institute for International Economics.

Keohane, Robert. 1984. *After Hegemony: Cooperation and Discord in the World Political Economy*. Princeton, NJ: Princeton University Press.

Keohane, Robert O., and Craig N. Murphy. 2004. "International Institutions." In Mary Hawkesworth and Maurice Kogan (eds.), *Encyclopedia of Government and Politics*. London and New York: Routledge, pp. 913–26.

Keohane, Robert O., and Joseph S. Nye. 2001. *Power and Interdependence*. 3rd ed. New York: Longman.

Khan, Mohsin S., and Sunil Sharma. 2003. "IMF Conditionality and Country Ownership of Adjustment Programs." *World Bank Research Observer* 18 (2): 227–48.

Kharas, Homi, Brian Pinto, and Sergei Ulatov. 2001. "An Analysis of Russia's 1998 Meltdown: Fundamentals and Market Signals." *Brookings Papers on Economic Activity* No. 1, pp. 1–50.

Killick, Tony. 1995. *IMF Programmes in Developing Countries: Design and Impact*. London and New York: Routledge.

Kindleberger, Charles P., and Robert Z. Aliber. 2005. *Manias, Panics and Crashes: A History of Financial Crises*. 5th ed. Hoboken, NJ: John Wiley & Sons.

Kodres, Laura, and Aditya Narain. 2010. *Redesigning the Contours of the Future Financial System*. IMF Staff Position Note No. 10/10. Washington, DC: International Monetary Fund.

Koremenos, Barbara, Charles Lipson, and Duncan Snidal. 2001. "The Rational Design of International Institutions." *International Organization* 55 (4): 761–99.

Korinek, Anton. 2011. "The New Economics of Prudential Capital Controls: A Research Agenda." *IMF Economic Review* 59 (3): 523–61.

Kose, M. Ayhan, Eswar S. Prasad, and Marco E. Terrones. 2003. "Financial Integration and Macroeconomic Volatility." *IMF Staff Papers* 50 (Special Issue): 119–42.

Kose, M. Ayhan, Eswar S. Prasad, Kenneth Rogoff, and Shang-Jin Wei. 2009. "Financial Globalization: A Reappraisal." *IMF Staff Papers* 56 (1): 8–62.

Kraft, Joseph. 1984. *The Mexican Rescue*. New York: Group of Thirty.

Krasner, Stephen D. 1983. *International Regimes*. Ithaca, NY, and London: Cornell University Press.

Krueger, Anne O. 2002. *A New Approach to Sovereign Debt Restructuring*. Washington, DC: International Monetary Fund.

Krugman, Paul. 1979. "A Model of Balance-of-Payments Crises." *Journal of Money, Credit and Banking* 11 (3): 311–25.

1994. "The Myth of Asia's Miracle." *Foreign Affairs* 73 (6): 62–78.

1996. "Are Currency Crises Self-Fulfilling?" In Ben S. Bernanke and Julio J. Rotemberg (eds.), *NBER Macroeconomics Annual*. Cambridge, MA: MIT Press, pp. 345–78.

2000. "Introduction." In Paul Krugman (ed.), *Currency Crises*. Chicago and London: University of Chicago Press, pp. 1–6.

Laeven, Luc, and Fabian Valencia. 2012. "Systemic Banking Crises: An Update." IMF Working Paper No. 12/163. Washington, DC: International Monetary Fund.

Lamfalussy, Alexandre. 1981. "Changing Attitudes towards Capital Movements." In Frances Cairncross (ed.), *Changing Perceptions of Economic Policy*. London and New York: Methuen, pp. 194–217.

2000. *Financial Crises in Emerging Markets: An Essay on Financial Globalisation and Fragility*. New Haven, CT, and London: Yale University Press.

Lane, Philip R., and Gian Maria Milesi-Ferretti. 2007. "The External Wealth of Nations Mark II: Revised and Extended Estimates of Foreign Assets and Liabilities, 1970–2004." *Journal of International Economics* 73 (2): 223–50.

2010. "The Cross-Country Incidence of the Global Crisis." IMF Working Paper No. 10/171. Washington, DC: International Monetary Fund.

League of Nations. 1944. *International Currency Experience: Lessons of the Inter-War Period*. Princeton, NJ: Princeton University Press.

Lee, Jaewoo, Gian Maria Milesi-Ferretti, Jonathan David Ostry, Alessandro Prati, and Luca Antonio Ricci. 2008. *Exchange Rate Assessments: CGER Methodologies*. IMF Occasional Paper No. 261. Washington, DC: International Monetary Fund.

Leiteritz, Ralf J. 2005. "Explaining Organisational Outcomes: The International Monetary Fund and Capital Account Liberalisation." *Journal of International Relations and Development* 8 (1): 1–26.

Lindert, Peter H., and Peter J. Morton. 1989. "How Sovereign Debt Has Worked." In Jeffrey D. Sachs (ed.), *Developing Country Debt and Economic Performance: The International Financial System*. Chicago and London: University of Chicago Press, pp. 39–106.

Lipsey, Phillip Y. 2003. "Japan's Asian Monetary Fund Proposal." *Stanford Journal of East Asian Affairs* 3 (1): 93–104.

Lipson, Charles. 1986. "Bankers' Dilemmas: Private Cooperation in Rescheduling Sovereign Debts." In Kenneth A. Oye (ed.), *Cooperation under Anarchy*. Princeton, NJ: Princeton University Press, pp. 200–25.

Lissakers, Karin. 1991. *Banks, Borrowers, and the Establishment: A Revisionist Account of the International Debt Crisis*. New York: Basic Books.

Lombardi, Domenico, and Ngaire Woods. 2008. "The Politics of Influence: An Analysis of IMF Surveillance." *Review of Political Economy* 15 (5): 711–39.

Loser, Claudio M., and Ewart S. Williams. 1997. "The Mexican Crisis and Its Aftermath: An IMF Perspective." In Sebastian Edwards and Moisés Naím (eds.), *Mexico 1994: Anatomy of an Emerging Market Crash*. Washington, DC: Carnegie Endowment for International Peace, pp. 259–73.

Lustig, Nora. 1997. "The United States to the Rescue: Financial Assistance to Mexico in 1982 and 1995." *CEPAL Review* issue 61: 41–62.

Lyne, Mona, Dan Nielson, and Michael Tierney. 2006. "Who Delegates? Alternative Models of Principals in Development Aid." In Darren G. Hawkins, David A. Lake, Daniel L. Nielsen, and Michael J. Tierney (eds.), *Delegation and Agency in International Organizations*. Cambridge and New York: Cambridge University Press, pp. 41–76.

Magud, Nicolas, and Carmen M. Reinhart. 2007. "Capital Controls: An Evaluation." In Sebastian Edwards (ed.), *Capital Controls and Capital Flows in Emerging Economies: Policies, Practices and Consequences*. Chicago and London: University of Chicago Press, pp. 645–74.

Makin, John. 1984. *The Global Debt Crisis: America's Growing Involvement*. New York: Basic Books.

Marchesi, Silvia, and Jonathan P. Thomas. 1999. "IMF Conditionality as a Screening Device." *Economic Journal* 109 (454): C111–C125.

Martin, Lisa. 1992. "Interests, Power and Multilateralism." *International Organization* 46 (4): 765–92.

——— 1999. "The Political Economy of International Cooperation." In Inge Kaul, Isabelle Grunberg, and Marc A. Stern (eds.), *Global Public Goods: International Cooperation in the 21st Century*. New York and Oxford: Oxford University Press, pp. 51–64.

——— 2006. "Distribution, Information, and Delegation to International Organizations: The Case of IMF Conditionality." In Darren G. Hawkins, David A. Lake, Daniel L. Nielson, and Michael J. Tierney (eds.), *Delegation and Agency in International Organizations*. Cambridge and New York: Cambridge University Press, pp. 140–64.

Masson, Paul R., and John C. Pattison. 2009. "Financial Regulatory Reform: Using Models of Cooperation to Evaluate Current Prospects for International Agreement." Available at http://ssrn.com/abstract=1414349.

Mateos y Lago, Isabelle, Rupa Duttagupta, and Rishi Goyal. 2009. *The Debate on the International Monetary System*. IMF Staff Position Note No. 09/26. Washington, DC: International Monetary Fund.

Mattione, Richard P. 1985. *OPEC's Investments and the International Financial System*. Washington, DC: Brookings Institution.

Mayer, Wolfgang, and Alexandros Mourmouras. 2004. "IMF Conditionality and the Theory of Special Interest Politics." *Comparative Economic Studies* 46 (3): 400–22.

——— 2005. "The Political Economy of IMF Conditionality: A Common Agency Model." *Review of Development Economics* 9 (4): 449–66.

——— 2008. "IMF Conditionality: An Approach Based on the Theory of Special Interest Politics." *Review of International Organizations* 3 (2): 105–21.

Meltzer, Allan H. 1998. "Asian Problems and the IMF." *Cato Journal* 17 (3): 267–74.

Mikesell, Raymond. 1994. *The Bretton Woods Debates: A Memoir*. Essay in International Finance No. 192. Princeton, NJ: Princeton University Press.

Miller, Calum. 2006. "Pathways through Financial Crisis: Turkey." *Global Governance* 12 (4): 449–64.

Mishkin, Frederic S. 2006. *The Next Great Globalization: How Disadvantaged Nations Can Harness Their Financial Systems to Get Rich*. Princeton, NJ, and Oxford: Princeton University Press.

——— 2011. "Over the Cliff: From the Subprime to the Global Financial Crisis." *Journal of Economic Perspectives* 25 (1): 49–70.

Mody, Ashoka, and Diego Saravia. 2006. "Catalysing Private Capital Flows: Do IMF Programmes Work as Commitment Devices?" *Economic Journal* 116 (513): 843–67.

Moggridge, D. E. 1992. *Maynard Keynes: An Economist's Biography*. London and New York: Routledge.

Montiel, Peter J. 1994. "Capital Mobility in Developing Countries: Some Measurement Issues and Empirical Estimates." *World Bank Economic Review* 8 (3): 311–50.

——— 2003a. *Macroeconomics in Emerging Markets*. Cambridge and New York: Cambridge University Press.

2003b. "Tight Money in a Post-Crisis Defense of the Exchange Rate: What Have We Learned?" *World Bank Research Observer* 18 (1): 1–23.

Moreno, Ramon. 2011. "Policymaking from a 'Macroprudential' Perspective in Emerging Market Economies." BIS Working Paper No. 336. Basel: Bank for International Settlements.

Morris, Stephen, and Hyun Song Shin. 1998. "Unique Equilibrium in a Model of Self-Fulfilling Currency Attacks." *American Economic Review* 88 (3): 587–97.

2006. "Catalytic Finance: When Does It Work?" *Journal of International Economics* 70 (1): 161–77.

Mundell, Robert A. 1963. "Capital Mobility and Stabilization Policy under Fixed and Flexible Exchange Rates." *Canadian Journal of Economics and Political Science* 29 (3): 475–85.

Mussa, Michael. 2002. *Argentina and the Fund: From Triumph to Tragedy*. Washington, DC: Institute for International Economics.

2006. "Follow the Money." In Michael Mussa (ed.), *C. Fred Bergsten and the World Economy*. Washington, DC: Peterson Institute for International Economics, pp. 275–312.

2007. "IMF Surveillance over China's Exchange Rate Policy." Paper presented at Conference on China's Exchange Rate Policy. Washington, DC: Peterson Institute for International Economics.

Mussa, Michael, and Miguel Savastano. 2000. "The IMF Approach to Economic Stabilization." In Ben S. Bernanke and Julio J. Rotemberg (eds.), *NBER Macroeconomics Annual 1999*. Cambridge, MA: MIT Press, pp. 79–122.

Mussa, Michael, Alexander K. Swoboda, Jeromin Zettelmeyer, and Olivier Jeanne. 2000. "Moderating Fluctuations in Capital Flows to Emerging Market Economies." In Peter Kenen and Alexander K. Swoboda (eds.), *Reforming the International Monetary and Financial System*. Washington, DC: International Monetary Fund, pp. 75–142.

Nelson, Rebecca M., Paul Belkin, and Derek E. Mix. 2010. *Greece's Debt Crisis: Overview, Policy Responses, and Implications*. Washington, DC: Congressional Research Service.

New York Times. 2008. "Rebuffed by China, Pakistan May Seek I.M.F. Aid." October 18.

Nsouli, Saleh M. 2006. "Petrodollar Recycling and Global Imbalances." Presentation at CESifo International Spring Conference. Available at www.imf.org.

Nsouli, Saleh M., Ruben Atoyan, and Alex Mourmouras. 2006. "Institutions, Program Implementation, and Macroeconomic Performance." In Ashoka Mody and Alessandro Rebucci (eds.), *IMF-Supported Programs: Recent Staff Research*. Washington, DC: International Monetary Fund, pp. 140–59.

Obstfeld, Maurice. 1994. "The Logic of Currency Crises." *Cahiers Économiques et Monétaires* No. 43, 189–213.

1996. "Models of Currency Crises with Self-Fulfilling Features." *European Economic Review* 40 (3–5): 1037–47.

2009a. "International Finance and Growth in Developing Countries: What Have We Learned?" *IMF Staff Papers* 56 (1): 63–111.

2009b. "Lender of Last Resort in a Globalized World." *Monetary and Economic Studies* 27 (1): 35–52.

Obstfeld, Maurice, and Alan M. Taylor. 2004. *Global Capital Markets: Integration, Crisis, and Growth*. Cambridge and New York: Cambridge University Press.

Odling-Smee, John. 2006. "The IMF and Russia in the 1990s." *IMF Staff Papers* 53 (1): 151–94.

Olson, Mancur. 1965. *The Logic of Collective Action*. Cambridge, MA, and London: Harvard University Press.

Ortiz Martinez, Guillermo. 1998. "What Lessons Does the Mexican Crisis Hold for Recovery in Asia?" *Finance & Development* 35 (2): 6–9.

Ostry, Jonathan D., Atish R. Ghosh, Karl Habermeier, Marcos Chamon, Mahvash S. Qureshi, and Dennis B. S. Reinhardt. 2010. *Capital Inflows: The Role of Controls*. IMF Staff Position Note No. 10/04. Washington, DC: International Monetary Fund.

Ostry, Jonathan D., Atish R. Ghosh, Karl Habermeier, Luc Laeven, Marcos Chamon, Mahvash S. Qureshi, and Annanmaria Kokenyne. 2011. *Managing Capital Inflows: What Tools to Use?* IMF Staff Discussion Note No. 11/06. Washington, DC: International Monetary Fund.

Özatay, Fatih, and Güven Sak. 2002. "Banking Sector Fragility and Turkey's 2000–01 Financial Crisis." *Brookings Trade Forum*, pp. 21–160.

Pattison, John C. 2006. "International Financial Cooperation and the Number of Adherents: The Basel Committee and Capital Regulation." *Open Economies Review* 17 (4–5): 443–58.

Pilbeam, Keith. 2006. *International Finance*. 3rd ed. Houndmills, Basingstroke, Hampshire, UK, and New York: Palgrave Macmillan.

Pinto, Brian, Evsey Gurvich, and Sergei Ulatov. 2005. "Lessons from the Russian Crisis of 1998 and Recovery." In Joshua Aizenman and Brian Pinto (eds.), *Managing Economic Volatility and Crises: A Practitioner's Guide*. Cambridge and New York: Cambridge University Press, pp. 406–38.

Polak, Jacques J. 1957. "Monetary Analysis of Income Formation and Payments Problems." *IMF Staff Papers* 6 (3): 1–50.

1991. *The Changing Nature of IMF Conditionality*. Essay in International Finance No. 184. Princeton, NJ: Princeton University Press.

1998. "The IMF Monetary Model at 40." *Economic Modelling* 15 (3): 395–410.

Powell, Andrew. 2002. "Argentina's Avoidable Crisis: Bad Luck, Bad Economics, Bad Politics, Bad Advice." *Brookings Trade Forum*, pp. 1–58.

2004. "Basel II and Developing Countries: Sailing through the Sea of Standards." World Bank Policy Research Working Paper No. 3387. Washington, DC: World Bank.

Pradhan, Mahmood, Ravi Balakrishnan, Reza Baqir, Geoffrey Heenan, Sylwia Nowak, Ceyda Oner, and Sanjaya Panth. 2011. *Policy Responses to Capital Flows in Emerging Markets*. IMF Staff Discussion Note No. 11/10. Washington, DC: International Monetary Fund.

Prasad, Eswar S., Kenneth Rogoff, Shang-Jin Wei, and M. Ayhan Kose. 2003. *Effects of Financial Globalization on Developing Countries: Some Empirical Evidence*. IMF Occasional Paper No. 220. Washington, DC: International Monetary Fund.

Putnam, Robert D., and Nicholas Bayne. 1987. *Hanging Together: Cooperation and Conflict in the Seven-Power Summits*. 2nd ed. Cambridge, MA: Harvard University Press.

Qian, Rong, Carmen M. Reinhart, and Kenneth S. Rogoff. 2010. "*On Graduation from Default, Inflation and Banking Crises: Elusive or Illusion?*" NBER Working Paper No. 16168. Cambridge, MA: National Bureau of Economic Research.

Quinn, Dennis P. 2003. "Capital Account Liberalization and Financial Globalization, 1890–1990: A Synoptic View." *International Journal of Finance and Economics* 8 (3): 189–204.

Quirk, Peter J., and Owen Evans. 1995. *Capital Account Convertibility: Review of Experience and Implications for IMF Policies.* Occasional Paper No. 131. Washington, DC: International Monetary Fund.

Radelet, Steven, and Jeffrey D. Sachs. 1998. "The East Asian Financial Crisis: Diagnosis, Remedies, Prospects." *Brookings Papers on Economic Activity* No. 1, pp. 1–74.

2000. "The Onset of the East Asian Financial Crisis." In Paul Krugman (ed.), *Currency Crises*. Chicago and London: University of Chicago Press, pp. 105–53.

Rajan, Raghuram G. 2005. "Has Financial Development Made the World Riskier?" In Federal Reserve Bank of Kansas City (ed.), *The Greenspan Era: Lessons for the Future*. Kansas City, MO: Federal Bank of Kansas City, pp. 313–69.

Rajan, Raghuram G., and Luigi Zingales. 2003. *Saving Capitalism from the Capitalists: Unleashing the Power of Financial Markets to Create Wealth and Spread Opportunities*. New York: Crown Business.

Reinhart, Carmen M., and Kenneth S. Rogoff. 2009. *This Time Is Different: Eight Centuries of Financial Folly*. Princeton, NJ, and Oxford: Princeton University Press.

Rieffel, Lex. 2003. *Restructuring Sovereign Debt: The Case for Ad Hoc Machinery*. Washington, DC: Brookings Institution.

Rodrik, Dani. 1996. "Why Is There Multilateral Lending?" In Michael Bruno and Boris Pleskovic (eds.), *Annual World Bank Conference on Development Economics 1995*. Washington, DC: World Bank, pp. 167–93.

2009. "A Plan B for Global Finance." *Economist*. March 1.

2010a. "The End of an Era in Finance." Project Syndicate. Available at www.project-syndicate.org.

2010b. *The Globalization Paradox: Democracy and the Future of the World Economy*. New York and London: W. W. Norton.

Rogoff, Kenneth S. 2010. "The IMF Does Europe." Project Syndicate. Available at www.project-syndicate.org.

Rojas-Suarez, Liliana. 2008. "Volatility: Prudential Regulation, Standards and Codes." In José María Fanelli (ed.), *Macroeconomic Volatility, Institutions and Financial Architectures: The Developing World Experience*. Houndmills, Basingstroke, Hampshire, UK, and New York: Palgrave Macmillan, pp. 73–100.

Rolfe, Sidney E., and James Burtle. 1973. *The Great Wheel: The World Monetary System*. New York: Quadrangle/New York Times Book Company.

Rottier, Stéphane, and Nicolas Véron. 2010. *Not All Financial Regulation Is Global*. Peterson Institute for International Economics No. PB10-22. Washington, DC: Peterson Institute for International Economics.

Rowlands, Dane. 2001. "The Response of Other Lenders to the IMF." *Review of International Economics* 9 (3): 531–46.

Ruggie, John Gerard. 1982. "International Regimes, Transactions, and Change: Embedded Liberalism in the Postwar Economic Order." *International Organization* 36 (2): 379–415.

1992. "Multilateralism: The Anatomy of an Institution." *International Organization* 46 (3): 561–98.

Russett, Bruce M., and John D. Sullivan. 1971. "Collective Goods and International Organization." *International Organization* 25 (4): 845–65.

Sachs, Jeffrey D. 1989. "Introduction." In Jeffrey D. Sachs (ed.), *Developing Country Debt and Economic Performance*. Chicago and London: University of Chicago Press, pp. 1–35.

Sachs, Jeffrey, Aaron Tornell, and Andrés Velasco. 1996a. "The Collapse of the Mexican Peso: What Have We Learned?" *Economic Policy* No. 22, pp. 13–56.

1996b. "The Mexican Peso Crisis: Sudden Death or Death Foretold?" *Journal of International Economics* 41 (3–4): 265–83.

Sampson, Anthony. 1981. *The Money Lenders: Bankers and a World in Turmoil*. New York: Viking Press.

Sandler, Todd. 1977. "Impurity of Defense: An Application to the Economics of Appliances." *Kyklos* 30 (3): 273–84.

1997. *Global Challenges: An Approach to Environmental, Political, and Economic Problems*. Cambridge and New York: Cambridge University Press.

2004. *Global Collective Action*. Cambridge and New York: Cambridge University Press.

Sandler, Todd, and Jon Cauley. 1977. "The Design of Supranational Structures: An Economic Perspective." *International Studies Quarterly* 21 (2): 251–76.

Sarno, Lucio, and Mark P. Taylor. 1999. "Moral Hazard, Asset Price Bubbles, Capital Flows, and the East Asian Crisis: The First Tests." *Journal of International Money and Finance* 18 (4): 637–57.

Schneider, Benu. 2008. "Do Global Standards and Codes Prevent Financial Crises?" In José Antonio Campo and Joseph E. Stiglitz (eds.), *Capital Market Liberalization and Development*. Oxford and New York: Oxford University Press, pp. 319–54.

Schwartz, Anna J. 1989. "International Debts: What's Fact and What's Fiction." *Economic Inquiry* 27 (1): 1–19.

1998. "International Financial Crises: Myths and Realities." *Cato Journal* 17 (3): 251–6.

Scott, Hal S. 2007. "International Finance: Rule Choices for Global Financial Markets." In Andrew T. Guzman and Alan O. Sykes (eds.), *Research Handbook in International Economic Law*. Cheltenham, UK, and Northampton, MA: Edward Elgar, pp. 361–417.

Servén, Luis, and Guillermo Perry. 2005. "Argentina's Macroeconomic Collapse: Causes and Lessons." In Joshua Aizenman and Brian Pinto (eds.), *Managing Economic Volatility and Crises: A Practitioner's Guide*. Cambridge and New York: Cambridge University Press, pp. 439–70.

Setser, Brad, and Anna Gelpern. 2006. "Pathways through Financial Crisis: Argentina." *Global Governance* 12 (4): 465–87.

Shakow, Alexander. 2008. *"The Role of the International Monetary and Financial Committee in IMF Governance."* Independent Evaluation Office Background Paper No. 08/03. Washington, DC: International Monetary Fund.

Simmons, Beth A. 2001. "The International Politics of Harmonization: The Case of Capital Market Regulation." *International Organization* 55 (3): 589–620.

Simmons, Beth A., and Zachary Elkins. 2004. "The Globalization of Liberalization: Policy Diffusion in the International Political Economy." *American Political Science Review* 98 (1): 171–89.

Singer, David Andrew. 2007. *Regulating Capital: Setting Standards for the International Financial System*. Ithaca, NY, and London: Cornell University Press.

Skidelsky, Robert A. 2000. *John Maynard Keynes: Fighting for Britain*. London: Macmillan.

Solomon, Robert. 1982. *The International Monetary System, 1945–1981*. 2nd ed. New York: Harper & Row.

Stiglitz, Joseph E. 2000. "Capital Market Liberalization, Economic Growth, and Instability." *World Development* 28 (6): 1075–86.

   2002. *Globalization and Its Discontents*. New York and London: W. W. Norton.

   2008. "Capital Market Liberalization, Globalization, and the IMF." In José Antonio Ocampo and Joseph E. Stiglitz (eds.), *Capital Market Liberalization and Development*. Oxford and New York: Oxford University Press, pp. 76–100.

   2010. "Risk and Global Economic Architecture: Why Full Financial Integration May Be Undesirable." *American Economic Review* 100 (2): 388–92.

Stiglitz, Joseph E., and Members of a UN Commission of Financial Experts. 2010. *The Stiglitz Report: Reforming the International Monetary and Financial Systems in the Wake of the Global Crisis*. New York and London: New Press.

Stone, Randall W. 2011. *Controlling Institutions: International Organizations and the Global Economy*. Cambridge and New York: Cambridge University Press.

Sturzenegger, Federico, and Jeromin Zettelmeyer. 2006. *Debt Defaults and Lessons from a Decade of Crises*. Cambridge and New York: Cambridge University Press.

Subbarao, Duvvuri. 2010. "Volatility in Capital Flows: Some Perspectives." Speech at High-Level Conference on the International Monetary System organized by the Swiss National Bank and IMF on May 11, 2010. Available at http://www.bis.org/review.

Subramanian, Arvind. 2009. "The IMF Balance Sheet." *Real Time Economics Watch*. Available at www.iie.com/realtime.

Summer, Peter M. 2005. "What Caused the Great Moderation? Some Cross-Country Evidence." Federal Reserve Bank of Kansas City *Economic Review* 90 (3): 5–32.

Summers, Lawrence H. 1999a. "Reflections on Managing Global Integration." *Journal of Economic Perspectives* 13 (2): 3–18.

Summers, Lawrence. 1999b. "The Right Kind of IMF for a Stable Global Financial System." Speech at the London School of Business. Available at www.ustreas.gov.

Sussangkarn, Chalongphob. 2010. "The Chiang Mai Initiative Multilateralization: Origin, Development and Outlook." ADBI Working Paper No. 230. Tokyo: Asian Development Bank Institute.

Tarullo, Daniel K. 2008. *Banking on Basel*. Washington, DC: Peterson Institute for International Economics.

Taylor, John B. 2002. "Sovereign Debt Restructuring: A U.S. Perspective." Speech at Institute for International Economics, Washington, DC. Available at www.piie.org.

Truman, Edwin M. (ed.). 2006. *Reforming the IMF for the 21st Century*. Washington, DC: Institute for International Economics.

Truman, Edwin M. 2008. "On What Terms Is the IMF Worth Funding?" Peterson Institute for International Economics Working Paper No. 08–11. Washington, DC: Peterson Institute for International Economics.

Union of International Associations. 2008. *Yearbook of International Organizations*. Munich: K. G. Saur Verlag.

United Nations Industrial Development Organization. 2008. *Public Goods for Economic Development*. Vienna: United Nations Industrial Development Organization.

United States General Accountability Office. 1996. *Mexico's Financial Crisis: Origins, Awareness, Assistance, and Initial Efforts to Recover*. Washington, DC: United States General Accountability Office.

2009. *International Monetary Fund Lending Programs Allow for Negotiations and Are Consistent with Economic Literature*. GAO Report No. 10–144. Washington, DC: General Accountability Office.

Vaubel, Roland. 1986. "A Public Choice Approach to International Organizations." *Public Choice* 51 (1): 39–57.

1991. "The Political Economy of the International Monetary Fund: A Public Choice Analysis." In Roland Vaubel and Thomas D. Willett (eds.), *The Political Economy of International Organizations*. Boulder, CO: Westview Press, pp. 204–44.

1994. "The Political Economy of the IMF: A Public Choice Analysis." In Doug Bandow and Ian Vásquez (eds.), *Perpetuating Poverty: The World Bank, the IMF, and the Developing World*. Washington, DC: Cato Institute, pp. 37–55.

2006. "Principal-Agent Problems in International Organizations." *Review of International Organizations* 1 (2): 125–38.

Vines, David. 2003. "John Maynard Keynes 1937–1946: The Creation of International Macroeconomics: Review Article." *Economic Journal* 113 (488): F338–F361.

Volcker, Paul A., and Toyoo Gyohten. 1992. *Changing Fortunes: The World's Money and the Threat to American Leadership*. New York: Times Books.

Vreeland, James Raymond. 2007. *The International Monetary Fund: Politics of Conditional Lending*. London and New York: Routledge.

Wade, Robert. 1998. "The Asian Debt-and-Development Crisis of 1997–?: Causes and Consequences." *World Development* 26 (8): 1535–53.

Wall Street Journal. 2009. "Mr. Rajan Was Unpopular (but Prescient) at Greenspan Party." January 2.

Weaver, Catherine. 2010. "The Politics of Performance Evaluation: Independent Evaluation at the International Monetary Fund." *Review of International Organizations* 5 (3): 365–85.

Weithöner, Thomas. 2006. "How Can IMF Policy Eliminate Country Moral Hazard and Account for Externalities?" *Journal of International Money and Finance* 25 (8): 1257–76.

White, William R. 2006. "Procyclicality in the Financial System: Do We Need a New Macrofinancial Stabilisation Framework?" BIS Working Paper No. 193. Basel: Bank for International Settlements.

Williamson, John. 1976. "The Benefits and Costs of an International Monetary Nonsystem." In Edward M. Bernstein *et al.*, *Reflections on Jamaica*. Essay in International Finance No. 115. Princeton, NJ: Princeton University Press.

1990. "What Washington Means by Policy Reform." In John Williamson (ed.), *Latin American Readjustment: How Much Has Happened*. Washington, DC: Institute for International Economics, pp. 5–20.

2004. "The Years of Emerging Market Crises: A Review of Feldstein." *Journal of Economic Literature* 42 (3): 822–37.

Wolf, Martin. 2008. *Fixing Global Finance*. Baltimore, MD: Johns Hopkins University Press.

Wood, Duncan. 2005. *Governing Global Banking: The Basel Committee and the Politics of Financial Globalisation*. Aldershot, UK, and Burlington, VT: Ashgate.

Woods, Ngaire. 2006. *The Globalizers: The IMF, the World Bank and Their Borrowers*. Ithaca, NY, and London: Cornell University Press.

World Bank. 1993. *The East Asian Miracle: Economic Growth and Public Policy*. Washington, DC: World Bank.

2007. *Global Development Finance 2007*. Washington, DC: World Bank.

World Bank. Independent Evaluation Group. 2010. *The World Bank Group's Response to the Global Economic Crisis: Phase 1*. Washington, DC: World Bank.

Wyplosz, Charles. 1999. "International Financial Instability." In Inge Kaul, Grunberg, Isabelle and Marc A. Stern (eds.), *Global Public Goods: International Cooperation in the 21st Century*. New York and Oxford: Oxford University Press, pp. 152–89.

Zhou, Xiaochuan. 2009. *Reform the International Monetary System*. Available at www.pbc.fov.cn/publish/english.

Index

Abdelal, Rawi, 83–84, 85
Abiad, Abdul, 78
absorption model, 30
Adams, Timothy, 166
Ad Hoc Committee of the Board of Governors
 on Reform of the International Monetary
 System and Related Issues, 36–37, 41,
 85, 138
agency theory, 10–13
 in democratic states, 11
 IGOs and, 11–12
 overview, 10
 public choice analysis, 12–13
 "slippage," 10
 social constructivist analysis, 12–13
Aggarwal, Vinod K., 55–56
aggregation technology, 5–6
Aliber, Robert Z., 7, 9
Allen, William A., 6
American Insurance General (AIG), 168–169
Arab Monetary Fund, 151
Argentina
 assistance from IMF, 45, 130
 capital account liberalization in, 80
 capital flows in, 128
 Convertibility Plan, 127–128, 129, 130
 currency crisis (See Argentina currency
  crisis)
 current account deficits in, 127, 128
 debt crisis of 1980s in, 54, 58, 62
 EFFs in, 127, 129
 GDP in, 130
 inflation in, 127
 SBAs in, 127, 129
 sovereign debt in, 128, 129
 SRFs in, 129

Argentina currency crisis
 appraisal of IMF actions, 132–133
 bond spreads and, 129
 Brazil currency crisis, effect of, 128
 devaluation of currency, 127–130
 East Asia currency crisis, effect of, 128
 Executive Board and, 129, 132
 G7 and, 121, 132, 133
 overview, 16, 121
 Russian currency crisis, effect of, 128
 Spain and, 129
 UK and, 132
 US and, 132–133
 World Bank and, 128
Article IV consultations
 financial sector, emphasis on, 138
 with Mexico, 57, 104
 multilateral, 164
 policy advice during, 141
 publication of, 167
 Staff Reports, 163
 "sudden stops" and, 142–143
 with Thailand, 108
Articles of Agreement
 Bretton Woods system and, 31
 broader membership support, necessity of, 195
 capital account liberalization under, 73, 78,
  83–86
 capital controls under, 23
 capital flows under, 41–42
 crisis prevention and management
  under, 192
 East Asia currency crisis and, 108, 119
 enforcing compliance with, 50, 51, 101
 exchange rate arrangements under, 13, 35,
  37–39

227

CPSIA information can be obtained
at www.ICGtesting.com
Printed in the USA
FSOW02n1823060115
4379FS